T0158095

The Sinclairs of Scotland

By Robert Sinclair

AuthorHouse™ UK Ltd.
1663 Liberty Drive
Bloomington, IN 47403 USA
www.authorhouse.co.uk
Phone: 0800.197.4150

Published by AuthorHouse 06/05/2013

ISBN: 978-1-4817-9570-8 (sc)
ISBN: 978-1-4817-9623-1 (e)

This book is printed on acid-free paper.

Castle Sinclair and Girnigoe[5.1] is a castle located on a rocky promontory jutting out into Sinclair's Bay[Ch 1] about 3 miles north of Wick on the east coast of Caithness, Scotland. It is one of the earliest seats of Clan Sinclair.[Ch 3] The castle, an L-plan crow-stepped gabled[1/1] tower house, is a ruin and is being restored by its owner, The Clan Sinclair Trust[2/1]. It is the only castle in Scotland to be listed by The World Monuments Fund.[3/1] This once im-pregnable medieval/renaissance stronghold, is now the most spectacular ruin in the North of Scotland. On 21st Oct. 1601, George Sinclair, 5th Earl of Caithness,[Ch 4] was, by an Act of Parliament, allowed to change the name of Girnigoe Castle to Sinclair Castle.

Table of Contents

1. Introduction 1
1.1 Overview 1
1.2 The origin of surnames 2
1.3 The French town of Saint-Clare-sur-epte 3
1.4 Clan progenitors 4
1.5 Sinclairs Bay 6

2. The Clan System 7
2.1 Clan organisation 9
2.1.1 Clan membership 9
2.1.2 Inheritance and authority 10
2.1.3 Legal process 11
2.1.4 Social ties 11
2.1.5 Clan management 12
2.1.6 Disputes and disorder 12
2.2. Lowland clans 13
2.3 History 15
2.3.1 Origins 15
2.3.2 Civil wars and Jacobitism 16
2.3.3 Decline of the Clan system 17
2.4 Clan symbols 18
2.4.1 Tartan 18
2.4.2 Crest badge 19
2.4.3 Clan Badge 19

3. Clan Sinclair 21
3.1 Origins of the clan 22
3.2 Profile 22
3.2.1 Places of Interest 25
3.2.2 The Sinclair tartans and crest 26

3.3 The Sinclairs/McNokairds 26
3.3.1 The early Sinclairs/McNokairds of Argyll 26
3.3.2 The Sinclairs/McNokairds on the island of Islay 30
3.4 Septs 32
3.4.1 Budge 32
3.4.2 Caird 32
3.4.3 Clouston 33
3.4.4 Clyne 33
3.4.5 Laird 33
3.4.6 Linklater 34
3.4.7 Lyall 34
3.4.8 Mason 34
3.4.9 Purdie 35
3.4.10 Snoddy 35
3.4.11 Peace 35
3.5 Archives 35
3.6 Scottish-Norwegian Wars 35
3.6.1 The Battle of Largs 35
3.6.1.1 Background 36
3.6.1.2 Events 37
3.6.1.3 Aftermath 38
3.6.1.4 Historical views 39
3.6.1.5 Viking festival in Largs 39
3.6.2 The Battle of Lewes 39
3.7 Wars of Scottish Independence 41
3.7.1 The Battle of Dunbar 41
3.7.1.1 Background 41
3.7.1.2 Battle 41
3.7.1.3 Aftermath 42
3.7.2 The Battle of Roslin 43
3.7.3 The Battle of Loudoun Hill 45
3.7.3.1 A Royal Fugitive 45
3.7.3.2 Return of the King 46
3.7.3.3 Loudoun Hill 47
3.7.4 The Battle of Bannockburn 48
3.7.4.1 Prelude 49
3.7.4.2 Edward comes north 49
3.7.4.3 Preparations 50
3.7.4.4 First day of battle 52
3.7.4.5 Second day of battle 54

3.7.4.6 Retreat........56
3.7.4.7 Legacy........56
3.7.4.8 Bannockburn Heritage Centre........57
3.7.5 The Battle of Donibristle (1317)........57
3.7.6 The Battle of Teba........57
3.7.6.1 War on the frontier of Granada........57
3.7.6.2 Scottish knights errant........58
3.7.6.3 March to Teba........58
3.7.6.4 The siege........59
3.7.6.5 The Battle........60
3.7.6.6 Aftermath........61
3.7.7 The Battle of Neville's Cross........61
3.7.7.1 Background........61
3.7.7.2 The Battle........62
3.7.7.3 Aftermath........63
3.8 16th century clan conflicts and Anglo–Scottish wars........64
3.8.1 Battle of Flodden or Flodden Field (1513)........64
3.8.1.1 Background........65
3.8.1.2 Invasion........65
3.8.1.3 The Battle........66
3.8.1.4 Tactics and aftermath........67
3.8.1.5 Casualties........68
3.8.1.6 Battlefield today........69
3.8.2 The Battle of SomersDale/Summerdale (May 1529)........69
3.8.2.1 The Sinclair uprising........69
3.8.2.2 The witch's prophecy........70
3.8.2.3 The battle by the loch........70
3.8.2.4 James Sinclair's pardon........71
3.8.3 The Battle of Solway Moss........71
3.8.3.1 Context........71
3.8.3.2 The Battle........71
3.8.4 The Battle of Dail-Riabhach........72
3.8.5 The Battle of Allt Camhna........73
3.8.5.1 Background........73
3.8.5.2 Account of The Battle of Allt Camhna........74
3.8.5.3 Aftermarth........75
3.8.6 Other events (1568–1592)........75
3.9 17th century clan conflicts and Civil War........76
3.9.1 Battle of Kringen (1612)........76
3.9.1.1 Background........76

3.9.1.2 Order of battle....77
3.9.1.3. Combat operations....77
3.9.1.4 Aftermath and legacy....78
3.9.1.5 In literature and music....79
3.9.2 The Battle of Carbisdale....79
3.9.2.1 Charles and Montrose....79
3.9.2.2 Landing in Orkney....80
3.9.2.3 Strachan's Ride....81
3.9.2.4 Montrose Moves South....81
3.9.2.5 Carbisdale....82
3.9.2.6 Death and Transfiguration....83
3.9.3 The Battle of Dunbar....83
3.9.3.1 Background....84
3.9.3.2 The Battle....85
3.9.3.3 The aftermath....86
3.9.3.4 Footnotes....86
3.9.4 The Battle of Worcester....87
3.9.4.1 Invasion of England....88
3.9.4.2 Worcester campaign....89
3.9.4.3 The Battle....90
3.9.4.4 Aftermath....93
3.9.4.5 Legacy....94
3.9.5 The Battle of Altimarlach - Scotland's last Clan Battle....94
3.9.6 Other events (1601–1698)....96
3.10 18th century and Jacobite Risings....96
3.10.1 1715 Jacobite Uprisings....97
3.10.1.1 The Battle of Sheriffmuir....97
3.10.1.1.1 History....97
3.10.1.1.2 Robert Burns and "The Battle of Sherramuir"....98
3.10.2 1745 Jacobite Rising....99
3.10.2.1 The Battle of Culloden....99
3.10.3 Colonial Wars....100
3.10.3.1 The Battle of the Plains of Abraham....100
3.10.3.2 The Battle of Charlestown....101
3.10.3.2.1 Background....101
3.10.3.2.2 Battle....101
3.10.3.2.3 Aftermath....102
3.10.4 Other events (1708–1761)....103

4. The Sinclair Barony and Earldoms 105
4.1 The Barony of Roslyn 105
4.1.1 William "The Seemly" Sinclair 1st Baron (b. 1028–d. 1093) 105
4.1.2 Henry Sinclair 2nd Baron (b. 1060–d. 1110) 106
4.1.3 Sir Henry St Clair 3rd Baron (d. 1214) 106
4.1.4 Sir William St Clair, 4th Baron (d. 1243) 106
4.1.5 Sir Henry St Clair, 5th Baron (d. 1270) 106
4.1.6 Sir William St Clair, 6th Baron (d. 1297) 107
4.1.7 Henry Sinclair (1275–1331) 7th Baron 107
4.1.8 William Sinclair 8th Baron (d. 1358) 107
4.1.9 Henry I 9th Baron (b. 1345–d. 1400) 107
4.1.10 Sir Henry St Clair 10th Baron (d. 1420) 108
4.1.11 William Sinclair 11th Baron (b.1420–d.1484) 109
4.1.12 Sir Oliver St Clair 12th Baron (d. 1525) 110
4.1.13 Sir William St Clair 13th Baron (d.1554) 110
4.1.14 Sir William St Clair 14th Baron (d. 1602) 110
4.1.15 Sir William St Clair 15th Baron (d. 1610) 111
4.1.16 Sir William St Clair 16th Baron (d. 1650) 111
4.1.17 Sir John St Clair 17th Baron (d. 1690) 111
4.1.18 Sir James St Clair, 18th Baron (d.1706) 111
4.1.19 Sir William St Clair, 19th Baron (d. 1778) 111
4.1.20 Subsequent title holders (Non-Sinclair) 112
4.1.20.1 Alexander Wedderburn St Clair 1st Earl (d. 1805) 112
4.1.20.2 Sir James St Clair-Erskine 2nd Earl (d. 1837) 113
4.1.20.3 James Alexander St Clair-Erskine 3rd Earl (d. 1866) 113
4.1.20.4 Francis Robert St Clair-Erskine 4th Earl (d. 1890) 113
4.1.20.5 James Francis Harry St Clair-Erskine 5th Earl (d. 1939) . 114
4.1.20.6 Anthony Hugh Francis Harry St Clair-Erskine, 6th Earl (d.1977) 114
4.1.20.7 Peter St Clair-Erskine, 7th and current Earl 114
4.2 The Earldom of Orkney 114
4.2.1 Norse Earls of Orkney (9th century–1231) 115
4.2.2 Scottish Earls under the Norwegian Crown 118
4.2.3 The Strathearn and Sinclair Earls 118
4.2.3.1 Maol Íosa (Strathearn 1330–1334; Caithness 1331–1334) 1331–1350 119
4.2.3.2 Erengisle Suneson (Orkney only) 1353–1357 (d. 26th Dec. 1392) 119

4.2.3.3 Alexander de l'Ard, (Caithness only) 1350–1375 120
4.2.3.4 Henry I Sinclair 1s Earl (b. 1345 –d. 1400) 120
4.2.3.5 Henry II Sinclair 2nd Earl (1375–1420) 120
4.2.3.6 Wiliiam Sinclair 3rd Earl (1404–1484) 121
4.3 The Earldom of Caithness 121
4.3.1 1st Creation (1334) 121
4.3.2 2nd Creation (1335) 122
4.3.3 3rd Creation (1452) 122
4.3.4 Final creation (1455) 122
4.3.5 Disturbance to normal succession 127
4.3.6 William Sinclair 2nd Earl (b. 9th Sept. 1459–d. 1513) 127
4.3.7 John Sinclair 3rd Earl (d. 1529) 128
4.3.8 George Sinclair 4th Earl (d. 1582) 128
4.3.9 George Sinclair 5th Earl (b. 1566–d. 1643) 128
4.3.10 George Sinclair 6th Earl (d. 1677) 128
4.3.11 John Campbell 1st Earl of Breadalbane and Holland (b. 1613–d. 1717) 128
4.3.12 George Sinclair 7th Earl (d. 1698) 128
4.3.13 John Sinclair 8th Earl (d. 1705) 129
4.3.14 Alexander Sinclair 9th Earl (b. 1685–d. 1765) 129
4.3.15 William Sinclair 10th Earl (b. 1727–d. 1765) 129
4.3.16 John Sinclair 11th Earl (b. 1757–d. 1789) 129
4.3.17 James Sinclair 12th Earl (b. 1766–d. 1823) 129
4.3.18 Alexander Campbell Sinclair 13th Earl (b. 1790–d. 1855) 129
4.3.19 James Sinclair 14th Earl (16th Aug. 1821 – 28th Mar. 1881) 129
4.3.20 George Sinclair 15th Earl (1858–1889) 129
4.3.21 James Augustus Sinclair 16th Earl (b. 1827–d. 1891) 130
4.3.22 John Sutherland Sinclair 17th Earl (b.1857–d. 1914) 130
4.3.23 Norman Macleod Sinclair 18th Earl (b. 1862–d. 1947) 130
4.3.24 Brigadier James Sinclair 19th Earl (1906–1965) 130
4.3.25 Malcolm Ian Sinclair 20th Earl (b. 3rd Nov. 1948) 131

5. Sinclair castles 133
5.1 Castle Sinclair Girnigoe 133
5.1.1 History 133
5.1.2 The Castle today 135
5.2 Roslin Castle 136
5.2.1 History 136
5.2.2 Architecture 137
5.2.3 Ruins 137

5.2.4 East Range 138
5.3 Rosslyn Chapel 138
5.4 The Castle of Mey 140
5.4.1 History 140
5.4.2 Royal residence 140
5.4.3 Ghost 141
5.5 Ackergill Tower 141
5.5.1 Early history 141
5.5.2 The Keiths and Sinclairs 142
5.5.3 The Dunbars Cont 142
5.5.4 The castle 143
5.6 Braal Castle 143
5.6.1 History 143
5.6.2 The castle 143
5.7 Dunbeath Castle 144
5.7.1 History 144
5.7.2 The castle 144
5.8 Keiss Castle 145
5.9 Castle of Old Wick 145
5.10 Thurso castle 145
5.11 Braal castle 146
5.11.1 History 146
5.11.2 The castle 146
5.12 Brims castle 147

Index 149

1. INTRODUCTION

1.1 Overview

This book presents a history of the Sinclairs since they first came to Britain from France in the 11th century. They arrived with William the Conqueror,[4/1] during the Norman[5/1] invasion[6/1], of England and settled there for a short time before moving to Scotland. Their roots can be traced back to the Norwegian Warlord Rollo.[7/1] Rollo (c. 846–c. 931), baptised Robert, and so sometimes numbered *Robert I,* to distinguish him from his descendants, was a Norse noble-man of Norwegian or Danish descent and founder and first ruler of the Viking,[8/1] principality in what soon became known as Normandy.[9/1] His descendants were The Dukes of Normandy.[10/1] Rollo is in fact, the great-great-great-grandfather of William the Conqueror. Through William, he is an ancestor of the present-day British royal family, as well as an ancestor of all current European monarchs and a great many pretenders to abolished European thrones.

Rollo on the Six Dukes statue in Falaise (Normandy) town square.

This is the first of a series of books about the Sinclairs. The first volume finishes with descriptions of the castles either owned or occupied by the Sinclairs. Also included is a description of the pre-Sinclair Earls of Orkney and Caithness since the Birth of Scotland in 843.[11/1] In all, there are 9 books in the series on different aspects of life in

Scotland for the Sinclairs. Below is a summary of what each book in the series contains:-

1.2 The origin of surnames

In Britain, hereditary surnames were adopted in the 13th and 14th centuries, initially by the aristocracy but eventually by everyone. By 1400 most English and Scottish people had acquired surnames, but many Scottish and Welsh people did not adopt surnames until the 17th century, or even later. Henry VIII (1491–1547),[12/1] ordered that marital births be recorded under the surname of the father. Most surnames of British origin fall into seven types:-

Occupations	Archer, Bailey, Baker, Brewer, Butcher, Carter, Chandler, Clark, Collier, Cooper, Cook, Carpenter, Dyer, Faulkner, Fisher, Fletcher, Fowler, Fuller, Glover, Hayward, Hawkins, Head, Hunt or Hunter, Judge, Knight, Miller, Mason, Page, Palmer, Parker, Porter, Sawyer, Slater, Smith, Taylor, Thatcher, Turner, Shoemaker, Walker, Weaver, Wood or Woodman and Wright (or variations such as Cartwright and Wainwright).
Personal characteristics	Short, Brown, Black, Whitehead, Young, Long and White etc.
Geographical features	Bridge, Camp, Hill, Bush, Lake, Lee, Wood, Holmes, Forest, Underwood, Hall, Brooks, Fields, Stone, Morley, Moore and Perry etc.
Place names	Washington, Everingham, Burton, London, Leighton, Hamilton, Sutton, Flint and Laughton etc.
Estate	For those descended from land-owners, the name of their holdings, manor or estate.
Patronymics,[13] matronymics,[14] or ancestral	Often from a person's given name. e.g. from male name: Richardson, Stephenson, Jones (Welsh for John), Williams, Jackson, Wilson, Thompson, Benson, Johnson, Harris, Evans, Simpson, Willis, Fox, Davies,

Reynolds, Adams, Dawson Lewis,Rogers, Murphy, Nicholson, Robinson, Powell, Ferguson, Davis, Edwards, Hudson, Roberts, Harrison, Watson, or female names Molson (from Moll for Mary), Madison (from Maud), Emmott (from Emma), Mariott (from Mary) or from a clan name (for those of Scottish origin, e.g., MacDonald, Forbes, Henderson, Armstrong, Grant, Cameron, Stewart, Douglas, Crawford, Campbell, Hunter) with "Mac" Scottish Gaelic,[15/1] for son.

The original meaning of the name may no longer be obvious in modern English, (e.g. a Cooper is one who makes barrels and the name Tillotson is a matronymic from a diminutive for Matilda). A much smaller category of names relates to religion, though some of this category are also occupations. The names Bishop, Priest or Abbot for example, may indicate that an ancestor worked for a bishop, a priest or an abbot respectively, or possibly took such a role in a popular religious play. Spelling of names in past centuries is often assumed to be a deliberate choice by a family, but due to very low literacy rates, many families could not provide the spelling of their surname and so the scribe, clerk, minister or official, would write down the name on the basis of how it was spoken or how they heard it. This results in a great many variations, some of which occurred when families moved to another country (e.g. Wagner becoming Wagoner or Whaley becoming Wheally). With the increase in bureaucracy, officially-recorded spellings tended to become the standard for a given family.

1.3 The French town of Saint-Clare-sur-epte

Saint-Clair-sur-Epte

Sinclair is one of the oldest surnames in Europe and can be traced back through centuries of history. It has its origins in Saint-Clair-sur-Epte,[16/1] in normandy,[9/2] France and is in turn derived from a hermit called *St. Clare, St. Clere* or *St. Clair*, who became a local saint. He lived near the town that is now called St. Clair sur l'Epte. His feast day is 16th July. In 1999, an emissary of the Sinclair family attended St. Clair's feast in the town. The Epte is a river in Seine Mari-time and Eure in Normandy, France. It is a tributary of The Seine. The river rises in Seine-Maritime in The Pays de Bray, near Forges-les-Eaux. The river empties into the Seine, not far from Giverny.[17] In 911, The Treaty of Saint-Clair-sur-Epte,[18/1] established the river as the historical boundary of Normandy and Île-de-France. were nine saints in all at different times and places named *Clarus.* (The Sinclair namesake, St. Clair, is not to be confused with Saint Clare or Sainte Claire in French. She was the founder of the Poor Clares, a monastic order associated with the Franciscans of St. Francis of Assisi. She is the namesake of Santa Clara, California, just as Francis is the namesake of San Francisco California, where Spanish missionaries left their names).

1.4 Clan progenitors

The Sinclairs first came to England (before they came to Scotland) with William the Conqueror,[4/2] during his invasion of England. They arrived in Scotland in the reign of Malcolm Canmore, as differences had arisen between them and those who held sway in England at the time. They considered that they had not been adequately rewarded for services which they had performed. That was the reason why they left England and took up their abode in Scotland. There was another cause that might have induced them to settle in Scotland. They knew that it was the policy of Malcolm Canmore to get some of these Norman,[5/2] Barons to his kingdom. On that account, they no doubt calculated that fortune would favour them more in Scotland than in England. It is unnecessary to state that they were well received at the Scottish court. The first of the name who it is believed took up his residence in Scotland was William de Sancto Claro,[19/1] a son of Waldernus Compte de St. Claro [20/1]

Portrait of William the Conqueror, painted ca. 1620 by an unknown artist. National Portrait Gallery, London

and Margaret,[21] daughter of Richard, Duke of Normandy.[10/2] He is considered to be the progenitor [22/1] of the clan. Extensive tracts of land were given to them and in this way The Barony [Ch 4] and lands of Rosslyn [23/1] came into their possession. Chief, Sir Henry Sinclair, 2nd Baron of Rosslyn,[Ch 4] (1060-1110), led a successful attack on England at The Battle of Alnwick (1093).[24/1] Chief Henry of Saint Clair/Sinclair, 3rd Baron of Rosslyn,[Ch 4] obtained a charter for the lands of Herdmanston [25/1] in Haddingtonshire in 1160. Sir William de St.Clair, was involved in negotiating the marriage of Yolande de Dreux,[26/1] with King Alexander III. He signed the "Ragman Roll" [27] of King Edward I of England [28/1] in 1296.

Malcolm III

His heir, Henry, was initially loyal to the English King but then supported Robert the Bruce,and,fought,at,The Battle of Bannockburn.[Ch 3] The king granted him lands in The Pentlands,[29/1] south of Edinburgh. Whilst escorting the heart of Robert the Bruce on a Crusade to the Holy Land in 1330, Sir William Sinclair was killed in Spain fighting off a marauding party of Moorish warriors.[30/1] In 1379, Sir Henry Sinclair claimed The Earldom of Orkney,[4.2] through his mother and received it from King Haco of Norway.[31] Sir Henry Sinclair was also Admiral of Scotland.[32/1] In 1455 the family received land in Caithness. The Earldom of Orkney was later resigned in 1470, by order of King James III of Scotland. The Chief of Clan Sinclair,[Ch. 3] split the family lands, giving the lands of Caithness to his elder son and the lands of Rosslyn, to the younger. It was around this time that the spelling *Sinclair* came into general use. Later much of the Sinclair land was sold off to pay debts. Later generations regained the land by an Order of Parliament. On 3rd April 1592, George 5th Earl of Caithness,[Ch 4] resigned Earldom in return for novodamus.[33/1] On Dec.11th 1592, his son William Sinclair of Mey,[34/1] was knighted by King James IV of Scotland.

In Argyllshire and the West of Scotland, a branch of the clan was known by the Gaelic,[15/2] "Clann-na-Cearda" or "Children of the Craft", from their principal occupation of metal working. So, in Gaelic (Argyll) the Sinclairs were referred to as "Mac na Ceardadh" and elsewhere in Scotland the gaelic spelling of Sinclair is "Singlear". The Sinclairs were frequently engaged in clan warfare alongside the Gunns, and emerged as a powerful and influential clan in the north of Scotland. It is the most frequently found name in Orkney. It can be said that the courage of the Sinclairs was considerable, when, in 1513, the Chief marched them out to engage an enemy much superior in tactical strength on Flodden Field.[Ch 3] The day ended in disaster for the clansmen. Sir John Sinclair of Ulbster,[35/1] in the true spirit of a good Highland Chief, was one of the first to raise a fencible regiment in 1794. The Clan Badge,[Ch 2] is a Cock and the motto "Commit thy work to God".

1.5 Sinclairs Bay

Sinclairs Bay is a small remote, left leaf of a tear drop shaped, coastal embayment, on the east coast of Scotland, in east Caithness, Scotland. It's coastline falls entirely within the Scottish council area of Highland. Starting in the north, at Ness Head, the bay is bounded by Freswick Bay, and overlooked by Skirza Head, the bay proper sweeps south in a long elliptical curve, before sweeping east to pass the the remains Castle Sinclair,[5.1] and terminating at Noss Head Lighthouse. Sinclairs Bay has two primary geological features. Starting at the coastal village of Keiss,[5.8] running northeast, a stony beach and coastal crags, become cliffs that are increasingly sheer the further north. South of Keiss, the cliffs even out in a large white sandy beach, called Keiss Beach, forming large Dunes further south. At Ackergill Tower, the beach again becomes stony and eventually forms into a series of cliffs and crags, further east.

Sinclairs Bay

2. The Clan System

The Highland Clans in the 1745 Rising

Scottish clans (from Gaelic [15/3] *clann* (progeny [36]) give a sense of identity and shared descent to people in Scotland [37] and to their relations throughout the world with a formal structure of Clan Chiefs [38] recognised by the court of The Lord Lyon King of Arms,[39/1] which acts as an authority concerning matters of Heraldry [40/1] and Coat of Arms.[41/1]

The Clan system was the effective means of government in the Highlands of Scotland from sometime before the year 1000 AD until it was essentially eliminated by the British in 1745. It grew out of the similar system of Celtic, Ireland, from whence the Scots, came The clans are even older than Scotland itself, and many people - especially expatriates living abroad - regard them as a vital part of the country's heritage.This age-old system of family groupings has given many Scots their surnames, provided a great amount of family pride, and produced a fierce sense of community which still exists to this day. Most Highlanders would have felt allegiance to their clan first and their country second. They believed in it so much that they were prepared to die for it - which is just as well, because that's often exactly what happened The big difference between the clans and the feudal,[42/1] society which existed in most of lowland Scotland was that the latter was based entirely on a hierarchy built around the ownership of land. The clan system was very different because it was built around relationships. After the ending of the Lordship of the Isles, in 1493 - some clans became far more powerful and assertive than others. The revoking of the Lordship left a power vacuum, for instance, which was quickly filled by the Argyll-based Campbells.

Most clans have their own tartan patterns usually dating from the 19th century, and members of the clan may wear kilts, plaids, sashes, ties, scarves or other items of clothing, made of the appropriate tartan as a badge of membership, and as a uniform where appropriate. The modern image of clans each with their "own" tartan and specific land, was promulgated by the Scottish author Sir Walter Scott and others. Historically, tartan designs were associated with Lowland and Highland districts, whose weavers tended to produce cloth patterns favoured in those districts. By process of social evolution, it followed that the clans/families prominent in a particular district would wear the tartan of that district, and it was but a short step for that community to become identified by it. Clans generally identify with geographical areas originally controlled by the Chiefs, sometimes with an ancestral castle, and clan gatherings form a regular part of the social scene. The most notable gathering of recent times was "The Gathering 2009" which included a "clan convention" in the Scottish Parliament.

2.1 Clan organisation

Chief = Supreme Leader and Lawgiver

↓

The Tanist,[43/1]
Nominated by the Chief
Tanistry was a system of succession by a previously elected member of the Clan or family.

↓

Commander/Military Leader

↓

Chieftains
(Heads of various branches or Septs,[44] of the clan, always appointed if the Chief were old or infirm)

↓

Gentlemen
(Those who could claim a blood connection with the Chief)

↓

Clansmen
The greatest in numbers —
In times of peace, the clansmen did the manual work; in times of war, they fought for their chief

2.1.1 Clan membership

The word *clann* in Scottish Gaelic,[15/4] can mean offspring, children or descendants. Each clan was a large group of people, theoretically an extended family, supposedly descended from one progenitor,[22/2] and all owing allegiance to the clan chief. It also included a large group of loosely-related Septs–dependent families–all of whom looked to the clan chief as their head and their protector. According to the former Lord Lyon,[39/2] Sir Thomas Innes of Learney,[45/1] a clan is a community which is distinguished by heraldry,[40/2] and recognised by the Sovereign. Learney considered clans to be a "noble corporation" because the arms borne by a clan chief are granted or otherwise recognised by the Lord Lyon as an Officer of the Crown, thus conferring royal recognition of the entire clan. Clans with recognised chiefs are therefore considered a noble community under Scots law. A group without a chief, recognised by the Sovereign through the Lord Lyon,[39/3] has no official standing under Scottish law. Claimants to the title of chief are expected to be recognised by the Lord Lyon, as the rightful heir to the undifferenced arms,[46] of the ancestor of the clan, of which the claimant seeks to be recognized as chief. A chief of a clan, is the only person who is entitled to bear the undifferenced arms of the ancestral founder of the clan. The clan is considered to be the chief's heritable estate and The Chief's Seal of Arms,[47] is the seal of the clan as a "noble corporation". Under Scots law, the chief is recognised as the head of the clan, and serves as the lawful representative of the clan community.

Historically, a clan was made up of everyone who lived on the chief's territory, or on territory of those who owed allegiance to the said chief. Through time, with the constant changes of "clan boundaries", migration or regime changes, clans would be made up of large numbers of members who were unrelated and who bore different surnames. Often those living on a chief's lands would, over time, adopt the clan surname. A chief could add to his clan by adopting other families and also had the legal right to outlaw anyone from his clan, including members of his own family. Today, anyone who has the chief's surname, is automatically considered to be a member of the chief's clan. Also, anyone who offers allegiance to a chief becomes a member of the chief's clan unless the chief decides not to accept that persons allegiance. The only rule is that it is up to the chief whom he may decide to accept as a member of his clan.

2.1.2 Inheritance and authority

The Highland,[48] clan system incorporated the Celtic/Norse,[49] traditions of heri- tage, as well as Norman Feudal society.[42/2] Chieftains and petty kings under the suzerainty,[50] of a High King,[51] (ard rí) ruled Gaelic Alba,[52/1] with all such offices being filled through election by an assembly. Usually the candidate was nominated by the current office holder on the approach of death and his heir-elect was known as the tanist, from the Gaelic *tànaiste* or second, with the system being known as tanistry.[43/2] This system combined a hereditary element with the consent of those ruled and while the succession in clans later followed the feudal rule of primogeniture,[53/1] the concept of authority coming from the clan, continued. Thus the collective heritage of the clan, the *dùthchas*, gave the right to settle the land to which the chiefs and leading gentry provided protection and authority, as trustees for the people. This was combined with the complementary concept of *òighreachd,* where the chieftain's authority came from charters granted by The Feudal,[42/4] Scottish Crown, where individual heritage was warranted. While dùthchas held precedence in the medieval,[54/1] period, the balance shifted, as the mainly lowland Scots law became increasingly important in shaping the structure of clanship.

2.1.3 Legal process

To settle criminal and civil disputes within clans, both sides put their case to an arbitration panel drawn from the leading gentry of the clan and presided over by the chief. Similarly, in disputes between clans, the chiefs served as procurators (legal agents) for the disputants in their clan, and put the case to an arbitration panel of equal numbers of gentry from each clan, presided over by a neighbouring chief or landlord. There was no appeal from the decision which awarded reparations, called *assythment*, to the wronged party. The decision was recorded in a convenient Royal or Burgh court. This compensation took account of the age, responsibilities and status of the victim as well as the nature of the crime, and once paid, precluded any further action for redress against the perpetrator. To speed this process, clans made standing provisions for arbitration and regularly contracted bonds of friendship between the clans which had the force of law, and were recorded in a convenient court.

2.1.4 Social ties

Fosterage and manrent, were the most important forms of social bonding in the clans. In fosterage, the chief's children were brought up by favoured members of the leading clan gentry (traditionally the mother's brother or similar, i.e. in another clan), whose children in turn were brought up by other favoured members of the clan (again the mother's brother or the like - i.e. in another clan). This brought about intense ties and reinforced inter-clan cohesion. Manrent was a bond contracted by the heads of families looking to the chief for territorial protection, though not living on the estates of the clan elite. These bonds were reinforced by *calps*, death duties paid to the chief as a mark of personal allegiance by the family when their head died, usually in the form of their best cow or horse. Although calps were banned by Parliament in 1617, manrent continued covertly to pay for protection. Less durably, marriage alliances reinforced kinship between clans. These were contracts involving the exchange of livestock, money and rent, *tocher* for the bride and *dowry* for the groom.

2.1.5 Clan management

Payments of rents and calps from those living on clan estates and calps alone from families living elsewhere, were channelled through tacksmen.[55/1] These lesser gentry acted as estate managers, allocating the run-rig,[56] strips of land, lending seed-corn and tools and arranging droving of cattle to the Lowlands for sale, taking a minor share of the payments made to the clan nobility, The Fine.[57/1] They had the important military role of mobilising *The Clan Host,* both when required for warfare and more commonly, for a large turn out of followers for weddings and funerals. Also, traditionally in August, for hunts which included sports for the followers, the predecessors of the modern Highland games. From the late 16th century, The Scottish Privy Council,[58/1] recognising the need for co-operation, required clan leaders to provide bonds of surety for the conduct of anyone on their territory and to attend regularly in Edinburgh, encouraging a tendency to become absentee landlords. With an increase in droving, tacksmen acquired the wealth to finance the gentry's debts secured against their estates, hence acquiring the land. By the 1680s, this led to the land in ownership largely coinciding with the collective 'duthchas' for the first time. The tacksmen became responsible for the bonds of surety, leading to a decline in banditry and feuding.

2.1.6 Disputes and disorder

Where the oighreachd,[Ch 2] land owned by the clan elite or Fine did not match the common heritage of the duthchas,[Ch 2] this led to territorial disputes and warfare. The Fine resented their clansmen paying rent to other landlords, while acquisitive clans used disputes to expand their territories. Ferocious feuds, such as that between the Clan Gordon and the Clan Forbes lasted for centuries, causing heavy casualties on both sides. On the western seaboard, clans became involved with the wars of the Irish Gaels,[59] against the Tudor English,[60] and a military caste called

The buannachan,[61] developed, seasonally fighting in Ireland as mercenaries and living off their clans as minor gentry. This was brought to an end with the Irish Plantations,[62] of King James VI of Scotland and I of England. During that century, law increasingly settled disputes and the last feud leading to a battle was at Mulroy in Lochaber on August 4th 1688.[63] Reiving,[64/1] had been a rite of passage, *the creach,* where young men took livestock from neighbouring clans. By the 17th century, this had declined and most reiving was for *spreidh* (cattle), where up to 10 men raided the adjoining Lowlands, the livestock taken, usually being recoverable on payment of tascal (information money) and guarantee of no prosecution. Some clans offered the Lowlanders protection against such raids on terms not dissimilar to blackmail. Although by the late 17th century disorder declined, reiving persisted with the growth of cateran,[65] bands of up to 50 bandits, usually led by a renegade of the gentry who had thrown off the constraints of the clan system. As well as preying off the clans, caterans acted as mercenaries for Lowland lairds,[66] pursuing disputes amongst themselves.

2.2. Lowland clans

It is quite acceptable to refer to the great Lowland families as *clans* also, since the Scots themselves appear to have used both terms interchangeably. Until the early 19th century, most of the Lowland and Border clans did not identify themselves by specific family tartans, other than that of their local district, nor did they wear the kilt, or play The Great Highland Pipes, (although they would be familiar with the widely used Lowland,[67] or Border or Northumbrian Pipes), but afterwards, they adopted these characteristics of Highland culture as a form of clan identification, which they continue to use to the present day. The Lowlands had been Brythonic Celtic,[68] with the southeast becoming Anglian,[69] and Galloway,[70/1] and the western seaboard becoming Norse/Gaelic.[71/1] Then, by 1034, The Kingdom of Alba,[52/2] had expanded to bring all but the last area under Gaelic Celtic,[72] rule. From the accession of King David I (1124), the traditional social patterns of much of Eastern Scotland began to be altered, particularly with the growth of Burghs,[73] and the settlement of Norman feudal families,[42/3] on Royal Demesne,[74] lands. This process was of course very slow, but its cumulative effect over centuries, was to undermine the integrity of Gaelic,[15/5] in the areas affected, areas which later became known collectively as the

Lowlands, though to a large extent Galloway,[70/24] and Carrick,[75/1] where Galwegian Gaelic,[76] survived into the 17th century, were not affected as much as elsewhere until very late. However aristocratic Gaelic clans did survive, especially in Galloway (e.g. Macdowall, MacLellan, MacCann), Carrick (e.g. Kennedy) and Fife (e.g. MacDuff). The term clan was still being used of Lowland families at the end of the 16th century, and while aristocrats may have been increasingly likely to use the word family, the terms remained interchangeable. An Act of the Scottish Parliament of 1597 talks of the "Chiftanis and chieffis of all clannis...duelland in the hielands or bordouris" – thus using the word clan and chief to describe both Highland and Border families. The act goes on to list the various Lowland clans, including the Maxwells,[A4] Johnstons,[A4] Turnbulls,[A4] and other famous Border Reivers,[64/2] names. Further, Sir George MacKenzie,[A4] of Rosehaugh,[77] the Lord Advocate (Attorney General) writing in 1680 said "By the term 'chief' we call the representative of the family from the word chef or head and in the Irish (Gaelic) with us the chief of the family is called the head of the clan". So it can be seen that all along the words chief or head and clan or family are interchangeable. It is therefore quite correct to talk of the MacDonald family or the Stirling clan.

The idea that Highlanders should be listed as clans, while the Lowlanders should be termed as families, was merely a 19th century convention. By the late 18th century the Lowlands were integrated into the British system with an uneasy relationship to the Highlanders. The total population of Lowlanders diminished drastically in some parts of the south as a direct result of The Agricultural Revolution,[78] which resulted in The Lowland Clearances,[79] and the subsequent emigration of large numbers of Lowland Scots. However, with the revival of interest in Gaeldom, and the visit of King George IV,[80/1] to Scotland in 1822, there was a new enthusiasm amongst Lowlanders for identification with pan-Scottish culture. Consequently, Lowland families and aristocrats now appear on clan lists with their own tartans, in some cases with a claim to ancestry from the Highland area - and as a result, more Lowland/Border clans than ever now have their own clan societies, websites and annual reunions. No doubt this has economically benifited traditional industries, such as manufacturers of tartan cloth and other clan items and has been encouraged by the immense growth of Internet genealogical research in the last few years of the 20th century. Regrettably, this last development has also led to certain companies springing up to exploit public enthusiasm, by marketing supposed heraldic devices,[40/3] and "family" coats-of-arms.[41/2]

2.3 History

2.3.1 Origins

The Senchus fer n-Alban,[81/1] lists three main kin groups in Dál Riata,[82] in Scotland, with a fourth being added later:-

The Cenél nGabráin,[83] in Kintyre,[84/1]	Supposedly the descendants of Gabrán mac Domangairt.[85]
The Cenél nÓengusa,[86] in Islay [87/1] and Jura,,[88]	Supposedly the descendants of Óengus Mór mac Eirc.[89]
The Cenél Loairn,[90/1] in Lorne,[91/1]	Perhaps also Mull,[92] and Ardnamurchan,[93/1] Supposedly the descendants of Loarn mac Eirc.[94]
The Cenél Comgaill,[95] in Cowal [96/1] and Bute,[97]	A later addition, supposedly the descendants of Comgaill mac Domangairt.[98]

The Senchus does not list any kindreds in Ireland. Among the Cenél Loairn it lists the Airgíalla, although whether this should be understood as being Irish settlers or simply another tribe to whom the label was applied, is unclear. The meaning of Airgíalla, 'hostage givers', adds to the uncertainty, although it must be observed that only one grouping in Ireland was apparently given this name and it is therefore very rare. There is no reason to suppose that this is a complete or accurate list. Some clans such as Clan Campbell,[A4] and Clan Donald, claim ancient Celtic mythologial progenitors,[22/3] mentioned in The Fenian, cycle,[99] with another group including Clan MacSween, Clan Lamont, Clan MacEwen of Otter, Clan Maclachlan and Clan MacNeil, tracing their ancestry back to the 5th century Niall of the Nine Hostages,[100] legendary High King of Ireland, through the O'Neill dynasty of Cenél nEógain,[101] (Kings of Ailech,[102]). Others such as Clan MacAulay, Clan Mackinon, Clan Grant and Clan Gregor claim descent from the Scots King Kenneth MacAlpin, who made himself King of the Picts in 843,[11/2] founding the Kingdom called after the name of the land Alba,[52/3] (modern-day Scotland). The Macdonalds, and MacDougalls claim descent from Somerled, the half Gael/Norse,[71/2] Manx Lord of the Isles, in the mid-11th century. Though the clans had always been a feature of pre-Christian Scotland, and Ireland, they first emerged into English consciousness from the turmoil of the 12th and 13th centuries. That is, when the Scottish crown pacified northern rebellions and reconqered areas taken by the Norse and after the fall of Macbeth,[103] when the crown became increasingly Anglo-Norman.[104/1] This turmoil created opportunities for Norse, Scottish and English warlords and their kin to dominate areas, and the instability of The Wars of Scottish Independence,[3.7] brought in warlords with Norman,[5/3] and Flemish,[105] ancestry, founding clans such as the Chisholms,and Menzies.

2.3.2 Civil wars and Jacobitism

As The Civil Wars of The Three Kingdoms,[106] broke out in the early 17th century, The Covenanters,[107] were supported by the territorially ambitious Argyll Clan Campbell,[A4] and the Clan Sutherland,[A4] both powerful Highland clans, as well as some clans of the central Highlands opposed to The Royalist House of Huntly.[108] While some clans remained neutral, others led by Montrose,[109] supported the Royalist cause, projecting their feudal,[42/4] obligations to clan chiefs onto The Royal House of Stuart, resisting the demands of The Covenanters, for commitment and reacting to the ambitions of the larger clans. In The Wars of 1644–47,[110] the most prominent Royalist clan were Clan Donald, led by Alasdair MacColla. With the restoration of Charles II,[111] Episcopalianism,[112] became widespread among clans, as it suited the hierarchical clan structure and encouraged obedience to royal authority, while some other clans were converted by catholic missions. In 1682, James Duke of York, Charles' brother, instituted The Commission for Pacifying the Highlands, which worked in co-operation with the clan chiefs in maintaining order as well as redressing Campbell acquisitiveness and when he became King James VII, the retained popularity with Highlanders. All these factors contributed to continuing support for the Stuarts, when James (the last catholic monarch to reign over England Scotland and Ireland) was deposed by William of Orange in The "Glorious Revolution.", Clan support, their remoteness from authority and the ready mobilisation of *the clan hosts,* made the Highlands the starting point for the Jacobite,[113/1] Risings. In Scottish Jacobite ideology the Highlander symbolised patriotic purity, as against the corruption of the Union and as early as 1689, some Lowlanders wore "Highland habit" in the Jacobite army. In contrast, despite relying on support from Presbyterian,[114/1] clans the government depicted Highlanders as frightening savages who ate babies.

2.3.3 Decline of the Clan system

Successive Scottish governments had portrayed the clans as bandits, needing occasional military expeditions to keep them in check and extract taxes. As Highlanders became associated with Jacobitism and rebellion, the government made repeated efforts to curb the clans, culminating with brutal repression after The Battle of Culloden.[Ch 3] This followed in 1746 with The Act of Proscription,[115] further measures making restrictions on their ability to bear arms, traditional dress, culture and even music. The Heritable Jurisdictions Act,[116] removed the feudal,[42/5] authority the Clan Chieftains had once enjoyed. With the failure of Jacobitism, the clan chiefs and gentry increasingly became landlords, losing the traditional obligations of clanship. They were incorporated into the British aristocracy, looking to the clan lands mainly to provide them with a suitable income. From around 1725, clansmen had been emigrating to North America; both clan gentry looking to re-establish their lifestyle or as victims of raids on the Hebrides looking for cheap labour. Increasing demand in Britain for cattle and sheep led to higher rents, with surplus clan population leaving in the mass migration later known as the Highland Clearances, finally undermining the traditional clan system. Shortly before or after The Dress Act,[117] restricting kilt wearing was repealed in 1782, Highland aristocrats set up Highland Societies in Edinburgh and other centres including London and Aberdeen - landowners' clubs with aims including "improvements" (which others would later call the Highland Clearances). Clubs like The Celtic Society of Edinburgh, included Highland chieftains and Lowlanders taking an interest in the clans. The success of the historical novels of Sir Walter Scott, as well as the pomp surrounding the visit of King George IV,[80/2] to Scotland in 1822, spurred 19th century interest in the clans and a re-awakening of Scottish culture and pride.

2.4 Clan symbols

The revival of interest and demand for clan ancestry, has led to the production of lists and maps,[p. 24] covering the whole of Scotland, giving clan names and showing territories, sometimes with the appropriate tartans. While some lists and clan maps confine their area to the Highlands, others also show Lowland clans or families. Territorial areas and allegiances changed over time, and there are also differing decisions on which (smaller) clans and families should be omitted. This list of Clans contains clans registered with The Lord Lyon Court.[39/3] The Lord Lyon Court defines a clan or family as a legally recognised group, but does not differentiate between Families and Clans, as it recognises both terms as being interchangeable. Clans or families thought to have had a Chief in the past but not currently recognised by the Lord Lyon, are listed as Armigerous Clans.[118]

2.4.1 Tartan

Ever since the Victorian "tartan craze", tartans, and "clan tartans", have been an important part of a Scottish clans identity. Almost all Scottish clans have more than one tartan attributed to their surname. Although there are no rules on who can or cannot wear a particular tartan, it is possible for anyone to create a tartan and name it almost any name they wish. The only person with the authority to make a clan's tartan "official", is the chief. In some cases, following such recognition from the clan chief, tartan appears in the heraldry,[40/4] of a clan chief, then the Lord Lyon considers it to be the "proper" tartan of the clan. Originally there appears to have been no association of tartans with specific clans; instead, highland tartans were produced to various designs by local weavers and any identification was purely regional, but the idea of a clan-specific tartan gained currency in the late 18th century and in 1815, The Highland Society of London, began the naming of clan-specific tartans. Many clan tartans derive from a 19th century hoax, known as the Vestiarium Scoticum.[121] The Vestiarium was composed by the "Sobieski Stuarts",[122] who passed it off as a reproduction of an ancient manuscript of clan tartans. It has since been proven a forgery, but despite this, the designs are still highly regarded and they continue to serve their purpose to identify the clan in question.

2.4.2 Crest badge

A sign of allegiance to a certain clan chief is the wearing of a crest badge. The crest badge, suitable for a clansman or clanswoman, consists of the chief's heraldic crest encircled with a strap and buckle and which contains the chief's heraldic motto or slogan. Although it is common to speak of "clan crests", there is no such thing in Scotland (and indeed all of UK), only individuals, not clans, possess a Heraldic Coat of Arms.[41/3] Even though any clansmen and clanswomen may purchase crest badges and wear them to show their allegiance to his or her clan, the heraldic crest and motto always belong to the chief alone. In principle, these badges should only be used with the permission of the clan chief and The Lyon Court,[39/4] has intervened in cases where permission has been withheld. Scottish crest badges, much like clan-specific tartans, do not have a long history and owe much to Victorian era romanticism, having only been worn on the bonnet since the 19th century.

2.4.3 Clan Badge

Clan badges are another means of showing one's allegiance to a Scottish clan. These badges, sometimes called plant badges, consist of a sprig of a particular plant. They are usually worn in a bonnet behind the Scottish crest badge. They can also be attached at the shoulder of a lady's tartan sash, or be tied to a pole and used as a standard. Clans which are connected historically or that occupied lands in the same general area may share the same clan badge. According to popular lore, clan badges were used by Scottish clans as a form of identification in battle. However, the badges attributed to clans today, can be completely unsuitable for even modern clan gatherings. Clan badges are commonly referred to as the original clan symbol, however Thomas Innes of Learney,[44/2] claimed the heraldic flags,[123] of clan chiefs would have been have been the earliest means of identifying Scottish clans in battle or at large gatherings.

3. Clan Sinclair

Crest badge	

Crest: *A cock rampant*	
Motto: *Revela Domino opera tua*	
Profile	
District	*Caithness*
Plant badge	*Gorse* [124]
Pipe music	*"The Sinclair's March"*
Gaelic name	*Mac na Ceardadh or Singlear*

Clan Sinclair is a Highland Scottish clan of Norman,[5/4] origin, who held lands in the north of Scotland, the Orkney Islands and the Lothians, which they received from the Kings of Scotland. The chiefs of the clan, were The Barons of Roslin,[Ch 4] and later became The Earls of Orkney,[Ch 4] and later still, The Earls of Caithness.[Ch 4]

3.1 Origins of the clan

The Sinclairs were a noble family, which had its origins in Saint-clair-sur-epte,[16/2] in Normandy,[9/3] in France. They first came to England (before they came to Scotland) with William the Conqueror,[4/3] during his invasion of England. The name was originally "Saint-Clair", (taken from Saint-Clair-sur-epte). William of Saint Clair,,accompanied,Saint Margaret of Scotland,[125/1] daughter of Edward the Exile,[126/1] to Scotland in 1068, where she eventually married Malcolm III of Scotland. In return for his efforts, the king supposedly granted Sinclair The Barony of Roslin,[4.1] Scotland "in free heritage". Chief Sir Henry Sinclair, 2nd Baron of Roslin (1060–1110),[Ch 4] led a successful attack on England at The Battle of Alnwick (1093).[24/2] One of the earliest recorded Sinclairs in Scotland was Chief Henry of Saint-Clair/Sinclair, 3rd Baron of Roslin,[Ch 4] who obtained a charter for the lands of Herdmanston,[25/2] in Haddingtonshire in 1160. Chief William Saint Clair/ Sinclair, 4th Baron of Roslin,[Ch 4] witnessed a charter granted by King Stephen of England,[127] in 1135.

3.2 Profile

Clan Chief (current 2011)	Malcolm Ian Sinclair, 20th Earl of Caithness.
Chiefs motto	Commit thy work to God (sometimes styled as Latin "Revela Domino opera tua").
Clan plant badge	Whin (Gorse).
Crest badge	The crest badge is made up of the chief's heraldic crest and motto.
Lands	Midlothian, Orkney and Caithness.
Gaelic Name	Mac na Ceardadh or Singlear.

"No family in Europe beneath the rank of royalty boasts a higher antiquity, a nobler illustration, or a more romantic interest than that of St. Clair" Sir Bernard Burke,[128]–'A Genealogical and Heraldic Dictionary of the Peerage and Baronetage'. *"The Lordly line of high St. Clair"*– Sir Walter Scott. In olden times surnames were not used but the key family figure in the late 9th Century was a Norwegian, Rognvald,[Ch 4] Jarl,[129/1] of Moeri,[130/1] who, with King Harald Fairhair,[131/1] conquered the Orkney Isles and later Caithness and was created Jarl or Earl. One of his sons Einar,[4.2] succeeded to the title and established the line of Norse Jarls, most of whom owed allegance to both the Scandinavian and Scottish Monarchs, until 1470. Another Rollo,[7/2] conquered Neustria (Normandy) in France and his direct descendent was the 7th Duke of Normandy,[10/2] William the Conqueror, [4/3] who became King of England.

The name Sinclair probably comes from St Clair-sur-epte,[16/3] in Normandy,[9/3] and was established in Scotland in the 11th century when William St Clair, a close relative of William the Conqueror, was given the life Barony of Rosslyn, [23/3] near Edinburgh for services to the king. The link of the name Sinclair to Caithness and Orkney was established in the mid 14th century when Sir William St Clair,[Ch 4] of Roslin married Isabella daughter and heiress of Malise V,[132/1] Earl of Caithness. Although Caithness and Orkney is considered 'home' for the Clan, Sinclair families are found not just throughout the UK but worldwide. The main Scottish branches of the family (2011) are headed by the Earl of Caithness,[Ch 4] Earl of Rosslyn,[Ch 4] Lord Sinclair, Viscount Thurso and Sir Patrick Sinclair of Dunbeath.[133/1] However, given its history it is not surprising to find branches of the family in Norway, Sweden, France and Germany. Equally, Sinclairs have played and are still playing a prominent role in the history of Australia, Canada, New Zealand, South Africa and the United States of America.

Henry St Clair, 7th Baron of Rosslyn,[Ch 4] with his brother William his son William, and his kinsman John St Clair of Herdmanston,[25/3] and a Gregory St Clair, rendered homage to Edward I of England,[28/2] in 1296. However, in company with Sir Symon Fraser[134/1] of Neidpath Castle,[135] and John Comyn,[136/1] Earl of Buchan, he later won the Battle of Roslin,[Ch 3] against the English in 1303. Thereafter, the St Clairs fought for Robert the Bruce and in 1317 received a grant of the lands of Pentland,[29/2] as a reward. Through his mother, Isabella Forteith of Strathearn, Sir Henry St Clair, 9th Baron of Rosslyn,[4.1.09] became 42nd Jarl,[129/2] and 1st St Clair Prince of Orkney,[137] owing allegiance not only to the Scottish Crown but to the rulers of Norway. From his castle in Kirkwall, he embarked upon several voyages, including one to the Faroe Islands and Greenland, and another to Nova Scotia (Estotiland) and North America. His grandson, 3rd St Clair Prince of Orkney, had three marriages, the first to Lady Margaret Douglas, granddaughter of Robert III, by whom he had a son and four daughters, one of whom married the Duke of Albany, brother of James III. By the second marriage to Lady Marjorie Sutherland, a great-great-granddaughter of Robert I, he had six sons and seven daughters. After her death it is thought that he married for a third time, but the records are vague.

Apart from his building Rosslyn Chapel,[Ch 5] two significant actions influenced the fortunes of the St Clair family during the tenure of Prince William. In 1455, he exchanged The Earldom of Nithsdale,[138] which he had inherited through his mother, for The Earldom of Caithness.[Ch 4] In 1469, following the marriage of James III and Princess Margaret of Denmark,[139] the Orkney Islands were formally annexed by the Scottish Crown and William handed over The Earldom of Orkney,[Ch 4] in exchange for Ravenscraig Castle,[140/1] and lands in Fife. This meant that future St Clairs were ineligible to style themselves 'Prince,' and when Prince William died, his lands and titles were dispersed among his children, his eldest son by his first marriage acquiring the Dysart Barony,[141/1] his eldest son by his second marriage acquiring Rosslyn, and the second son by his second marriage becoming 2nd St Clair Earl of Caithness.[Ch 4]

It was at this time that the Caithness branch of the family began to spell their name Sinclair, although the Rosslyn,[23/2] branch continued with St Clair. The 2nd Earl of Caithness fought and died at the Battle of Flodden,[Ch 3] with 600 Highland Sinclairs. His descendants thereafter were of a wild disposition, the 4th Earl imprisoning and starving to death his own son for making peace with Clan Moray without his approval. George 6th Earl of Caithness,[Ch 4] burdened with inherited debts, was obliged to sell off parcels of family land. He died childless in 1676, whereupon the Caithness title eventually passed to George Sinclair of Keiss.[142/1] The 19th Earl of Caithness (1906–1965) was Commander-in-Chief of the newly independent Ceylon (Sri Lanka). Malcolm, 20th Earl of Caithness,[Ch 4],(1948-),served as Minister of State at the Home Office and Paymaster General in Margaret Thatcher's Government. Sir William St Clair of Rosslyn, (d.1331), son of the 6th Baron of Rosslyn,[Ch 4] accompanied Sir James Douglas,[143/1] on his expedition to Spain with the heart of Robert I.

William St Clair (d.1337) was Bishop of Dunkeld. He crowned Edward Balliol,[144] and rallied Scots against the English attack on Dunfermline. John Sinclair (d.1566) officiated at the wedding of Mary Queen of Scots,[145/1] and Lord Darnley.[146/1] George Sinclair (d.1696) was Professor of Philosophy at Glasgow University and was associated with the invention of the Diving Bell. He was author of *Satan's Visible World Discovered.* Sir John Sinclair of Ulbster,[35/2] (1754-1835) became President of the Board of Agriculture in 1798. Robert, 4th Earl of Rosslyn,[Ch4] (d.1890) was Ambassador Extraordinary to Madrid. Sir Archibald Sinclair, 1st Viscount Thurso (1890–1970) was leader of the British Liberal Party from 1935 to 1945. He was Secretary of State for Air in the Churchill Administration.

3.2.1 Places of Interest

Roslin, Midlothian	This picturesque village sprang up beside the 14th century castle and 15th century chapel, built by the St. Clairs of Rosslyn.[23/4] Rosslyn Chapel,[Ch 5] has recently attracted world wide interest from featuring in the best-selling novel, *The Da Vinci Code.*[147]
Castle of Mey,[5.4] Caithness	Built in 1568 by George, 5th Earl of Caithness. It is today probably best known for having been the private home and retreat of Her Majesty Queen Elizabeth the Queen Mother.
Keiss Castle,[5.8] Keiss, Caithness	Remnants of a small 16th century tower can be seen here. The 19th century castle nearby was the home of Sir William Sinclair, Founder and Pastor of the first Baptist Church in Scotland.
Noss Head, Wick, Caithness	The ruins of castles Sinclair.[5.1] (15th century) and Girnigoe (17th century) can be seen here. The estates were invaded in 1697 by Campbell of Glenorchy,[148/1] and both castles were destroyed.
Thurso Castle,[5.10] Thurso, Caithness	Sir John Sinclair of Ulbster,[35/2] (1754-1835), the well known agricultural improver, lived here.

3.2.2 The Sinclair tartans and crest

There are four main forms of Sinclair tartan; two red (formal) and two green (hunting).

Sinclair Hunting (Green) Ancient tartan
A subtle blend of blues/blue greens/ greys with white and red stripes

Sinclair Hunting (Green) Modern tartan
A bold blend of greens/blue greens with white and red stripes

Sinclair red ancient tartan
A subtle blend of blues, purples, pinks with white stripes

Sinclair red modern tartan
A bold blend of blues, purples, reds with white stripes

Sinclair Plant Badge - Whin (Gorse)
A yellow shrub

Sinclair Crest Badge

3.3 The Sinclairs/McNokairds

3.3.1 The early Sinclairs/McNokairds of Argyll

Were the Sinclairs of Argyllshire a totally different clan or tribe, or could there have been a connection between them and the Sinclairs, who came to England with William the Conqueror,[4/4] from Normandy [9/4] in 1066 (thus alluding to Viking [8/4] ancestry)? Perhaps they came from a totally different origin, one taking these artisans back to an earlier history in the Middle East? There were definitely 'Sinclairs' living in the area near Oban as early as the late 17th century. One practical explanation for these men in Argyll, might be the fact that Sir John Campbell of Glenorchy [148/2] had been made the Earl of Caithness in the 1670s after he had foreclosed on the debts of his Sinclair relative. This could have given Glenorchy plenty of time to choose some of the willing Sinclair men of Caithness for better employment in Argyll. One Duncan Sinclair was a tacksman,[55/3] (overseer) on a Campbell estate, while there is evidence of others being soldiers with Argyll regiments, in battles as far away as Spain, North America and South Africa. This might be a reasonable justification for finding Sinclairs in Argyllshire, but they were small in number compared to the MacNacaerds, who also occupied the area in that time frame and earlier.

Argyllshire is a very large county and the topography is extremely rugged. Old Scottish documents such as parish records and tenant lists, show that there were several MacNacaerds in some of the most remote and isolated areas, as well as the more populated towns and villages. Their occupations range from agricultural labourers to a burgess,[149/1] in Inverary,[150/1] but strangely, as yet, none have been found to be such an artisan as George Black describes in his book *"Scottish surnames: Their meaning and origin"*. Records of the name appear as early as 1297 (when Gregor Makenkerd agreed to serve Edward I of England,[28/2] in France). However, the name gradually converted to Sinclair in the early 18th century and within a few decades the name of MacNacaerd all but disappeared from the hills and glens of Argyll. If the MacNacaerds of Argyll were originally such craftsmen, where did they come from? Where did they learn this trade? Why would all the descendants of the original craftsmen decide to change their name from the Gaelic,[15/2] McNacaerd, to the Anglicized Sinclair, after several centuries of being employed in many different occupations? How would the McNacaerds, even in those remote areas of the Highlands and the Islands, have come up with the same name?

Was the name change imposed on them following the unsuccessful rebellions of the first half of the 18th century, in an effort to eradicate Gaelic,[15/2] names, bagpipes, and even tartans?[5.6] Can it really be as simple as the word, "tinkler" rhymes with the Gaelic pronunciation of "Sinclair"? Why not "Campbell", the name of their landlords and overlords? How is it possible that the McNokairds of Argyll became known by the surname

Sinclair? For it is certain that the McNokairds of Argyll and their descendants became Sinclairs in the late 17th and early 18th centuries. The transformation of the name McNokaird to Sinclair was not as strange and convoluted as may first appear. Instead the transition can be easily shown, its various stages occurring through the three languages that have been used in Scotland over the centuries: Gaelic,[15/4] Scots and English. The name change took place on both a phonetic level and a literal, or meaning, level. The same transformation occurred with the *Gaelic Mac an fhucadair*, which meant *son of the fuller of cloth.* The phonetic Scots spelling became MacNucator, while the Scots meaning was 'wauker'. The English version of this name became Walker. Thus, many of the Walkers in Scotland, descend from the clan Mac an fhucadair. According to George F. Black's Surnames of Scotland: Their Meaning, Origin and History, McNokaird roots are in the Gaelic "Mac na cearda", which means son of the smith. Specifically, a cerd worked in brass. Anciently, the ceard was a craftsman par excellence. Black states that these craftsmen created many of the fine old Highland plaid brooches of brass which are exhibited at Edinburgh's Scottish National Museum of Antiquities. However, *"the term was degraded and applied to the poorest class of itinerant artificers, patchers of pots and pans and equated with Scots tinker."* Black then quotes part of Robert Burns' poem The Jolly Beggar, which goes:-

"When thus the caird address'd her:
My bonie lass, I work in brass,
A tinkler is my station:
I've travell'd round all Christian ground
In this my occupation;
I've taen the gold, an been enrolled
In many a noble squadron;
But vain they search'd when off I march'd
To go an clout the cauldron."

So at the time Robert Burns wrote the poem (1780s - 1790s) we know that the term *caird* was still associated with *tinkler.* One can imagine that this nickname derived from the actual tinkling sound made by the pots and pans as they were being re-shaped, pounded, molded and patched. *'Tinkler'* replaced *ceard* and came to be negatively associated with wandering gypsy-like pot-patchers. The word has further been refined to the English *'tinker'.*

'Tinkler was found only once in the Argyll parish records as a surname: Duncan Tinkler, son of Duncan Tinkler and Cristin NcTaylor was christened on 6th Sept. 1668 in Inveraray,[150/2] and Glenaray.[151] No further reference to this family was found. A handful of other Tinklers were found in Renfrew and Stirling. Therefore, it seems "*tinkler*" became a slang term, while Sinclair became the surname for those descendants of the early Mac na ceards or McNokairds. The McNokairds lived in northern Argyll and into present-day Perth as well, whose western borders adjoin Argyll.

An article printed in The Kist,[152] made reference to Sinclairs, known as Mcnokairds, who lived at Coulfochan, at the foot of Shira Glen,[153] in Argyll. *"Their land stretched from the south end of the Dhuloch to Portinstonich, where the salmon for the table at Inveraray Castle was netted. The house of the Sinclairs has long since disappeared but was probably sited near the present-day lodge house at the Boshang Gate, entrance to the Castle avenue. This family were not really Sinclairs at all but McNokairds."* Parish registers in Inveraray & Glenaray, are some of the earliest extant for Argyll. Available documentation does not show Sinclairs living in Coulfochan but instead reveal that McNokairds did, indeed live in Coulfochan: Donald McNokaird and Ann McNokaird, of Cualfochan, christened their son Duncan on 25th Apr. 1860, while Duncan McNokerd and Mary McInturner lived in Cuilfochan in 1704. Other residences for McNokairds noted in parish registers include, Brenthoill/Bromhoil, Auchinbreck, Bralockan, Killian, Penmore, Bracherban and Stronshiray (spelling questionnable on all).

Analysis of families in Argyll reveal two in particular that appear to be the closest thing to "proof'" of the name change. The first family is that of Malcolm McNokaird and Ann Crawford, who were "of Stronshiray" in Inveraray, & Glenaray, parishes.Their first three children (daughters) were: Jonet, christened 17th Apr. 1705; Margaret, christened 4th May 1707; and Mary, christened 30th May 1708. Then Malcolm Sinclair and Ann Crawford "of Stronshiray", had the following two sons christened under the name Sinclair, not McNokaird: Donald Sinclair, christened 7th March 1721; and Patrick Sinclair, christened 25th August 1723. The coincidence of same names and same locale, with the only variation being the surnames of McNokaird and Sinclair, cannot be quickly dismissed. Indeed, it suggests a definite time period when Malcolm's surname underwent its transformation. (The gaps in birth years of children, is explained away by many years when christening records weren't kept and various other losses). The second suggestion or "proof'", was also found in parish registers and is illustrated in the following: Archibald Sinclair, son of Neil Sinclair married Janet Reid, sister of John Reid on 14th November 1720. When Archibald Sinclair and Janet Reid christened their daughter Mary, on 13th Nov. 1721, the witnesses were recorded as John Reid and Neil McNokaird. It appears that the father Neil was known interchangeably as both Sinclair and McNokaird. McNokairds were found extensively in the parish records for Perth as well, under the spelling McIncaird. (A few McNokairds were also found in Stirling and Moray Shires). The same name change took place in Perth as well, although the use of the McNokaird name continued here later than it did in Argyll.

It was in Perth parish records, that definitive proof of the name change was discovered. Donald Mcnakeard, "alias Sinclar", married Kathren Anderson, on 8th Dec. 1739, in Kenmore,[154] parish, Perth. Six years later, John Sinclair, born to Donald Sinclair "alias McIncaird" and Katrine Anderson, was christened 7th January 1746, in Kenmore. The distinction that Donald was known by both names, first McNakeard and later by Sinclair, leaves no doubt that the name change did take place. The use of the surname McNokaird died out by about 1750. The parish registers and other records show the rising use of Sinclair in its place.

The increase of Sinclair appearances in Argyll records is due to this change-over, more than sudden populations of Sinclairs appearing in Argyll. The name transformation also explains the close relationship between the "Sinclairs" of Argyll and the Campbells, at a time when the Campbells and members of the traditional Clan Sinclair,[Ch. 3] were engaged in a dispute over the title and lands of Caithness. This dispute culminated in The Bloody Battle at Altimarlach,[Ch 3] near Wick,[155/1] between these two clans. It is certain that some of the Sinclairs in Argyll (possibly those listed as 'strangers' in the Cowal peninsula,[96/4]), came in response to advertisements and demand for labour and were members of the traditional clan Sinclair whose origins can be found in Caithness, the Orkneys and Lothian. However, most of the Sinclairs in Argyll are descendants of the craftsmen par excellence, who were members of the clan *Mac na cearda.*

3.3.2 The Sinclairs/McNokairds on the island of Islay

Situated near the southern end of the Hebrides, the Isle of Islay,[87/3] has long been reknowned for its fine peaty whiskys and good farmland. Historically however, Islay was the pivotal centre of the prosperous north Atlantic islands, including parts of Ireland and the Argyllshire mainland which became The Seat of Lords of the Isles. The ruling MacDonalds, owed allegiance of their mainland possessions to The King of the Scots, but to The King of Norway for their island possessions. Once the MacDonalds were defeated at The Battle of Largs,[Ch 3] in 1263, the islands were eventually ceded to Scotland. Yet, they maintained power in that part of Scotland as *Angus MacDonald* was a strong ally of Robert the Bruce. *"He was always a follower of King Robert the Bruce in all his wars, assisting him with his men in recovering the hold of Dundonald and another castle in Carrick,*[75/2] *from the English. The King stayed with him half a year in Sadell in Kintyre,*[84/2] *sent his galleys and men with him to Ireland, transported Edward Bruce,*[156/1] *very often to Ireland and furnished him with necessaries for his expedition."* It is believed that MacDonald supplied Bruce with 1,500 warriors at Bannockburn,[Ch 3] for which he was handsomly rewarded, including the post of Honour (The Right of the Royal Standard). Thus the MacDonalds 'reigned' and held court at Finlaggan,[157/1] a splendid castle built on an island loch on Islay, and where Council sat and administered their domain until the early 17th century, when it came into the hands of The Earl of Argyll.

What has this to do with 'Sinclair'? There is no documentary evidence that there was Sinclair on Islay prior to 1745 but many by that name thereafter. However, the name *Gilchrist McNarkerde* appears as early as 1541 in The Exchequer Rolls of Scotland,[158/1] (rentals), for a property called Braid in the west of Islay and several tenants with the surname of MacNokaird, occur in later rentals on the adjacent farm, Gearach, near the site of the castle at Finlaggan. Could this Gilchrist McNarkerde tenant have been a craftsman of such fine brooches and metalwork now displayed in the Museum of Antiquities in Edinburgh? Most of the records indicate that the jewellery was found the same parish where this man lived and there is coincidentally, a small valley called the *Gleann na Cairdaich*, or *Glen of the Smiddy*, only a mile to the north of Braid. Who else would employ such artisans and craftsmen of fine jewellery and metalwork but the powerful Lords of the Isles?, The earliest Islay,[87/3] "Sinclair" record found, was an inscription on a gravestone near Bridgend for an Archibald Sinclair who died in 1749 age, 35 years. Since this is the crucial time between the use of both names, it was important to find out who this early Sinclair was and where he came from. Was he an 'incomer' or a native to the island - a man who changed his Gaelic,[15/3] surname to an English translation? Mentioned in the 1741 tenant list, was an Archibald McNakaird, of Nerebie farm in Kilarrow,[159] parish. The Stent Book,[160] recording of municipal proceedings on Islay in 1745, calls for the appointment of Archibald McNokard in Neriby, to search neighbouring houses for stolen property. If this is the same person as Archibald Sinclair who died in 1749, it might appear that his neighbours were not at all pleased to be spied upon! This Archibald's grandson, also named 'Archibald Sinclair', eventually left Islay for Glasgow and started his own printing establishment in 1848.

3.4 Septs

The clan has the following septs:-

3.4.1 Budge

The Budges of Trotternish,[161] Skye, are descended from a very old Caithness family, who settled originally on the lands of Toftingall,[162] Caithness, around the 14th or 15th century. According to Hugh Macdonald, a Skye Sennachie,[163] to The House of Sleat,[164] who wrote in the reign of Charles II, the Budges came to Scotland from Ireland as part of the dowry of Margaret, daughter of Guy O'Kane, an Irish chieftain, when she married Angus Og of Islay,[165] the friend of Robert Bruce. Her "tocher" consisted of 140 men of different surnames from her father's kingdom. Listed among these are the Butikes and Budges of Caithness. The coat of arms [41/3] was recor- ded in The Public Register of all Arms and Bearings in Scotland,[166] *Vol.i, folio 119*, on 8th Feb. 1703, in the name of Donald Budge of Toftingall.

3.4.2 Caird

This interesting surname is derived from the Gaelic,[15/3] "ceard", meaning a craftsman, an artistan and later a travelling tinker. In an ancient Irish manuscript, *Cerdd*, is referred to as a "worker in brass". Many of the fine old Highland plaid brooches of brass, specimens of which are shown in *The Scottish National Museum of Antiquities* in Edinburgh, are believed to be the work of men of this class. Individuals bearing this surname are found recorded as early as the 13th Century. The first recorded spelling of the family name is shown to be that of Gilfolan Kerd, which was dated 1275, in a "Calendar of Documents relating to Scotland", during the reign of King Alexander 111 of Scotland 1249–1286.

3.4.3 Clouston

The surname of Clouston was a locational name 'of Clouston' in Stenness, Orkney. Local names usually denoted where a man held his land and indicated where he actually lived. The name was originally derived from the Old Norman Klostaor and was brought into Scotland in the wake of the Norman Invasion of 1066.[6/2] Early records of the name mention William Cloustath (councilman), who was recorded in Stenness in the year 1500.

3.4.4 Clyne

The word "clyne" is derived from Gaelic, "claon", meaning slope or hillside. As a surname it is not officially recognised as a Sept but it comes from the place named Clyne in Sutherlandshire. Spelling variations include Clyne, Clynde and Cline. Sir William Clyne is the first recorded chief of the family line, in the year 1315. Sir Wiliam held the lands of Cathboll,[167] in Tarbat,[168] of the Bishop of Moray.[169] In 1456 William of Clyne oversaw the transition of the Earldom of Sutherland to John, the son and Heir of Robert, the 6th Earl of Sutherland. Another related branch also of Caithness, were notable for their presence at Culloden in 1745.[Ch 3]

3.4.5 Laird

Conventionally Lairds are first recorded in the south of Scotland in the 13th century, when one Roger Lawird of Berwick, made an agreement with the Abbey of Kelso relating to his land of Waldefgat,[170] in 1257. William Laird of Glenhuntly had a Grant of Arms from The Lord King of Arms,[39/3] in 1777. William was one of the shipbuilding family, later to establish themselves in Birkenhead. Glenhuntly was in the area of the Port of Glagow, in Renfrewshire. William Laird's Arms have The Stag's Head of Rollo,[7/2] as the crest. Rollo was a real warlord. He was a Viking,[8/2] with a large following and raided in the North Sea to the extent that the French King granted him the land that became Normandy,[9/2] and gave rise to the Norman people.[5/4] It was the Vikings who dominated the seas in the 900s and 1000s and their domination continued until The Battle of Largs.[Ch 3] For 600 years, Scotland down to Perth was part of the Kingdom of Norway. So perhaps the Arms referred to, are those of William Laird of Glenhuntly and the warlord is a memory of Rollo, which points back to Norway. It is the Sinclairs who are the direct descendants of Rollo. So it is possible the Lairds, in Caithness at least, have always been alongside the Sinclairs.

3.4.6 Linklater

The Linklater surname was a habitation name, taken on from one of the places so named in the Orkneys. The place name derived from the Old Norse "lyng" meaning "heather" and "klettr", or "rock" which were combined to make the Old Norse name "Lynglettr." First found in the Orkneys, where the original form of the name was Linklet. Today, Linklet and Linklater are both located in the Orkney Islands. Linklater is located in South Ronalday, while Linklet is located on North Ronaldsay. Records of Linklater in South Ronaldsay date back as far as 1500, where it appears as Linclet and Linklet in 1596. Linklater was also found in North Sandwick, where it was listed as Lynkclet in 1500.

3.4.7 Lyall

This most interesting surname, found early in Scotland, may derive from two possible sources. Firstly, it may come from the Old Norse personal name "Liulfr", composed of an uncertain first element and "ulfr", wolf. Alternatively the surname maybe a hypocoristic,[171] of "Lyon", which comes from two possible origins, from either the personal name,"Leo", which was also a nickname from the Latin "leo", lion, or from a place called Lyons (-la-Foret) in Eure, Normandy,[9/4] recorded in the 1st Century B.C. as "Lugdunum", from Gaulish elements, meaning "raven" and "hill fort". The name is also found in the modern idiom as Lyal, Lyel, Lyell and Liell. The first recorded spelling of the family name, is shown to be that of Johannes filius Lyelli, which which was dated 1329, "The Exchequer Rolls of Scotland 1264-1600",[157/2] during the reign of King Robert Bruce, ruler of Scotland, 1306–1329.

3.4.8 Mason

The surname Mason derives from the occupation of stonemason (the word itself coming from the French masson). A mason was generally recognized as someone who had already served his time as an apprentice to a master craftsman. Mason craft guilds may have been the origin of the freemasonry,[172] which began in Scotland in the early 18th century, but there is no strong evidence that this was the case.

3.4.9 Purdie

This surname, Purdie, was a nickname of French origin - pourdieu - meaning 'By God's grace'. The name was brought into England in the wake of the Norman Conquest of 1066.[6/4]

3.4.10 Snoddy

Snoddy was first used in the Scottish/English Borderlands by The Strathclyde Briton. The first Snoddy family lived at the town of Snodgrass, in the county of Ayrshire. The name of this place is derived from the Northern Old English word snod, meaning smooth and grass, meaning grass. Medieval,[54/6] Scottish names are rife with variations. This is due to the fact that scribes in that era spelled according to the sound of words rather than any set of rules. Snoddy has been spelled Snodgrass, Snodgers, Snedgrass, Snadgrass and others. First found in Ayrshire, where they held a family seat from very ancient times, some say well before The Norman Conquest,[6/2] and the arrival of Duke William at Hastings,[4/2] in 1066 A.D.

3.4.11 Peace

Spelling variations of this family name include Peace, Pease, Paise and others. First found in the Orkney islands where they held a family seat from early times. The first records of the Peace family appeared on the early census rolls taken by the early Kings of Scotland, to determine the rate of taxation of their subjects.

3.5 Archives

The archives for The Sinclair Family Papers, are maintained by the Archives of the University of Glasgow (GUAS).

3.6 Scottish-Norwegian Wars

3.6.1 The Battle of Largs

Chief Sir Henry Sinclair, 5th Baron of Roslin (1190– 1270),[Ch 4] led the soldiers of King Alexander III of Scotland, to repel the last Norwegian invasion. Today, a column marks the spot where the battle took place. Every September a Viking,[8/2] festival celebrates the event. It was an engagement fought between the armies of Norway and Scotland, near the present-day town of Largs in North Ayrshire, on the Firth of Clyde in Scotland, on 2nd Oct. 1263. It was the most important military engagement of the Scottish-Norwegian War. The Norwegian forces were led by King Håkon Håkonsson,[173/1] and the Scottish forces by King Alexander III. The result was inconclusive but in the long term favoured the Scots.

3.6.1.1 Background

The Kingdom of Súðreyjar ("Southern Islands"), comprising the Inner and Outer Hebrides and Kintyre [84/2] and the Kingdom of Man, had been under the suzerainty,[50/2] of Norway since about 1100, its kings vassals [174/1] of the King of Norway. Since the 1240s, the Scottish King Alexander II, had been attempting to buy the islands from the Norwegian King Håkon Håkonsson, but he consistently refused. Alexander's successor, Alexander III, continued this policy but again, King Håkon refused. In the summer of 1262, Scottish forces under the Earl of Ross, launched raids against the Isle of Skye. News of this reached the Norwegian King, together with reports that the Scottish king was planning to conquer all the islands. Håkon responded by equipping a large conscripted leidang-fleet.[175/1] According to Icelandic annals Håkon led *the biggest fleet everto leave Norway* which left Bergen for Scotland in July 1263. In the Hebrides, *Håkon's*,[173/1] fleet linked up with the forces of King Magnus III of Man,[176/1] and King Dubhghall mac Ruaidhri of the Hebrides.[177/1] Historians estimate that the size of his fleet after this was probably over 120 ships, with a force of between 12,000 and 20,000 After establishing control of the Hebrides, King Håkon anchored his fleet by the Isle of Arran,[178] in the Firth of Clyde where he was approached by envoys from the Scottish King, opening peace talks. The talks dragged on without producing results and in the end Håkon broke off the talks. He sent the Kings Magnus and Dougal, with 40 ships,

Map of the Firth of Clyde area

Loch Long

up Loch Long and into Loch Lomond with a part of the fleet to loot. The main body of the fleet moved closer to the mainland between the islands of Cumbrae [179] and Largs,[180] Cunninghame.[181]

3.6.1.2 Events

While anchored here, the Norwegian fleet was surprised by stormy weather. Five longships,[182/1] and a trading cog,[183] were driven ashore on the mainland by the storm. They were attacked with ranged weapons by a small number of Scots, but no serious fighting ensued. The next day, 2nd October, King Håkon went ashore with some of his lendmenn,[184] presumably to stave off further attacks, until the stranded ships could be brought free. The lendmann, Ogmund Crouchdance,[185/1] took control of a hill overlooking the beach with about 200 men, the force on the beach probably numbered about 600 more. During the day a Scottish army approached. The Scottish army was divided into three parts, the right led by Alexander Stewart High Steward of Scotland,[186/1] consisting of men from, Argyll, Atholl,[187/1] Lennox,[188/1] and Galloway,[188/1] the left led by Patrick de Dunbar, Earl of Dunbar consisting of men from Lothian, Fife, Merse,[189] and Berwick and the centre led by King Alexander III, consisting of men of Perth, Angus, Mearns,[190] and the northern counties.

The saga states that the Scottish force included 500 knights in armour on horseback, and a large body of foot soldiers so that the Norwegians were out-numbered ten to one. If the saga is accurate it would mean the Scottish army numbered about 8,000 men, compared to the 800 Norwegian troops onshore. However, it has been suggested that this was merely referring to a particular Norwegian stand, not the entire Norwegian force, as it is unlikely that the Scots had 8000 troops.

King Håkon,[173/3] was transported to safety on board his ship. Ogmund Crouchdance's,[185/3] force on the hill started to retreat toward the beach, in order not to be cut off. While retreating down the hill, they were attacked by the vanguard of the Scottish force. The retreat was in danger of becoming a rout, as the Norwegians on the beach started scrambling to get into their boats to get back to their ships. Several boats sank as a result of overcrowding. However, the Norwegians managed to restore order in their ranks and make a stand on the beach. King Håkon was unable to send large reinforcements on land because of the storm, but one ship from the main fleet managed to reach the shore. When the ship arrived, the Scots withdrew back up the hill. There followed a lengthy, long-distance battle, with bows and stone-throwing but the Scottish force ultimately retreated, whereupon the Norwegians immediately boarded their boats and withdrew to the main fleet.

3.6.1.3 Aftermath

The saga implies that the Scottish cavalry had not been in action and it is also doubtful whether the full body of the foot soldiers was brought to bear. Similarly the main body of the Norwegian force were on board their ships, prevented by the storm from joining battle. The Norwegians went back on land the day after to retrieve their dead and burn the stranded long-ships,[182/3] which they were able to do unmolested. The saga names seven of the Norwegian casualties. It also names one dead Scottish knight, Perus, but also states that the Norwegians could not know how many Scots had been killed, as they had already retrieved their bodies. Within a few days the Norwegian fleet left the Firth of Clyde. Winter approaching, the army was short of provisions and with a large Scottish force intact on land, looting for provisions was not a tenable option Håkon,[173/3] sailed North. His vassals,[174/3] Magnus III,[176/3] and Dougal,[177/2] went back to their own holdings and Håkon went to Orkney for the winter. Most of his leidang-fleet,[175/2] sailed back to Norway. Largs had not been a crushing military defeat for Håkon but it meant that he had not been able to win a decisive victory before the winter, something he would probably have had to do, in order to achieve his objectives. As it was, it remains an open question whether Håkon would have been able to renew the fighting in the spring of 1264. He fell ill while staying in the Bishop's Palace in Kirkwall and died on 15th Dec. 1263. The following year, King Alexander III, successfully invaded the Hebrides. In 1265, negotiations between Scottish envoys and Håkon's successor, King Magnus the Lawmender,[191] led to agreement that suzerainty,[50/2] over the Hebrides and Man, was to pass to the Scottish King, in return for a lump sum of 4000 marks and subsequently 100 marks annually in perpetuity. This was confirmed in The Treaty of Perth,[192] signed in 1266. Norway retained control over Orkney.

Long ship

3.6.1.4 Historical views

Scottish historians of later centuries, grossly exaggerated the scale of The Battle of Largs. George Buchanan, in the 16th century, claimed that the Norwegians had landed 20,000 men, of whom 16,000 had been killed along with 5,000 Scots. Today, historians view the encounter as hardly a battle at all, but merely a skirmish. The main source to the battle, is a lengthy passage in Håkon Håkonssons saga. This saga was written on order of King Håkon's son Magnus and so obviously presents the events, purely from the Norwegian perspective. However, as it was written within five years of the events and in all likelihood based on conversations with participants in the battle, it is considered a fairly reliable source, as regards factual details. Interpretation of these facts have varied widely however, with the battle traditionally being seen as a Scottish victory in Scotland and a Norwegian victory in Norway. Modern-day historians generally agree, that the "battle" amounted to something of a draw. In the long run however, this result was satisfactory for the Scots, whereas the Norwegians needed to win.

3.6.1.5 Viking festival in Largs

The battle is commemorated in modern-day Largs by a monument at the sea-front, in the shape of a tall cylinder with a conical top akin to a Round Tower – inevitably, it is known as "The Pencil". Once a year, Largs holds a Viking festival, which used to be a Scottish celebration of the defence of their land but has now been turned into a friendly celebration of both nations, with dignitaries of Norway making regular attendances, symbolizing friendship between the two countries. The festival includes a parade, stalls, food, armoury and a symbolic battle re-enactment of the landing of the Norwegians at the pencil.

The Largs "Pencil" stands just over a mile south of the town centre.

3.6.2 The Battle of Lewes

Simon de Montfort, 6th Earl of Leicester,[193/1] England, had gained great influence over other barons and bishops. They drew up The Provisions of Oxford.[194/1] Henry III,[195/1] objected. Civil war broke out. The rebellious barons won, capturing the King. After years of conflict, the Crown was returned to his son Edward. King Alexander III of Scotland,had ordered Sir William Sinclair to assist King Henry III in a bloody victory. Sinclair escaped unharmed. The Battle was one of two main battles of the conflict, known as The Second Barons' War.[196] It took place at Lewes in Sussex, on 14th May 1264. It marked the high point of the career of Simon de Montfort, 6th Earl of Leicester, and made him the "uncrowned King of England". The battle occurred because of the vacillation of King Henry III, who was refusing to honour the terms of The Provisions of Oxford, an agreement he had signed with his barons led by Montfort in 1258.The King was encamped at St. Pancras Priory with a force of infantry but his son, Prince Edward (later King Edward I,[28/3]) commanded the cavalry at Lewes Castle,[197] a mile to the north. A night march enabled Montfort's forces to surprise Prince Edward and take the high ground of the Sussex Downs overlooking the town of Lewes, in preparation for battle. They wore white crosses as their distinguishing emblem. The royalist army, perhaps as much as twice the size of Montfort's, was led by Edward on the right and the King's brother Richard of Cornwall on the left, while the King himself commanded the central battalion. Having led his men out from the castle to meet the enemy, Edward gained early success but unwisely pursued a retreating force to the north, thus sacrificing the chance of overall victory. Meanwhile, Montfort defeated the remainder of the royal army led by the king and Cornwall. On being defeated, Cornwall decided to take refuge in the Priory. He was unable to reach the Priory so he hid in a windmill where, upon his discovery, he was taunted with cries of *"Come down, come down, thou wicked miller!"*. All three royals were eventually captured and by imprisoning the King, Montfort, became the de facto ruler of England. The King was forced to sign the so-called Mise of Lewes.[198] Though the document has not survived, it is clear that Henry was forced to accept The Provisions of Oxford,[194/2] while Prince Edward remained hostage to the barons. This put Montfort in a position of ultimate power, which would last until Prince Edward's escape and and Montfort's subsequent defeat at The Battle of Evesham,[199] in August 1265.

Monument to the Battle of Lewes

3.7 Wars of Scottish Independence

3.7.1 The Battle of Dunbar

Sir William Sinclair of Rosslyn,[23/4] was captured and died later, probably in The Tower of London.[200/1] Henry his son was also captured and later sent to St. Briavel Castle.[201] The Battle was the only significant field action in the campaign of 1296 to punish King John Balliol,for his refusal to support English military action in France.

3.7.1.1 Background

After the sack of Berwick-upon-Tweed, Edward rushed to complete the conquest of Scotland, but remained in the town for a month, supervising the strengthening of its defences. On 5th April, he received a message from King John renouncing his homage, to which he remarked, more in contempt than anger, "O foolish knave! What folly he commits. If he will not come to us we will go to him." The next objective in the campaign was the Earl of March's castle at Dunbar, a few miles up the coast from Berwick. March was with the English, but his wife, Marjory Comyn, sister of the Earl of Buchan, (John Comyn,[136/2]) did not share her husband's political loyalties and allowed her fellow Scots to occupy the castle. Edward,[28/2] sent one of his chief lieutenants, John de Warenne, 6th Earl of Surrey,[202/1] John Balliol's, own father-in-law, northwards with a strong force of knights to invest the stronghold. The defenders sent messages to King John, bivouacked with the main body of his army at nearby Haddington, asking for urgent assistance. In response the army, or a large part of it, advanced to the rescue of Dunbar. John, who was showing even less skill as a commander than he had as a king, did not accompany it. The campaign of 1296 was now to enter its final phase.

3.7.1.2 Battle

There is little evidence to suggest that Dunbar was anything other than an action between two bodies of mounted men-at-arms (armoured cavalry). Surrey's, force seems to have comprised one formation (out of four) of the English cavalry; the Scots force lead in part by Comyns probably represented the greater part of their cavalry element. The two forces came in sight of each other on 27th April. The Scots occupied a strong position on some high ground to the west. To meet them, Surrey's cavalry had to cross a gully intersected by the Spot Burn. As they did so their ranks broke up, and the Scots, deluded into thinking the English were leaving the field, abandoned their position in a disorderly downhill charge, only to find that Surrey's forces had reformed on Spottsmuir and were advancing in perfect order. The English routed the disorganised Scots in a single charge. The action was brief and probably not very bloody, since the only casualty of any note was a minor Lothian knight, Sir Patrick Graham, though about 100 Scottish lords, knights and men-at-arms were taken prisoner. According to one English source over ten thousand Scots died at The Battle of Dunbar, however this is probably a confusion with the casualties incurred at the storming of Berwick. The survivors fled westwards to the safety of Selkirk Forest. The following day King Edward appeared in person and Dunbar castle surrendered. Some important prisoners were taken: John Comyn, Earl of Buchan,[136/3] and the earls of Atholl,[187/2] Ross and Menteith,[203/1] together with 130 knights and esquires. All were sent into captivity in England.

3.7.1.3 Aftermath

The battle of Dunbar effectively ended the war of 1296 with the English winning. The remainder of the campaign was little more than a grand mopping-up operation. James, the hereditary High Steward of Scotland,[186/2] surrendered the important fortress at Roxburgh without attempting a defence, and others were quick to follow his example. Only Edinburgh Castle,[204] held out for a week against Edward's siege engines.[205] A Scottish garrison sent out to help King John, who had fled north to Forfar, were told to provide for their own safety. Edward himself, true to his word, advanced into central and northern Scotland in pursuit of King John. Stirling Castle,[206/1] which guarded the vital passage across the River Forth was deserted save for a janitor who stayed behind to hand the keys to the English. John reached Perth on 21st June, where he received messages from Edward asking for peace. John Balliol, in surrendering, submitted himself to a protracted abasement. At Kincardine Castle on 2nd July he confessed to rebellion and prayed for forgiveness. Five days later in the kirkyard of Stracathro he abandoned the treaty with the French. The final humiliation came at Montrose on 8th July. Dressed for the occasion John was ceremoniously stripped of the vestments of royalty. Anthony Bek, the Bishop of Durham ripped the red and gold arms of Scotland from his surcoat, thus bequeathing to history the nickname *Toom Tabard* (empty coat) He and his son Edward were sent south into captivity. Soon after, the English king followed, carrying in his train The Stone of Scone,[207] and other relics of Scottish nationhood.

3.7.2 The Battle of Roslin

Scots under Henry Sinclair and John Comyn III,[208] Lord of Badenoch,[209/1] defeated an English force at Roslin Glen,[210] in two or possibly three separate engagements. It was a battle of The First War of Scottish Independence, taking place on 24th February 1303 at Roslin,[23/3] Scotland. Three thousand troops, under Sir John Comyn, hid in the woods on the west bank of the River Esk whilst the remaining five thousand commanded by Sir Symon Fraser,[134/2] crossed the river and circled to the southeast, guided by the Prior. It was dark and cloudy early on 24th February as they formed a crescent formation behind Sir John Seagrave's,[211/1] encampment, on high ground east of the river, before gradually tightening the crescent on the sleeping encampment. The Scots were able to maintain the element of surprise until the very last moment when they fell upon the camp with such ferocity that many English were killed in their sleep. In the confusion some English tried to escape into the forest towards the southwest, the flat area or haugh below the castle, only to be confronted by Comyn's,[208/2] force that had lain in ambush. The English losses were so great and so sudden that Seagrave surrendered himself and the survivors to avoid total annihilation. The Scots had won the first phase of the battle at very little cost. The few wounded were tended to by the women of the Sinclairs of Rosslyn,[23/11] in the grounds of the castle, where Rosslyn Chapel now stands.

After a hasty meal, the Scots took up their second battle positions, to the northwest of Roslin. They formed a line of battle on the summit of the Langhill and watched the second English force, under Ralph de Confrey,[212/1] approach from the direction of the Ramsay's castle of Dalhousie,[213] having abandoned their siege. With virtually no knowledge of the area or terrain, the English army charged up the Langhill, only to be met by volleys of arrows from the Scottish archers which broke the charge, and threw the English into total confusion. This caused the charging English soldiers to wheel towards the north little realising that they were heading towards a steep ravine, with a stream at its foot. The force of numbers in the rout created a juggernaut effect and most of the fleeing English fell or were pushed over the precipice, onto the troops and horses that had already fallen; driven by Scots pikes,[214/1] and archers to their deaths, and in such numbers that it is said the burn became choked with the dead and dying. Heavy cavalry horses, soldiers with weapons and equipment, became a deadly entangled mass. Ralph de Confrey, the commander of the force died with his men at the bottom of the ravine. The carnage was so terrible that very few survived. Most of the English captives had to be killed upon hearing of the approach of the third section of the English force, as the Scots lacked the men to guard them and it was too dangerous to risk having them alive to their rear. The Scots then moved northeast along the River Esk and positioned themselves near the top of a steep bank overlooking the River Esk, close by the village of Polton. Now exhausted by their efforts; a march through the night with little food or rest and two fierce conflicts, even with the elation of victory, they were at the point of collapse. Prior Abernethy,[215] had foreseen such an eventuality and in the morning before the second engagement, he had sent a small party of his Cistercians,[216] to erect a huge St Andrew's Cross, made of wood and canvas, on the highest point on the Pentland Hills.[29/3] Being February the sun was low in the sky, illuminating the cross on the hill, giving it the appearance of a fiery cross. The Prior delivered an inspiring address reminding them of the English King's persecution of Scotland, of the sacking of Berwick, the desecration of Scone Abbey,[217] and the history of the Scots nation before instructing the Scots to turn towards the Pentlands, pointing out the cross and saying that it was a sign from the Lord that they were fighting under the banner of heaven. Calling them to kneel in prayer the prior gave them benediction and absolution from their sins. Thus so inspired the Scots awaited the next battle refreshed, if not physically certainly spiritually.

Unaware of the destruction of Ralph de Confreys,[212/2] force, the English third group under Sir Robert Neville, had come on from Borthwick Castle,[218] near Catcune in the valley of Gorebridge, by way of Rosewell and along the river valley, making their way along the cart-road, which followed the glen. Making full use of the topography, the Scots positioned themselves at Mountmarle overlooking the road; to the west and right of the English force. To the east and left of the English were the steep cliffs of the Glen, dropping down vertically some one hundred feet to the River Esk. From their elevated position the Scottish archers wreaked havoc; creating panic in the English ranks. The ensuing Scottish charge down from the high ground further panicked the English and drove them over the precipitous cliffs to their deaths.

Thousands were killed without ever being able to strike a blow; many were killed their swords unsheathed. So incredible had been the carnage that day that Sir Symon Fraser,[134/2] the Scottish Commander, called on his troops to give quarter and allow the few survivors to escape with their lives. So total was the victory it was later claimed, only ten per cent of the entire English force ever made it back to England. Sir John Seagrave,[211/2] and Ralph de Manton, the English paymaster and other captured knights who survived, were ransomed. Soldiers who were captured were released without their weapons and allowed to return south of the border after they had sworn an oath never again to take up arms against Scotland. Despite the unsupported claims of the 15th century chronicler, Walter Bower, there is no evidence to indicate that Roslin was a battle between large armies, but a clash between relatively modest forces of men-at-arms; the sort of action that was absolutely typical of Scottish-English warfare in the late 13th and early 14th centuries. It would seem that there were at least two and possibly three separate actions, resulting in a clear victory for the Scots.

3.7.3 The Battle of Loudoun Hill

Scots under Henry Sinclair defeat the English. The / Battle was fought in May 1307 between a Scots force led by Robert Bruce, and the English commanded by Aymer de Valence.[219/1] It took place beneath Loudoun Hill, in Ayrshire, and ended in a victory for Bruce. It was Bruce's first major military victory.

Commemorative Loudoun Hill summit stone

3.7.3.1 A Royal Fugitive

Bruce and Valence had first met in combat the previous year, at The Battle of Methven,[220/1] just outside Perth, where Bruce's lack of preparedness and his somewhat conventional military tactics, had brought him to the edge of disaster and beyond. His army virtually disintegrated under Valence's rapid onslaught, with many of Bruce's leading supportersfalling captive. What was left of his force was mauled for a second time soon after this, by the Macdougalls,[A4] of Lorn,[91/2] allies of the English, at The Battle of

Dalrigh.[221] As an organised military force, the army of Scotland ceased to exist, and the king took to the heather as a fugitive. For a time he took refuge in Dunaverty Castle,[222] near Mull of Kintyre,[223] but with his enemies closing in once more, he sailed out of the light of history into the mist of legend, seeking refuge on Rathlin Island near the coast of Ulster according to some and the Orkney Isles according to others: into a cave inhabited by a spider. Supposedly, Bruce watched the small spider try to spin a line across a seemingly impossibly wide gap. As Bruce watched, the spider tried and tried and tried. "Foolish spider" thought Bruce, but continued to watch. Suddenly, the spider succeeded in leaping across the gap with its thread.

Bruce considered this and took it as an encouragement that he too should continue to persevere regardless of seemingly hopeless circumstances and he later came out of hiding. It is doubtful if the story is true however.

3.7.3.2 Return of the King

When he reappeared in Feb. 1307, he was set to take his greatest gamble. From the island of Arran in the Firth of Clyde he crossed to his own Earldom of Carrick,[75/2] in Ayrshire, landing near Turnberry, where he knew the local people would be sympathetic, but where all the strongholds were held by the English. A similar landing by his brothers Thomas and Alexander in Galloway,[70/3] met with disaster on the shores of Loch Ryan at the hands of Dougal MacDougal,[224] the principal Balliol, adherent in the region. Thomas and Alexander's little army of Irish and Islemen was destroyed and they were sent as captives to Carlisle, where they were later executed, on the orders of Edward I.[28/3] But against all the odds Robert,survived and with remarkable tenacity, soon established himself in the hill country of Carrick and Gallo- way.[70/3] From the feudal,[42/4] warlord, who had been overthrown at The Battle of Methven,[220/2] Bruce was in the process of transforming into one of history's great guerilla captains. Bruce had learned well the sharp lesson delivered at Methven. Never again would he allow himself to be trapped by a stronger enemy. His greatest weapon was his intimate knowledge of the Scottish countryside, which he used to his advantage time and again.

Even at the future Battle of Bannockburn,[Ch 3] where he temporarily abandoned his guerilla war, he chose his ground with genius, allowing his small army to operate at maximum advantage. As well as making good use of the country's natural defences, he made sure that his force was as mobile as possible. Bruce was now fully aware that he could rarely expect to get the better of the English in open battle. His army was often weak in numbers and ill-equipped. It would be best used in small hit-and-run raids allowing the best use of limited resources. He would keep the initiative and prevent the enemy from bringing his superior strength to bear. Whenever possible, crops would be destroyed and livestock removed from the path of the enemy's advance, denying him fresh supplies and fodder for the heavy war horses. Most important of all, Bruce recognised the seasonal nature of English invasions, which swept over the country like summer tides only to withdraw before the onset of winter.

3.7.3.3 Loudoun Hill

Bruce had enemies in all directions but managed to evade them, winning his first small success at Glen Trool,[225] where he ambushed an English cavalry force led by Philip Mowbray,[226] sweeping down from the steep hillsides and driving them off with heavy losses. He then slipped through the gap in the enemy ring passing through the moors by Dalmellington to Muirkirk, appearing in the north of Ayrshire in early May, where his army was strengthened by fresh recruits. Here he soon encountered his old enemy, Aymer de Valence,[219/2] commanding the main English force in the area. In preparing to meet him, he took up a position on 10th May at Loudoun Hill some 10 miles east of Kilmarnock and about 3 miles east of Darvel, both in Ayrshire. With all care Bruce scouted the ground and made the necessary preparations. John Barbour describes his actions in his rhyming chronicle:-

> *"The king upon the other side,*
> *Whose prudence was his valour's guide,*
> *Rode out to see and chose his ground.*
> *The highway took its course, he found,*
> *Upon a medow, smooth and dry.*
> *But close on either side therby*
> *A bog extended, deep and broad,*
> *That from the highway, where men rode,*
> *Was full a bowshot either side."*

Valence's only approach was over the highway, through the bog where the parallel ditches Bruce's men dug outwards from the marsh, restricted his room for deployment still further, effectively neutralising his advantage in numbers. He was forced at attack, along a narrow constricted front upwards, towards the waiting enemy spears. It was a battle reminiscent in some ways of The Battle of Stirling Bridge, with the same 'filtering' effect at work.

> *"The king's men met them at the dyke,*
> *So stoutly that the most warlike,*
> *And strongest of them fell to the ground.*
> *Then could be heard a dreadful sound*
> *As spears on armour rudely shattered,*
>
> *And cries and groans the wounded uttered.*
> *For those that first engaged in fight*
> *Battled and fought with all their might.*
> *Their shouts and cries rose loud and clear;*
> *A grevious noise it was to hear."*

As Bruce's spearmen pressed downhill on the disorganised English knights, they fought with such vigour that the rear ranks began to flee in panic. A hundred or more were killed in the battle. Amyer de Valence,[219/3] managed to escape the carnage and fled to the safety of Bothwell Castle.[227] Three days after The Battle of Loudoun Hill, Bruce defeated another English force under the Earl of Gloucester. But the greatest boost to his cause came two months later. At Burgh-on-Sands just short of the Scottish border, Edward I,[28/4] died.

3.7.4 The Battle of Bannockburn

The Clan Sinclair,[Ch. 3] fight in support of Robert the Bruce, of Scotland. After the battle, Robert the Bruce gave William Sinclair his sword. The battle (*Blàr Allt a' Bhonnaich* in Scottish Gaelic,[15/7]) (24th June 1314), was a significant Scottish victory in The Wars of Scottish Independence.[Ch 3] Indeed, it was the decisive battle in The First War of Scottish Independence.

3.7.4.1 Prelude

Around Lent of 1314, Edward Bruce,[156/2] brother of the Scottish king, began The Siege of Stirling Castle which was commanded by Sir Philip Mowbray.[226/2] Unable to make any headway Bruce agreed to a pact with Mowbray - if no relief came by midsummer 1314, the castle would surrender to Bruce. It was now two years since an English army had come to Scotland, and King Edward II of England.[228/1] had recently been on the verge of war with his barons after the murder of Piers Gaveston,[229] in the summer of 1312. Stirling was of vital strategic importance and its loss would be a serious embarrassment to the English. The time allowed in the Bruce-Mowbray pact, was ample for Edward to gather a powerful army. According to the historian and poet John Barbour, King Robert Bruce rebuked the folly of his brother, even though Dundee had probably fallen to the Scots through a similar arrangement in 1312. Mowbray had a breathing space and looked forward to the summer of 1314. In England, Edward and his barons reached an uneasy peace and made ready.

3.7.4.2 Edward comes north

Edward came to Scotland in the high summer of 1314 with the preliminary aim of relieving Stirling Castle:[206/1] the real purpose of course was to find and destroy the Scottish army in the field, and thus end the war. England, for once was largely united in this ambition, although some of Edward's greatest magnates and former enemies, headed by his cousin, Thomas of Lancaster, did not attend in person, sending the minimum number of troops they were required to by feudal law.[42/4] Even so the force that left Berwick-upon-Tweed, on 17th June 1314, was impressive: it comprised between 2,000–3,000 horse (likely closer to 2,000) and 16,000 foot, at least two or three times the size of the army Bruce had been able to gather. Edward was accompanied by many of the seasoned campaigners of the Scottish wars, headed by the Aymer de Valence,[219/3] 2nd Earl of Pembroke and veterans like Henry de Beaumont.[230/1] and Robert de Clifford,[231/1] 1st Baron de Clifford. The most irreconcilable of Bruce's.[A2.3] Scottish enemies also came: Ingram de Umfraville,[232] a former Guardian of Scotland,[233/1] and his kinsman the Earl of Angus as well as others of the MacDougalls, MacCanns and Sir John Comyn III.[208/3] Lord of Badenoch,[209] the only son of The Red Comyn,[234] who was born and raised in England, and was now returning to Scotland to avenge his father's killing by Bruce.

At Greyfriars Kirk in Dumfries, in 1306. This was a grand feudal [42/2] army, one of the last of its kind to leave England in the middle Ages. King Robert awaited its arrival south of Stirling near the Bannock Burn, in Scotland.

3.7.4.3 Preparations

The English army marched rapidly to reach Stirling before Mowbray's [226/3] agreement expired on 24th June. Edinburgh was reached on 19th June and by 22nd June it was at Falkirk, only 15 miles short of its objective. Edward's host followed the line of the old Roman road which ran through an ancient forest known as the Torwood, over the Bannockburn and into the New Park, a hunting preserve enclosed at the time of Alexander III. Bruce's army had been assembling in the Tor Wood, an area providing good natural cover from the middle of May. On Saturday 22nd June with his troops now organised into their respective commands, Bruce moved his army slightly to the north to the New Park, a more heavily wooded area, where his movements could be concealed and which if the occasion demanded, could provide cover for a withdrawal. Bruce's army, like William Wallace's before him, was chiefly composed of infantry armed with long spears. It was probably divided into three main formations. Thomas Randolph, 1st Earl of Moray,[235/1] commanded the vanguard which was stationed about a mile to the south of Stirling, near the church of St. Ninian, while the king commanded the rearguard, at the entrance to the New Park. His brother, Edward,[156/2] led the third division. According to the chronicler Barbour, there was a fourth, nominally under the youthful Walter the Steward,[236] but actually under the command of Sir James Douglas.[143/3] The army might have numbered as many as 9,000 men in all, but probably more of the order of 6,000 –7,000.

20th century illustration portraying Bruce reviewing his troops before the battle.

It was gathered from the whole of Scotland: knights and nobles, freemen and tenants, town dwellers and traders: men who could afford the arms and armour required. Barbour tells that King Robert turned away those, who were not adequately equipped. For most, such equipment would consist of a spear, a helmet, a thick padded jacket down to the knees and armoured gloves. It is highly probable that a large proportion of the spearmen had acquired more extensive armour given that the country had been at war for nearly twenty years. This is in contrast to the modern romantic notion of the Scots army which depicts its foot soldiers clad in kilts, painted woad,[237] and little else (Kilts were not worn until much later in any case). The balance of the army consisted of archers and men-at-arms. The Scottish archers used yew-stave longbows, and it is not to be thought that they had weaker or inferior bows but rather had inferior numbers. Consisting of possibly only 500 archers, they played little part in the battle. There is first hand evidence from the captured Carmelite friar, Robert Baston in his poem written just after the battle, that one or both sides employed slingers and crossbowmen. Each of these troop types was indistinguishable from their counterparts in France or England. Many of the Scottish men-at-arms (recruited from the nobility and the more prosperous burgesses,[149/2]) served on foot at Bannockburn. Since his landing at Ayrshire in 1307, King Robert had demonstrated time and time again that he was willing to take risks but these were always measured and calculated.

He had no intention of chancing all on the outcome of a day as had William Wallace at The Battle of Falkirk. Almost to the last minute he was prepared to withdraw. He was persuaded to remain by news of the poor state of morale in the English army. But undoubtedly, the most important factor in persuading him to make a stand was the ground before him. The Bannockburn, over which the English army had to cross on the way to Stirling and its sister streams, flowed over the Carse of Stirling. A carse is an area which is wet in winter but hard in summer and most of it was used for growing wheat, oats and barley. With the trees of the New Park covering Bruce's army to the west, the only approach, apart from the Pows to the east, was directly the old road from Falkirk. If this route, virtually the only solid ground on which heavy cavalry could be effectively deployed, were to be denied to the English, they would have no choice but to wheel right to the north-east on to the Carse. To force Edward to take this route, Bruce adopted tactics similar to those he used at The Battle of Loudon Hill,[Ch 3] Both sides of the road were peppered with small pits or 'pots', each three feet deep and covered with brush, which would force the enemy to bunch towards the centre of a dangerously constricted front. Once on the Carse, the English army would be caught in a kind of natural vise as the main action on 24th June showed, with waterways to the north, east, and south. Such natural advantages were not easily obtained, and were unlikely to occur again. There is some confusion over the exact site of the Battle of Bannockburn although most modernhistorians agree that the traditional site, where a visitor centre and statue have been erected, is not the correct one. Although a large number of possible alternatives have been proposed, most can be dismissed and two serious contenders can be considered: -

- The area of peaty ground known as *The Dryfield,* outside the village of Balquhide-*rock,* about three-quarters of a mile to the east of the traditional site and

- *The Carse of Balquhiderock*, about a mile and a half north-east of the traditional site accepted by the National Trust as the most likely candidate.

3.7.4.4 First day of battle

It was on the old road that the preliminary actions of the Battle of Bannockburn took place, on Sunday, 23rd June. For the English, things started to go wrong before the first blow had been struck. Sir Philip Mowbray,[226/3] the commander of Stirling Castle,[206/2] who had observed Bruce's,[A2.3] preparations on the road, appeared in Edward's,[28/4] camp early in the morning and warned of the dangers of approaching the Scots directly through the New Park. Mowbray also pointed out that there was no need to force a battle as Edward was now close enough to the castle to constitute a technical relief, in terms of the agreement with Edward Bruce.[156/3] But even if the king was disposed to act on Mowbray's advice it was already too late; for he was showing signs of losing control of his formidable but unwieldy host.

The vanguard under the earls of Gloucester and Hereford, appointed to joint command by Edward after a quarrel about who would take the lead — a compromise that satisfied no one — were already closing in on the Scots from the south, advancing in the same reckless manner that had

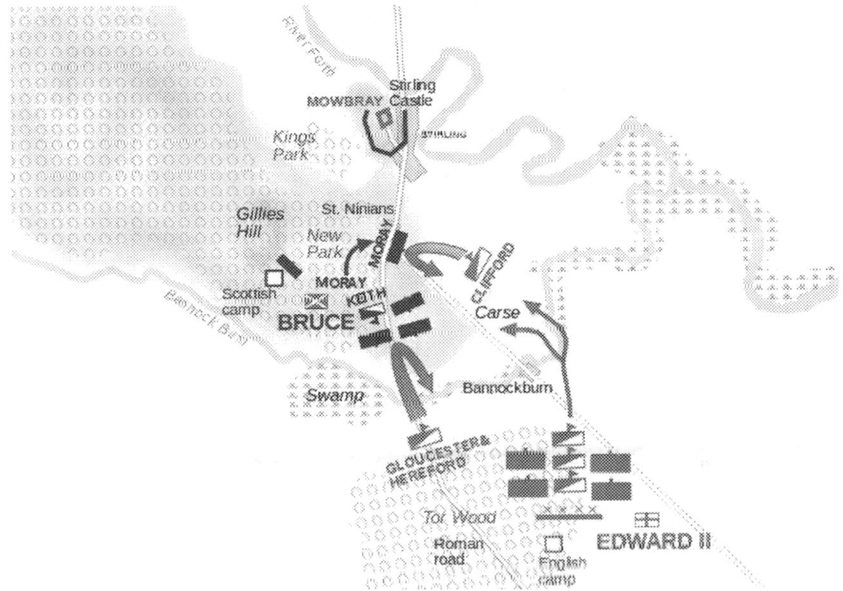

An interpretation of the battle of Bannockburn-first day

almost brought disaster at Falkirk. Following the line of the Roman road they crossed the ford over the Bannockburn, towards King Robert's division, at the opening of the New Park. There now occurred one of the most memorable episodes in Scottish history. Henry de Bohun,[238] nephew of the Earl of Hereford, was riding ahead of his companions, when he caught sight of the Scottish King. De Bohun lowered his lance and began a charge that carried him to lasting fame. King Robert was mounted on a small palfrey,[239] and armed only with a battle-axe. He had no armour on. As de Bohun's great war-horse thundered towards him he stood his ground, watched with mounting anxiety by his own army. With the Englishman only feet away, Bruce turned aside, stood in his stirrups and hit the knight so hard with his axe that he split his helmet and head in two. This small incident became, in a larger sense, a symbol of the war itself: the one side heavily armed but lacking agility; the other highly mobile and open to opportunity. Rebuked by his commanders for the enormous risk he had taken, the king only expressed regret that he had broken the shaft of his axe. Cheered by this heroic encounter, Bruce's division rushed forward to engage the main enemy force. For the English, so says the author of the Vita Edwardi Secundi (Life of Edward II,[228/5]), this was the beginning of their troubles. After some fierce fighting in which the Earl of Gloucester was knocked off his horse, the knights of the vanguard were forced to retreat to the TorWood. The Scots eager to pursue, were held back by the command of the king. In the meantime, another English cavalry force under Robert Clifford,[231/2] and Henry de Beaumont,[230/2] skirted the Scottish position to the east and rode towards Stirling, advancing as far as St. Ninians.

Bruce spotted the manoeuvre and ordered Randolph's,[235/2] schiltron,[240/1] to intercept. Randolph's action was a foretaste of the main contest the following day.

3.7.4.5 Second day of battle

Unsupported by archers, the horsemen were unable to make any impression on theScots spearmen, precisely what had happened in the opening stages of Falkirk. The difference now was that the schiltrons had learnt mobility and how to keep formation at the same time. The English squadron was broken, some seeking refuge in the nearby castle, others fleeing back to the army. The captives included Sir Thomas Gray, whose son and namesake later based his account of The Battle of Bannockburn in his book, *The Scalacronica*, on his father's memories.The English army was still approaching Stirling from the south. Bruce's, preparations had made the direct approach to Stirling too hazardous. Edward made the worst decision of all: he ordered the army to cross the Bannockburn, to the east of the New Park. Not long after daybreak on 24th June, the Scots spearmen began to move towards the English. Edward was surprised to see Robert's army emerge from the cover of the woods. As Bruce's army drew nearer, they paused and knelt in prayer. / Edward is supposed to have said in surprise "*They pray for mercy!*" "*For mercy, yes,*" one of his attendants replied, "*But from God, not you. These men will conquer or die.*" One of the English earls, Gloucester, asked the king to hurry up but the king accused him of cowardice. Angered, the earl mounted his horse and led the vanguard on a charge against the leading Scots spearmen commanded by Edward Bruce. Gloucester, who according to some accounts, had not bothered to don his surcoat, was killed in the forest of Scottish spears, along with some of the other knights. The very size and strength of the great army was beginning to work against the English king, as his army could not move quickly and lost a lot of time in getting into position. Bruce then committed his whole Scots army to an inexorable bloody push into the disorganized English mass, fighting side by side across a single front.

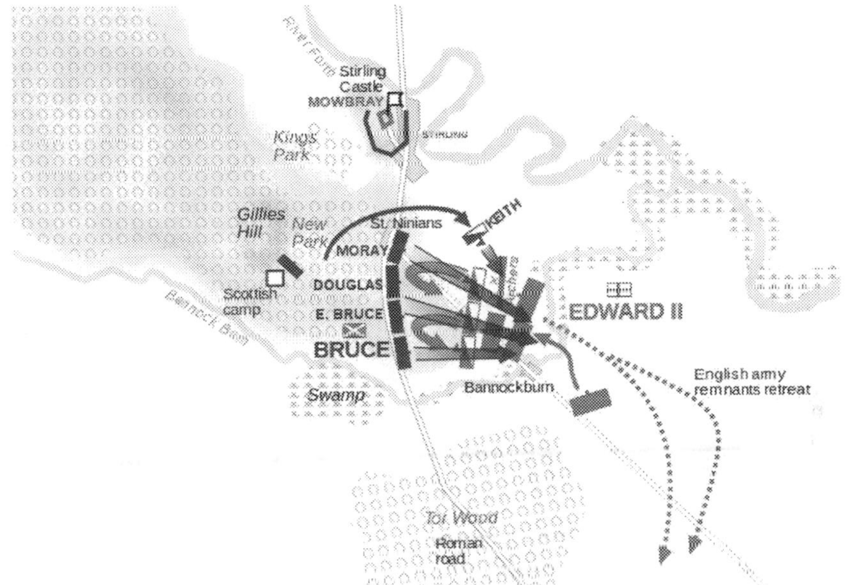

An interpretation of the battle of Bannockburn- second day

Edward's army was now so tightly packed that if a man fell, he risked being immediately crushed underfoot or suffocated and the English and Welsh long bowmen failed to get a clear shot in fear they might hit their own men. After some time, they moved to the side of Douglas's division and began shooting into its left but upon the command of Robert the Bruce, who oversaw this Scottish 500-horse light cavalry, under Robert Keith, dispersed them. The returning fleeing archers then caused the infantry itself to begin to flee. Later, the knights began to escape back across the Bannockburn. With the English formations beginning to break, a great shout went up from the Scots, *"Lay on! Lay on! Lay on! They fail!"* This cry was heard by Bruce's camp followers, who promptly gathered weapons and banners and charged forward. To the English army, close to exhaustion, this appeared to be a fresh reserve and they lost all hope. The English forces north of the Bannockburn broke into flight. Some tried to cross the River Forth where most drowned in the attempt. Others tried to get back across the Bannockburn but as they ran "tumbling one over the other" down the steep, slippery banks, a deadly crush ensued so that "*men could pass dry-shod upon the drowned bodies.*"

3.7.4.6 Retreat

Edward,[28/4] fled with his personal bodyguard ending the remaining order in the army; panic spread and defeat turned into a rout. He arrived eventually at Dunbar Castle,[241] from here he took ship to England. From the carnage of Bannockburn, the rest of the army tried to escape, to the safety of the English border, ninety miles to the south. Many were killed by the pursuing Scottish army or by the inhabitants of the countryside that they passed through. Historian Peter Reese says that, "only one sizeable group of men—all footsoldiers—made good their escape to England." These were a force of Welsh spearmen who were kept together by their commander Sir Maurice de Berkeley, and the majority of them reached Carlisle. Weighing up the available evidence, Reese concludes that "it seems doubtful if even a third of the footsoldiers returned to England." Out of 16,000 infantrymen this would give a total of about 11,000 killed. The English chronicler Thomas Walsingham gave the number of English men-at-arms who were killed as 700, while 500 more-at-arms were spared for ransom. The Scottish losses appear to have been comparatively light with only two knights among those killed.

3.7.4.7 Legacy

The modern Bannockburn monument

The victory was complete, and although full English recognition of Scottish independence was not achieved until more than ten years later, Robert Bruce's position as King was greatly strengthened by the outcome. A modern abstract monument stands in a field above the battle site where the warring parties are believed to have camped on the night before the battle. The monument consists of two hemicircular walls, depicting the opposing parties. Nearby, stands the 1960s statue of Bruce by Pilkington Jackson.. In 1932, The Bannockburn Preservation Committee, under Edward Bruce, 10th Earl of Elgin and Kincardine, presented lands to *The* National Trust for Scotland. Further lands

Statue of Robert the Bruce by Pilkington Jackson near Bannock-burn Heritage Centre

were purchased in 1960 and 1965 to facilitate visitor access. "Scots Wha Hae",[242] is the title of a patriotic poem by Robert Burns. The chorus of Scotland's unofficial national anthem, Flower of Scotland,[243] refers to Scotland's victory over Edward and the English at Bannockburn.

3.7.4.8 Bannockburn Heritage Centre

The National Trust for Scotland operates the Bannockburn Heritage Centre, which is open daily from March through October.

3.7.5 The Battle of Donibristle (1317)

William Sinclair, Bishop of Dunkeld, rallies Scots army to defeat an English invading force in Fife.

3.7.6 The Battle of Teba

Sir William Sinclair, heir to Henry and his brother John, are among the Scots killed attempting to carry Bruce's, heart to the Holy Land. They were buried in Rosslyn Chapel.[Ch 5] The battle took place in August 1330 in the valley below the fortress of Teba, now a town in the province of Malaga in Andalusia, southern Spain. The encounter occurred during the frontier campaign waged between 1327-1333 by Alfonso XI of Castile, against Muhammed IV, Sultan of Granada..

3.7.6.1 War on the frontier of Granada

On coming of age in 1325, King Alfonso declared war on the Muslim Kingdom of Granada and invited other Christian kings to join him in a new crusade. This project came to nothing but Alfonso nevertheless, proceeded with a campaign against the western frontier of Granada. In 1327, he captured the castles of Olvera, Pruna and Torre Alhaquime. In 1330, a second expedition was mounted, to attack the castle of Teba twenty five miles east of Olvera, and a key fortification in the defences of Malaga. Alfonso established his headquarters at Cordoba and sent word to his nobles and knights to concentrate there. A contingent of five hundred knights, was also sent by the King of Portugal. By the end of July Alfonso was preparing to march down the Roman road to Ecija, where an advance base would be set up.

3.7.6.2 Scottish knights errant

In 1329, as Robert the Bruce, King of Scots, lay dying, he made one last request of his friend and lieutenant, Sir James Douglas.[143/2] He charged that after his death, Sir James should take the king's embalmed heart and bear it with him on crusade, thus fulfilling the pledge that Bruce had been unable to honour in his lifetime. The projected campaign in Spain offered Sir James the ideal opportunity. In the spring of 1330, armed with a safe conduct from Edward III of England,[244/1] and a letter of recommendation to King Alfonso XI of Castile, Douglas set off from Berwick and sailed first to Sluys in Flanders. He was accompanied by one knight banneret,[245] six ordinary knights and twenty esquires. The company included Sir William de Keith, Sir William de St. Clair of Rosslyn,[23/8] and the brothers Sir Robert Logan of Restalrig,[246] and Sir Walter Logan. Others, alleged at one time or another to have accompanied Douglas are John de St. Clair, younger brother of Sir William, Sir Simon Lockhart of Lee, Sir Kenneth Moir, Sir William Borthwick, Sir Alan Cathcart and Sir Robert de Glen but all evidence is lacking. There appears to be no historical basis, for claims that any of these men were connected with The Order of the Knights Templar,[247] dissolved by Pope Clement V in 1312, eighteen years previously. At Sluys they remained for twelve days, with Douglas holding court on board ship, as if the late king were present. It may be he was awaiting news of the planned crusade. It would seem that when Douglas learned that despite the withdrawal of his allies, King Alfonso still intended to go to war, he finally set sail for Spain. After a stormy passage, the party arrived at the mouth of the Guadalquivir, probably sometime in late June and disembarked upstream at Seville.

3.7.6.3 March to Teba

Douglas,[143/2] presented his credentials to Alfonso XI. According to the chronicler Barbour, the King offered Douglas riches, fine horses and armour. Sir James declined these gifts, declaring that he and his men were prepared to offer their arms in the service of the king as humble pilgrims seeking absolution for their sins. Alfonso accepted and assigned experienced soldiers accustomed to the style of fighting on the Frontera, as advisors to Douglas and his fellow knights. While the Scots rested after their long voyage and waited for the expedition to depart, many foreign knights who had come to seek service with Alfonso of Castile, paid their respects to Douglas, including a number of Englishmen, who were particularly keen to meet the man who until recently had been their nemesis.

Alfonso formed up his army for the advance south. Barbour claims that Douglas was given command of the lead division, the *'vaward'* or vanguard. It may be more likely that he was put in charge of all the foreign knights in the Castilian arm. The Christian host, its size unknown, marched to Ecija, then to Osuna on the frontier. Once across the border Alfonso continued south to the meadows of Almargen, five miles west of Teba, from where he advanced to set up camp and invest the fortress. While waiting for his siege engines,[205/2] to come up from Ecija, Alfonso prepared for the Granadan forces in Malaga to react. These were under the command of Uthman bin Abi-l-Ulá, a Berber,[248/1] noble, fighting in the service of the sultans of Granada who set off with six thousand cavalry and an unknown number of infantry, to the relief of Teba. Marching up the Guadalhorce valley, Uthman's force crossed over into the valley of River Turon where they pitched camp between the citadel of Ardales, and the castle of Turon ten miles south of Teba.

3.7.6.4 The siege

Meanwhile, the siege engines arrived at Teba and operations began to open a breach in the walls of the castle. The Christian army was hampered by a lack of water and they were forced daily to drive their herds out of camp and eastwards down to the Guadalteba, an abundant river flowing two miles south of the castle. Uthman quickly identified this weakness and sent raiding parties to disrupt the watering details. Alfonso in turn, set up a defensive screen of patrols to hold them off, and there were regular costly skirmishes on the river and in the hills to the south. In one of these encounters it is possible that Sir James Douglas,[143/2] was killed. The 'Gran Cronica de Alfonso XI' refers to *"the death of a foreign count through his own error"*, although some commentators prefer to think Douglas died in a more decisive encounter some days later. Alfonso had other problems. The five hundred Portuguese knights declared their term of service was about to expire and withdrew, and one night the garrison of Teba sallied out to attack the siege lines and retired leaving a siege tower in flames. Uthman too faced difficulties. He had concluded he could not defeat the Christians in open battle and so devised a stratagem to force Alfonso to abandon the siege.

3.7.6.5 The Battle

15th century depiction of Battle of Teba

Under cover of darkness, three thousand Moorish,[30/2] cavalry, prepared to make a diversionary attack across the river, while Uthman took another three thousand upstream, to make a flank attack on Alfonso's camp. At dawn, Uthman's river contingent occupied the watering grounds of the Guadalteba. Alfonso, however, having been warned by his scouts of the enemy's movements, kept the main force of his army in camp while he sent troops to check the assault developing on the river. Some argue that Douglas and his contingent must have been part of this reinforcement. With battle joined, Uthman believed that his ruse was working and emerging from the valley where he and his men had been concealed, rode up to attack the Christian camp from the west. When he reached the col,[249] overlooking the Almargen valley he saw the camp bristling with Alonso's men armed and ready, while at the same time saw his men on the river downstream beginning to fall back. He instantly abandoned the attack and rode back to support his right flank but arrived only in time to join in the general rout. The Moors on the river, had been unable to withstand the weight of the Christian counter attack. When Alfonso, having seen Uthman's move east, sent a further 2000 men to intervene, the Granadan withdrawal turned into a rout. John Barbour, the chronicler describes Douglas and his contingent pursuing the fleeing enemy closely, until having outrun most of his men, Sir James finds himself out in front, with only ten or so followers. Too late, he turns back to rejoin the main body. The agile Moorish,[30/3] cavalry see their opportunity, rally and counter-attack. In the running fight that followed, Douglas.[143/2] is supposed to have seen Sir William St. Clair surrounded by a body of Moors, trying to fight his way free. With the few knights still with him, Douglas rode to the rescue but all were killed, including *'The Good Sir James'*, Sir William St Clair and the brothers, Sir Robert and Sir Walter Logan.

3.7.6.6 Aftermath

The Castilian forces pursued the Moorish army back to their camp in the Turon valley. The chance of a more comprehensive victory, was lost when the Christians stopped to loot the enemy tents and baggage. Despite further skirmishes, Uthman made no further attempt to raise the siege and shortly afterwards the garrison of Teba surrendered. The aged Berber,[248/2] general died some weeks later. Barbour tells how Douglas' body, together with the casket containing the embalmed heart of Bruce, were recovered after the battle. His bones, the flesh boiled off them and the casket were taken back to Scotland by Douglas' surviving companions. Douglas was buried at St Bride's Kirk at Douglas, South Lanarkshire. The battle was not decisive. While Teba remained secure in Castilian hands, the Guadalteba and Turon valleys continued debatable land, for the next hundred and fifty years. However, in response to Alfonso XI's victories of 1327-1330, The Marinid sultan of Morocco Abu Hasan sent forces in support of Muhammad IV, to re-establish control of the Straits. Gibraltar was re-captured from the Christians in 1333 but Abu Hasan's attempt to re-take Tarifa in 1340, led to his disastrous defeat by allied Christian forces at Rio Salado. This was the last intervention by North African powers in the defence of Muslim Granada.

3.7.7 The Battle of Neville's Cross

Sir John Sinclair of Herdmanston,[25/4] is taken prisoner after the battle.The Battle of Neville's Cross, took place to the west of Durham, England on 17th October 1346.

3.7.7.1 Background

By mid 1346, it was obvious that the English, under Edward III,[244/2] had every intention of breaking the Truce of Malestroit,[250] and resuming (what would be known later as) *The* Hundred Years' War *with* France. As a consequence of the Franco-Scottish Auld Alliance,[251/1] and Philip VI,[252/1] of France's fear of an impending English invasion of northern France (an area which the French were not yet prepared to defend), Philip VI sent David II of Scotland, numerous appeals for assistance, to blunt the coming English threat.

Though Philip VI's pleas became especially desperate in June 1346, (when the English were amassing troops in southern England), major Scottish action against England would not commence for some time — in fact, the Scots would not invade Northern England, until October 1346. On 7th October, the Scots entered England with approximately 12,000 men. They were expecting to find northern England relatively undefended because Edward III was by then, conducting a major campaign in France. (Philip VI went so far as to characterise northern England as a "defenceless void").

Unfortunately David II's strategic and tactical abilities were not up to the task of making good use of the Scots' element of surprise. Perhaps though, they did not feel the need for haste. After taking Liddesdale (and bypassing Carlisle after being paid protection money), the Scots moved on toward their ultimate goal of Durham and Yorkshire, after more than a week's march. Along the way, they sacked the priory of Hexham and burned the territory around their line of march (not unlike the English in France at the time). They arrived at Durham on 16th October and camped at Beaurepaire, where the Scots were offered £1,000 (£490,000 as of 2011) in protection money, to be paid on 18th October. Without the Scots' knowledge however, the English had already arrayed troops for just such an invasion. Once the Scots invaded, an army was quickly mobilised in Richmond under the supervision of William Zouche, the Archbishop of York. It was not however, a large army, and what men were available were split into two separate groups: 3,000-4000 men from Cumberland, Northumberland and Lancashire, with another 3,000 Yorkshiremen en route. Given the demands of The Siege of Calais,[253] no further men could be summoned for the defence of Northern England. Worse still, on 14th October. (while the Scots were sacking Hexham), the Archbishop decided not to wait for the Yorkshiremen and made haste toward Barnard Castle.

3.7.7.2 The Battle

The Scots only discovered the presence of the English army on the morning of 17th October. Troops, under command of William Douglas stumbled upon them in the morning mist during a raid south of Durham. The two rearward divisions of the English army drove the Scots off, with heavy Scottish casualties. Upon hearing Douglas's report, David II, led the Scottish army to high ground at Neville's Cross (site of an old Anglo-Saxon stone cross), where he prepared his army for battle. Both the Scots and English, arranged themselves in three battalions. Though the Scots were in what is considered a rather poor position (with various obstacles between them and the English position), they remembered well their defeats in The

Battle of Dupplin Moor,[254/1] and The Battle of Halidon Hill,[255/1] and thus took a defensive stance waiting, for the English to attack.

However, the English also took a defensive stance knowing they had the superior position and likely knowing that time was on their side. A stalemate resulted that lasted until the afternoon, when the English sent longbowmen forward to harass the Scottish lines. The archers succeeded in forcing the Scots to attack, but their initial hesitation in going on the offensive appears in hindsight to have been the correct decision. The Scots' poor position resulted in their formations falling apart as they advanced, allowing the English to deal easily with the Scottish attack. When it became clear that the battle was going in favour of the English, Robert Stewart and the Earl of March fled, abandoning David II's battalion to face the enemy alone. Late in the afternoon, the king's own battalion attempted to retreat but was unsuccessful and David II was captured (though not without difficulty) while the rest of the Scottish army, was pursued for more than twenty miles. Several Scottish nobles were killed, including:-

John Randolph	3rd Earl of Moray.
Niall Bruce of Carrick [75/3]	An illegitimate son of Robert the Bruce.
Lord David de la Hay	The Constable.
Maurice de Moravia	Earl of Strathearn.
Lord Robert Keith	The Great Marischal of Scotland.
Lord Thomas Charteris	The Chancellor.
Lord Robert de Peebles	The Chamberlain

Scottish chroniclers Andrew of Wyntoun and Walter Bower both wrote that 1,000 Scots were killed in the battle, while The Chronicle of Lanercost said that "*few English were killed.*"

3.7.7.3 Aftermath

David II, initially managed to escape. However, legend has it that while he was hiding under a bridge over the nearby River Browney, David's reflection was spotted in the water by a detachment of English soldiers that was out searching for him. David was then captured by John Copeland, the leader of the detachment. Later King Edward III,[244/3] ordered Copeland to bring the Scots king to Calais and hand him over. Edward then rewarded Copeland with a knighthood and a handsome annuity. King David was brought back to England and imprisoned, from 1346 to 1357 at Odiham Castle (King John's Castle) in Hampshire. After eleven years, he was released in return for a ransom of 100,000 marks (approximately £15 million in 2006). The Battle of Neville's Cross derives its name from a stone cross that Lord Neville paid to have erected on the battlefield to commemorate this remarkable victory. The fate of the unfortunate David II of Scotland is immortalised in Shakespeare's play Henry V. In Act 1 Scene 3 Henry says to the Archbishop of Canterbury:-

> *For you shall read that my great-grandfather / Never went with his forces into France / But that the Scot on his unfurnish'd kingdom / Came pouring, like the tide into a breach, With ample and brim fullness of his force; / Galling the gleaned land with hot essays, / Girding with grievous siege castles and towns; / That England, being empty of defence, / Hath shook and trembled at the ill neighbourhood.*

But the archbishop replies:-

> *She hath been then more fear'd than harm'd my liege; / For hear her but exampled by herself: / When all her chivalry hath been in France, / And she a mourning widow of her nobles, / She hath herself not only well defended, / But taken, and impounded as a stray, / The king of Scots; whom she did send to France, / To fill King Edward's fame with prisoner kings*

3.8 16th century clan conflicts and Anglo-Scottish wars

3.8.1 Battle of Flodden or Flodden Field (1513)

During The Anglo-Scottish Wars,[256] William Sinclair, 2nd Earl of Caithness,[Ch 4] was one of the nobles fighting for King James IV of Scotland. He previously sat in parliament. In battle, King James observed Sir William leading his followers, all wearing green. The King asked and found they were of Caithness, led by the Earl. King James wrote the renewal of Sir William's Earldom on a drumhead, the only parchment available. The drumhead was carried by runner to Sir William's lady. Sir William died in battle the next day, leaving the Earldom to his son John.[Ch 4] William,

2nd Earl, helped lead the right wing of the Scottish army that beat the English left wing. Unlike some, he returned to help the rest of the Scots and was killed. There was a loss of 300 Sinclairs, including George Sinclair of Keiss,[142/4] Henry, 3rd Lord Sinclair, Sir John Sinclair of Herdmanston,[25/6] The Bishop of Caithness, as well as King James IV of Scotland. The Battle was fought in the county of Northumberland in northern England, on 9th September 1513, between an invading Scots army under King James IV and an English army commanded by Thomas Howard, Earl of Surrey.[257/1] It ended in a victory for the English and was the largest battle (in terms of numbers) fought between the two nations.

3.8.1.1 Background

This conflict began when James IV, King of Scots, declared war on England to honour the Auld Alliance,[251/2] with France by diverting Henry VIII's,[12/7] English troops from their campaign against the French King Louis XII.[258/1] Henry VIII,[12/8] had also opened old wounds, by claiming to be the overlord of Scotland which angered the Scots and the King. At this time, England was involved in *The* War of the League of Cambrai – defending Italy and the Pope from the French as a member of the "Catholic League".

3.8.1.2 Invasion

Flodden Field

Western side of the battlefield, looking south-south-east from the monument erected in 1910. The Scottish army advanced down the ploughed field, the English down the grassy field in the foreground, and they met, presumably at the valley boundary between the two fields.

Using the pretext of revenge for the murder of Robert Kerr, a Warden of the Scottish East March,[259/1] who had been killed by "The bastard" Heron in 1508, James, invaded England with an army of about 30,000 men in 1513. In keeping with his understanding of the medieval code of chivalry, King James sent notice to the English, one month in advance of his intent to invade. This gave the English time to gather an army and as importantly, to retrieve the banner of Saint Cuthbert from the cathedral of Durham, a banner which had been carried by the English in victories against the Scots in

1138 and 1346. After a muster on the Burgh Muir of Edinburgh the Scottish host moved to Ellemford and camped and then crossed the River Tweed near Coldstream. By the 29th August, Norham Castle was taken and partly demolished. The Scots moved south capturing the castles of Etal and Ford. A later chronicler, Robert Lindsay of Pitscottie,[260] tells the story that James wasted valuable time at Ford enjoying the company of Lady Heron and her daughter.

3.8.1.3 The Battle

The battle actually took place near the village of Branxton, in the county of Northumberland, rather than at Flodden — hence the alternative name is *Battle of Branxton*. The Scots had previously been stationed at Flodden Edge, to the south of Branxton, which the Earl of Surrey,[257/2] compared to a fortress. Surrey moved to block off the Scots' route north and so James, was forced to move his army and artillery 2 miles to Branxton Hill. The Scottish artillery included; 5 great curtals; 2 great culverins,[261] 4 sakers,[262] and 6 great serpentines. When the armies were within 3 miles of each other, Surrey sent Rouge Croix Pursuivan,[263] to James, who answered that he would wait till noon. At 11 o'clock, Lord Howard's vanguard and artillery crossed the Twissell Bridge. (Pitscottie says the king would not allow the Scots artillery to fire on the vulnerable English during this manouevre). The Scots army was in good order in 5 formations after the Almain (German) manner. On Friday afternoon, the Scots host descended without speaking any word, to meet the English. According to an English report, first the groups commanded by the Earls of Huntly Arran and Crawford totalling 6000 men, engaged Lord Howard and were repulsed and mostly slain. Then James IV, himself leading a great force, came on to Surrey,[257/3] and Lord Darcy's son, who bore the brunt of the battle. Lennox and Argyll's commands were met by Sir Edward Stanley. James was killed within a spear length from Surrey and his body taken to Berwick. The *'rent surcoat of the King of Scots stained with blood'*, was sent to Henry VIII,[12/8] at Tournai. The biggest error the Scots made was placing their officers in the front line, medieval style. A Scottish letter of /January 1514 contrasts this loss of the nobility with the English great men, who took their stand with the reserves and at the rear. The English generals stayed behind the lines in the Renaissance style. The loss of so many Scottish officers, meant there was no one to coordinate a retreat.

3.8.1.4 Tactics and aftermath

Flodden was essentially a victory of bill,[264] used by the English, over the pike,[214/3] used by the Scots. As a weapon, the pike was effective only in a battle of movement, especially to withstand a cavalry charge The pike had become a Swiss weapon of choice and represented modern warfare. The hilly terrain of Northumber- land, the nature of the combat, and the slippery footing, did not allow it to be employed to best effect. Bishop Ruthall reported to Wolsey, *'the bills disappointed the Scots of their long spears, on which they relied.'* The infantrymen at Flodden, both Scots and English, had fought in a fashion that in essence would have been familiar to their ancestors and it has rightly been described, as the last great medieval battle in the British Isles. This was the last time that bill and pike would come together as equals in battle. Two years later, Francis I defeated the Swiss pikemen. at The Battle of Marignano,[265] using a combination of heavy cavalry and artillery, ushering in a new era in the history of war.

Thomas Howard, 2nd Duke of Norfolk was given an augmentation of honour to commemorate the Battle of Flodden Field

An official English diplomatic report, issued by Brian Tuke, noted the Scots' iron spears but concluded: *'the English halberdiers,[266] decided the whole affair, so that in the battle the bows and ordnance were of little use.'* Despite Tuke's comment (he was not present), tactically this battle was one of the first major engagements on the British Isles, where artillery was significantly deployed. John Lesley, writing sixty years later, noted the Scottish bullets flew over the English heads while the English cannon was effective, the one army placed so high and the other so low. The battle is considered the last decisive use of the longbow, yet through the 16th century, the English longbowmen continued to have success, as in The Battle of Pinkie Cleugh.[267] Many of these archers were recruited from Lancashire and Cheshire. Sir Richard Assheton raised one such company from Middleton, near Manchester.

In gratitude for his safe return he rebuilt St. Leonard's, the local parish church. It contains the unique "Flodden Window", depicting each of the archers, and the priest who accompanied them by name in stained glass. As a reward for his victory, Howard was subsequently restored to the title of "Duke of Norfolk", lost by his father's support for Richard III. [268] The arms of the Dukes of Norfolk still carry an augmentation of honour, awarded on account of their ancestor's victory at Flodden, a modified version of the Royal Coat of Arms of Scotland,[269] with an arrow through the lion's mouth. Soon after the battle there were legends that James IV, had survived; a Scottish merchant at Tournai, in October, claimed to have spoken with him, Lindsay of Pitscottie,[Ch 3] records two myths; "*thair cam four great men upon hors, and every ane of thame had ane wisp upoun thair spear headis, quhairby they might know one another and brought the king furth of the feild, upoun ane dun hackney*", and also that the king escaped from the field but was killed between Duns and Kelso. Similarly, John Lesley adds that the body to England was "*my lord Bonhard*" and James was seen in Kelso after the battle and then went secretly on pilgrimage in far nations. Every noble family in Scotland was supposed to have lost a member at Flodden. The deadare remembered by the song (and pipe tune) "The Flowers of the Forest";

> *We'll hae nae mair lilting, at the yowe-milking,*
> *Women and bairns are dowie and wae.*
> *Sighing and moaning, on ilka green loaning,*
> *The flowers of the forest are all wede away.*

3.8.1.5 Casualties

Surrey's,[257/4] army lost 1,500 men killed. There were various conflicting accounts of the Scottish loss. A contemporary French source, *The Gazette of the Battle of Flodden*, said that about 10,000 Scots were killed, a claim made by Henry VIII,[12/9] on 16th September while he was still uncertain of the death of James IV. Italian newsletters put the Scottish losses at 18 or 20 thousand and the English at 5000. Brian Tuke the English Clerk of the Signet, sent a newsletter stating 10,000 Scots killed and 10,000 escaped the field. Tuke reckoned the total Scottish invasion force to have been 60,000 and the English army at 40,000. George Buchanan wrote in his History of Scotland (published in 1582) that according to the lists that were compiled through- counties of Scotland, there were about 5,000 killed. A plaque on the monument to the 2nd Duke of Norfolk (as the Earl of Surrey became in 1514) at Thetford put the figure at 17,000. Notable men who died included Willliam Sinclair, 2nd Earl of Caithness. [Ch 4]

3.8.1.6 Battlefield today

The battlefield still looks much as it probably did at the time of the battle, but the burn and marsh which so badly hampered the Scots advance is now drained. A monument erected in 1910, is easily reached from Branxton village by following the the road past St Paul's Church. There is a small car park and a clearly marked and signposted battlefield trail with interpretive boards which make it easy to visualise the battle. Only the chancel arch remains of the medieval church where James IV's, body was said to have rested after the battle – the rest is Victorian, dating from 1849 and in the "Norman"[5/7] style.

3.8.2 The Battle of SomersDale/Summerdale (May 1529)

John Sinclair, 3rd Earl of Caithness (1490–1529),[Ch 4] died leading 500 men to help James Sinclair defend Orkney. He was succeeded by his son George 4th Earl of Caithness.[Ch 4] William, 4th Lord Sinclair, was taken prisoner The battle was, as any Orcadian should be able to tell you, the last pitched battle fought on Orkney soil. Although history, and local tradition, treats the confrontation as a battle, it was more likely to have been a brief, bloody, skirmish on the boundary of the parishes of Orphir and Stenness. After the transfer of Orkney to the Scottish Crown in 1468, the former Earldom property was rented to tacksmen.[55/3] These individuals collected the various skats,,[270] rents and other dues formerly paid to the Earls. Needless to say, some of the tacksmen were disliked and, in some cases, used their power unscrupulously. In 1489, Lord Henry Sinclair, was tacksman. After his death at the Battle of Flodden,[Ch 3] the tack was allowed to pass to his widow. Henry's son, William, was a minor at the time of his father's death, so his uncle, Lord William Sinclair of Warsetter, (Orkney) took over Henry's legal duties. On Warsetter's death, young William Sinclair was made Justice Depute of Orkney, but his behaviour soon led to trouble and eventually a revolt.

3.8.2.1 The Sinclair uprising

A body of udallers[271] led by James Sinclair of Brecks, (Orkney) refused to pay dues for three years. These men, who feared the encroachment of Scottish feudalism,[42/3] into Orkney, rebelled. James Sinclair, aided by his brother Edward (both illegitimate sons of Sinclair of Warsetter), led the uprising that led to the seizure of the Kirkwall Castle,[272] the Sinclair stronghold. A number of people were killed during the incident and William Sinclair fled from Orkney to take up refuge in Caithness. There, the exiled Sinclair made an appeal to the Crown, asking for assistance to quash the rebellion in Orkney. The following year, a Royal demand was made to the insurgents to hand over the castle. They refused. So, acting on Royal authority, William Sinclair, with the help of his kinsman John, Earl of Caithness, raised a force of around 500 men from Caithness and invaded Orkney. According to Orcadian tradition, the invading force landed in the parish of Orphir, on the north side of Scapa Flow.[273/1] But Sir James Sinclair, well aware that they were approaching, had gathered a large body of Orcadians to resist the invaders. Many traditional stories about the battle have been handed down over the ages.

3.8.2.2 The witch's prophecy

It was said that when the Earl of Caithness and his troops landed in Orphir a witch walked before them on the march. The crone,[274] unwound two balls of wool - one blue, the other red. The red ball was the first to run out and the witch assured the Earl that the side whose blood was spilled first would certainly be defeated. It would appear that the Earl put great faith in the witch's proclamation. So much so that he was determined to slay the first Orcadian he met - man, woman or child - to ensure his victory on the day. The first person he met was a defenceless young herd boy. The Caithness men fell on the hapless youth and murdered him. Only after the lad lay dead at their feet did they learn from the witch that their victim was no Orcadian - he was a Caithness boy who had taken refuge in Orkney. Unnerved by the incident, if tradition is to be believed, the Caithness men's actions had a major effect on their conduct at the battle.

3.8.2.3 The battle by the loch

The Earl's men marched up the valley on the west side of the Loch o' Kirbister, while James Sinclair's Orkney rebels followed a route to the east side of the loch. The two forces met at the valley of Summerdale and in the clash that followed, tradition says that the invaders were completely routed. The invaders cast their weapons into the Kirbister Loch and fled the carnage. But the few who survived the battle were pursued as the ran back to their boats and slaughtered. The Earl himself reached the farm of Oback and dashed in among the farm buildings to seek a hiding place, only to be met by a party of his enemies who slew him on the spot. It was said that the Earl's head was sent back to Caithness in defiance. Only one Orkneyman is said to have been killed on that day. His death was a tragic one; after the battle he dressed himself in clothes taken from a dead Caithness man and on his return home his mother, thinking he was one of the enemy, struck him on the head with a makeshift weapon - a stone in the foot of a stocking.

3.8.2.4 James Sinclair's pardon

But despite Sir James Sinclair blatant defiance of the Crown, the King of Scotland not only pardoned him but also gifted him a feudal,[42/9] grant of the islands of Sanday and Stronsay. Some maintain that this act of appeasement was made in order not to drive the islanders into the arms of King John of Norway and Denmark, who had pledged himself to redeem the mortgaged islands.

3.8.3 The Battle of Solway Moss

Scots, commanded by Oliver Sinclair of Pitcairns,[275/1] were beaten by the English and Oliver Sinclair was taken prisoner, he died in 1560. The Battle took place on Solway Moss near the River Esk on the English side of the Anglo - Scottish Border in November 1542 between forces from England and Scotland

3.8.3.1 Context

When Henry VIII,[12/5] of England broke from the Roman Catholic Church he asked James V of Scotland, his nephew, to do the same. James ignored his uncle's request and further insulted him by refusing to meet with Henry at York. Furious, Henry VIII sent troops against Scotland. In retaliation for the massive English raid into Scotland James responded by assigning Robert Lord Maxwell, the Scottish Warden of West March,,[259/3] the task of raising an army.

3.8.3.2 The Battle

On 24th November 1542, an army of 15,000-18,000 Scots advanced south. Maxwell, though never officially designated commander of the force, declared he would lead the attack in person. The Scots advance was met at

Solway Moss by Sir Thomas Wharton and his 3,000 men. Sir William Musgrove an English commander, reported that Maxwell was still in charge and fought with the rest of the Scottish nobles who dismounted on the bank of the River Esk. A report of Sir George Douglas of Pittendreich,[276] and later chronicle accounts say that with the earlier loss of Maxwell, Sir Oliver Sinclair de Pitcairns, James V's,[Ch 4] favourite, declared himself to be James's chosen commander. Unfortunately, the other commanders refused to accept his command and the command structure disintegrated. The battle was uncoordinated and is better described as a rout. The Scots were pursued by the English and found themselves penned in South of the River Esk on English territory between the river and the Moss, and surrendered themselves and their 10 field guns to the English cavalry. The Scots were *'beguiled by their own guiding'* according to one Scottish writer. Several hundred of the Scots may have drowned in the marshes and river. James, who was not present at the battle (he remained at Lochmaben), withdrew to Falkland Palace humiliated and ill with fever. He died there two weeks later at the age of thirty. According to George Douglas, in his delirium he lamented the capture of his banner and Oliver Sinclair at Solway Moss more than his other losses. He left behind a six-day-old daughter, Mary, Queen of Scots.[145/2]

Gervase Phillips has estimated that only about 7 Englishmen and 20 Scots were killed but 1,200 Scottish prisoners were taken including Sinclair, the Earls of Cassillis and Glencairn and Maxwell. Prisoners taken to England included Lord Gray and Stewart of Rosyth. A number of captured Scottish earls, lords and lairds were released; they sent hostages, called "pledges" into England in their place. These hostages and prisoners were mostly well treated in England as it was hoped that when they returned to Scotland after their ransoms were paid, they would further the English cause. However, a modern historian Marcus Merriman sees the battle and hostage-taking more as the culmination of James V's war rather than the beginning of Henry VIII's,[12/6] Rough Wooing.[277] He notes that the capture of so many Scottish nobles at the time of the birth and accession of Mary Queen of Scots did not affect Henry's policy or the Scottish lords's subsequent rejection of The Treaty of Greenwich,[278] in Dec. 1543.

3.8.4 The Battle of Dail-Riabhach

The Battle of Dial-Riabhach was a Scottish clan battle that took place in the year 1576. It was fought between members of the Highland Clan MacKay with the involvement of John Sinclair, 5th Earl of Caithness,[Ch 4] and chief of the Clan Sinclair.[Ch. 3] An account of the battle was written in the book *Conflicts of the Clans* published by the Foulis Press in 1764, taken from a manuscript from the time of *King* James VI of Scotland (1566 - 1625):

> *The year of God 1576, Y Roy Mackay of Strathnaver dying, there arose civil dissension in Strathnaver betwixt John Mackay (the son of Y Roy) and Neil Nawerigh (the said Y Roy's brother). John Mackay excludes his uncle Neil (who was thought to be righteous heir, and took possession of Strathnaver. Neil, again, alleging that his nephews John and Donald were bastards, doth claim these lands, and makes his refuge of John Earl of Caithness, of whom he did obtain a company of men, who were sent with Neil's four sons to invade Strathnaver. They take possession of the country from John Mackay, who being unable to resist their forces, retires to the Clan Chattan to seek their support, and leaves his brother Donald Mackay to defend the country as he might. Donald, in his brothers absence, surprised his* cousin-german,[279] *under silence of the night at Dail-Riabhach, and killed two of his cousins (the sons of Neil Nawerigh) with the most part of their company. Thereafter, Neil Nawerigh came and willingly surrendered himself to his nephews John and Donald, who caused apprehend their uncle Neil, and beheaded him at a place called Clash-nan-ceap in Strathnaver.*

3.8.5 The Battle of Allt Camhna

The Battle of Allt Camhna was a Scottish clan battle fought in 1586 between the Clan Gunn and Clan MacKay against the Clan Sinclair.[Ch. 3]

3.8.5.1 Background

In 1585 a meeting took place at Elgin Scotland between George Gordon, 1st Marquess of Huntly,[280/1] John Gordon, 12th Earl of Sutherland,[281/1] George Sinclair, 5th Earl of Caithness,[Ch 4] and Hugh MacKay of Strathnaver.[282/1] The purpose of the meeting was to repair relations which had become damaged between the Earl of Sutherland, Earl of Caithness and Hugh MacKay, in Assint,[283/1] both having gone there on the orders of the Earl of Caithness. It was decided at the meeting that the Clan Gunn should be "made away" because they were judged to be the principal authors of these "troubles and commotions". However both Hugh MacKay and George Sinclair, Earl of Caithness, were unwilling to attack their old allies the clan Gunn and therefore departed from the meeting at Elgin. In consequence, 1586 George Gordon, Marquess of Huntly came north to Sutherland, the lands of his cousin, John Gordon 12th Earl of Sutherland.[281/2] He sent a message to both Hugh Mackay George Sinclair, Earl of Caithness,[Ch 4] to meet him there. The Earl of Caithness met with the Gordon Earls of Huntly,[280/2] and Sutherland but MacKay,[282/2] did not and was denounced as a rebel by Sutherland. At this meeting an agreement was made that George Sinclair Earl of Caithness, Chief of Clan Sinclair,[Ch. 3] would expel the Clan Gunn from the lands of Sutherland and Caithness. The Clan Sinclair gathered under the command of Henry Sinclair, the uncle of William and Hugh MacKay. Having been informed of the proceedings at this meeting, the Clan Gunn gathered their forces and prepared for battle. They were joined by William MacKay and a strong force from the Clan MacKay. William MacKay proposed to attack the men of the Clan Sutherland but this was overuled by the Clan Gunn who opted to fight the Clan Sinclair of Caithness instead.

3.8.5.2 Account of The Battle of Allt Camhna

Historian Sir Robert Gordon (1580 – 1656) who was living at the time of the battle and was a close relative of John Gordon, Earl of Sutherland, wrote an account of the battle in his book the "Genealogical History of the Earldom of Sutherland":-

> *So having the advantage of the hill, they set upon the enemy with a resolute courage. The Caithness-men came short with their first flight of arrows; by contrary, the Guns spared their shot until they came hard to the enemy, which then they bestowed among them to great advantage. In the end the clan Gun overthrew the Caithness-men at Auldgown,[284] upon the borders of Caithness, the year 1586, and killed seven score of their most resolute men, with their captain Henry Sinclair, cousin to the Earl of Caithness, and uncle to Hugh and William MacKay. William MacKay was sore*

for the slaughter of his uncle, Henry Sinclair, whom he knew not to be there till he was slain; but afterwards in the chase William MacKay spared no man. The Caithness host had been all destroyed, had not the darkness of the night favoured their flight. Hugh MacKay was then in Caithness, with Earl George; but the inhabitants of Caithness understanding that his brother, William MacKay was with the clan Gun at the conflict of Auldgown, they sought for Hugh MacKay to slay him; whereupon he was forced in all haste to flee secretly into Strathnaver, thereby to eschew,[285] their present fury.

3.8.5.3 Aftermarth

Shortly after the Battle of Allt Camhna the Clan Gunn, was defeated at The Battle of Leckmelm,[286] by the Clan MacLeod, the Clan Sutherland, and the Clan Mackay.

3.8.6 Other events (1568–1592)

In 1568	Henry 3rd Lord Sinclair assisted Mary, Queen of Scots,[145/4] to escape from Lochleven Castle.[287]
In pursuit (1570)	John Sinclair, Master of Caithness, son of George Sinclair 4th Earl of Caithness,[C5.3.1] burned the local Cathedral in pursuit of men from the Clan Murray,[A7] who had taken refuge in the steeple. John was later imprisoned in Castle Sinclair Girnigoe,[5.1] by his father until 1577.
Battle near Wick,[155/2] (1588)	John Gordon, 12th Earl of Sutherland,[281/3] divorced his obnoxious Sinclair wife in 1573. He waged all out war with her father and Clan Sinclair,[Ch. 3] before gaining a decisive victory outside Wick in 1588, when more than a hundred Sinclair clansmen were killed in a pitched battle on the seashore. Earl Alexander later married Jean Gordon, the divorced wife of the Earl of Bothwell,[288] third husband to Mary Queen of Scots. The Sinclair's Girnigoe Castle withstood a siege by the Earl of Sutherland and his forces of the Clan Sutherland,[A4] in 1588. In 1589, George Sinclair, 4th Earl,[4.3.08] invades and ravishes the lands of the Clan Sutherland.

Resignation of Earldom (1592)	On 3rd April 1592, George, 5th Earl of Caithness,[Ch 4] resigned Earldom in return for novodamus.[33/2] On 11th Dec. 1592 his son William Sinclair of Mey,[289/1] was knighted by King James IV of Scotland.

3.9 17th century clan conflicts and Civil War

3.9.1 Battle of Kringen (1612)

An Adolph Tidemand paining representing Sinclair's forces landing in Norway

Battle of Kringen, (Slaget ved Kringen) 1612, Otta, Norway. George Sinclair was killed with most of his men in an ambush The Battle was a battle perpetrated by a Norwegian peasant militia against Scottish mercenary soldiers who were on their way to enlist in the Swedish army for The Kalmar War.[290] The battle has since become a part of folklore in Norway, giving names to local places in the Otta region. A longstanding misconception was that George Sinclair, chief of the Highland Clan Sinclair was the commander of the forces; in fact, he was subordinate to Lieutenant Colonel Alexander Ramsay.[291/1]

3.9.1.1 Background

Scottish forces were partly recruited, partly pressed into service by Sir James Spens, apparently against the preferences of James VI who was partial to the Danish side of the war. Two ships sailed from Dundee and Caithness in early August, met up on the Orkney Islands and sailed for Norway. Because sea routes had been blocked by Danish forces in the Kalmar War, the Scottish forces decided to follow a land route to Sweden that other Scottish and Dutch forces had successfully used. On 20th August the ships landed in Isjforden in Romsdal, though the pilot apparently through an act of sabotage, put the forces on shore in rough terrain. The soldiers proceeded to march up Romsdalen and down the valley of Gudbrandsdalen. Having been warned of the incursion and probably inflamed by a massacre of Norwegian conscripts at Nya Lödöse, and the events of Mönnichhoven-s march (Mönnichhoven-marsjen) earlier in July, the farmers and peasants of the Vågå, Lesja, Dovre, Fron, and Ringebu mobilized to meet the enemy. Legend has it that the sheriff of the area, Lars Gunnarson Hågå (b. approx. 1570, d. approx. 1650), came into the church in Dovre with a battle axe, struck it on the floor and shouted *"Let it be known-the enemy has come to our land!" (Gjev ljod - fienden har kome til landet!).*

3.9.1.2 Order of battle

As the Scottish forces progressed southward, they were followed by Norwegian scouts. Scottish forces included two companies on foot, commanded by George Sincair and Alexander Ramsay. In recent years it has been argued that the Scots were lightly armed, but this is not probable and the bodies were looted afterwards for weapons and belongings. The Norwegians were armed with swords, spears, axes, a few muskets and some crossbows. According to folklore, the force of the Scottish troops was between 900 and 1,100 or more but historians generally discount the estimate, placing the probable strength as low as 300. The strength of the Norwegian militia troops is estimated to about 500.

3.9.1.3. Combat operations

There are few entirely credible accounts of the battle but the oral history has two Norwegians on horseback following the Scottish troops, possibly on the other side of the valley. One was a woman by the name of Guri, known as Prillar-Guri to posterity; the other was an unnamed man. The man rode his horse facing backward, providing a distraction for the marching troops. When the Scots reached the narrowest section of the valley - Kringen - Guri blew in her horn signalling the ambush. According to folklore the Norwegian troops let loose logs and rocks down the valley, crushing the marching soldiers but this appears not be confirmed. It is known however, that they also shot at the soldiers with crossbows and muskets. Among the first to fall was George Sinclair, apparently shot by Berdon Sejelstad.[292] It is his name that is most commonly associated with the battle. Sinclair was a nephew of the Earl of Caithness and a historical figure in the Clan Sinclair.[Ch. 3]

Close combat ensued, the militiamen fighting with axes, scythes and presumably other improvised weapons. Most of the Scots were killed during the battle. Some may have escaped, but others were captured. All but 14 were summarily executed at Kvam in what is now Nord-Fron, the survivors then sent to Christiania for imprisonment. Those killed were thrown into a mass grave north of the Scottish barn at the local cemetery which later was called Skottehaugen (Scots barrow). Among these survivors were the officers Alexander Ramsay,[291/2] Sir Henry Bruce, James Moneypenny and James Scott. These were eventually repatriated, Ramsay being made the scapegoat for the defeat.

3.9.1.4 Aftermath and legacy

It is considered that this battle constituted a defense of Norwegian sovereignty, and was historically interpreted that way when the patriotic movement arose about 160 years later. A number of places were named after the Scottish incursion, notably along the route. The (Skottetoget), in which the soldiers were held captive, was destroyed by artillery fire and during the intense British-German hostilities at Kvam in 1940. The Gudbrandsdal War Museum at Kvam also has a display commemorating the battle which has a model of one of the Caithness Scots together with a Scots broadsword,[293] and attributed to the battle. Captured Scottish weapons including a pistol, a Lochaber axe,[294] and basket hilt claymores,[295] were put on display at the Gudbrandsdal War Museum Kvam to commemorate the battle. There is some evidence that many Scotsmen settled in Norway and farm names may confirm that. There is also a "Sinclair's Club" in Otta, / and there are regular re-enactments of the battle. Sinclair's grave is a local landmark, and though the Norwegians at the time sought to desecrate his memory by burying him outside the church walls he is now revered in the area.

Scottish barn Skottetogetat /...... Klomstad, Kvam in Hordaland county, Norway

Monument in Otta over the battle site.

Since there has been a historical connection between Norway and Scotland in general and Caithness in particular, the battle has become a matter of shared history between the two peoples. Part of The bunad,[296] design for this area - known as rutaliv - is reminiscent of the Sinclair red tartan.

3.9.1.5 In literature and music

Norwegian poet Edvard Storm wrote a poem that tells the story of the battle Zinklarvisa (Sinclair's Song). Henrik Wergeland wrote an historical tragedy, called "*The death of Sinclair*" (Sinklars død). The plotline concerns Sinclair and his Lady, telling of the fatal choices that led to the tragic deaths at Kringen. The Norwegian folk-rock band Folque's song Sinclairvise makes use of Storm's poem. The Faroese metal group Týr made a version of this song on their 2008 album Land, called *Sinklars Visa* In 2009 The Norwegian rock band Street Legal released an instrumental song called *The Battle of Kringen* on their album titled Bite the bullet.

3.9.2 The Battle of Carbisdale

Carbisdale loch in Carbisdale woods where the royalist army was cut down

James Graham, 1st Marquess of Montrose,[109/2] was defeated. He was supported by the Sinclairs and Major Sinclair helped Montrose to escape but he was later betrayed by MacLeod of Assynt,[283/2] imprisoned in Ardvreck Castle,[297/1] tried and killed. The Battle (also known as Invercarron) took place close to the Village of Culrain on April 27th 1650 and was part of The Wars of the Three Kingdoms.[106/2] (Part of the Scottish Civil War). It was fought by the Royalist Marquess of Montrose against the Scottish Government of the time, dominated by the Marquess of Argyll and a grouping of radical Covenanters,[107/2] known as *The* Kirk Party.

3.9.2.1 Charles and Montrose

After the execution of Charles I in January 1649, Scotland entered a period of complex political maneuvering. His son was immediately proclaimed as Charles II, in Edinburgh, though it was soon to be made clear to him that if he were ever to exercise real power he would be obliged to subscribe to a radical Presbyterian,[114/2] agenda. Amongst other things he would be required to take the Covenants of 1638 and 1643,,[298/1] a move his father had always resisted. In exile at the Hague Charles was anxious to take the quickest way back to the throne. He initially favoured calling on the assistance of the Catholic Irish authorities at Kilkenny, until this option was removed by Oliver Cromwell,[299/1] in the summer of 1649. In falling back on the Covenanters Charles hoped to put them in a more accommodating frame of mind. One way of doing this was to take the advice of the ultra-royalist Marquess of Montrose,[109/3] who had led a military campaign against the Covenanters,[107/1] in 1644 and 1645, enjoying some notable successes. On 22nd February 1649, Charles appointed Montrose as Lieutenant-Governor of Scotland and Captain General of all of his forces there. Although he was about to receive a deputation from the government in Edinburgh he was prepared to listen to Montrose's more militant advice, especially as there were already some stirrings against the Covenanters in northern Scotland.

3.9.2.2 Landing in Orkney

Throughout the course of the year Montrose kept busy using his commission in an attempt to raise troops and money in the German state of Brandenburg, as well as Sweden and Denmark. This met with limited success; but by September he had managed to raise and equip a small force of 80 officers and 100 Danish soldiers soldiers under the leadership of The Earl of Kinnoul.[300] These men were sent as an advance party to occupy the Orkney Isles, charged with recruiting local forces, while Montrose remained on the Continent employing professional troops. In March 1650 Montrose came in person landing at Kirkwall with some more foreign mercenaries to join his advance party and the Orcadian levies. Amongst his officers was Sir John Hurry his old opponent at The Battle of Auldearn,[301] in 1645. Altogether he had 40 horse, 500 mercenaries and 700 Orcadians, completely unskilled in the arts of war. On board his ship the Herderinnan, anchored in Scapa Flow,[273/2] Montrose issued his orders to Hurry at a conference on 9th April. He was instructed to cross to Caithness that same evening with part of the little army and advance to Ord of Caithness,[302/1] a high hill overhanging the sea just north of Kildonan. Montrose crossed with the rest of his force a few days later. Montrose had heard that the local Highland Scottish Clans of Munro, Ross and MacKenzie,were up in arms and were likely to join him although as it turned out, they did not. Montrose hoped to meet up with the Clan Munro,and Clan Ross. When none of the clans arrived he pressed on to Strathoikell and into the narrow valley of Carbisdale. For two days he waited in the valley for the Munros and Rosses. Waiting for them was his biggest mistake as the clans had sided with the Scottish government and Argyll had already set his counter plans in operation.

3.9.2.3 Strachan's Ride

In Edinburgh the Committee of Estates, the executive authority of the Scottish Parliament was soon aware that Montrose had crossed to the mainland. General David Leslie,[303/1] was instructed to take his forces north to prevent this incursion from developing into a major rising. A rendezvous was held at Brechin on 25th April. From here Colonel Archibald Strachan was sent ahead to gather the cavalry that had wintered in the north. He now had five troops of horse under his command, including three that had been with him at the rout of an anti-Covenanter,[107/4] army at Balvenie Castle,[304/1] near Dufftown in May 1649. This episode, known as the *'Bourd of Balvenie'*, convinced Strachan and the more extreme Covenanters that all that was needed to disperse the mighty was a small band of righteous men, after the example of Gideon in the Book of Judges. Strachan now rode on to Rossshire convinced that victory was already his.

3.9.2.4 Montrose Moves South

Montrose joined Sir John Hurry at the Ord of Caithness.[302/2] From here their combined force advanced along the coast to Dunrobin Castle,[305] garrisoned for the government by the tenants of the Earl of Sutherland as were the smaller fortresses at Skelbo Castle,[306] Skibo Castle.[307] and Dornoch Castle.[308] Avoiding these obstacles the royalists turned aside, marching up Strathfleet towards Strathoykell. The Oykell was forded just to the west of its junction with the Cassley and the trek continued along the southern bank. Montrose had counted on the support of the Mackenzies,but their chief the Earl of Seaforth was in exile, and even his brother Sir Thomas Mackenzie of Pluscardine,[309] who led the rising the previous year remained quiet. With no support in the hills the rebels continued back towards the coastal plain, halting at Carbisdale on the southern side of the Kyle of Sutherland on 27th April. By now Strachan was at Tain conferring with the Earl of Sutherland. Learning of Montrose's whereabouts he decided on an immediate surprise attack.

3.9.2.5 Carbisdale

Ardvreck Castle where Montrose surrendered to Neil Macleod of Assyant after the Battle of Carbisdale

Montrose's,[109/4] army was in a narrow glen, where the Culrain Burn flows into the Kyle of Sutherland. To his rear the ground rose up to the wooded hill of *Creag a' Choineachan.* With a good view of the surrounding countryside he would be able to deploy his men on the hill if subject to a sudden attack. Yet believing there was a small body of enemy horse in the area he failed to carry out a thorough reconnaissance, thus making the same mistake that led to the disaster at the Battle of Philiphaugh.[310] Strachan had now reached Wester Fern to the south-east of Carbisdale. On his onward march he still had the River Carron to cross by a ford which left him some miles short of the enemy position. A direct approach would only alert the royalists to his position. Fortunately much of the way was covered by thick broom,[311] which ended just before the Culrain Burn was reached. Close to the Burn Strachan concealed his men in a gully overshadowed by broom, allowing only a single troop to emerge into the open. Montrose sent his cavalry under Major John Lisle to investigate, while the infantry took cover in the woods of Creag a' Choineachan. Before these deployments were complete Strachan's whole force emerged and charged. Lisle was immediately overwhelmed as the Covenanters,[107/3] rode on towards the infantry. The Germans and Danes seeing their cavalry defeated, retreated into nearby Scroggie Wood. Here Clan Munro,and Clan Ross joined in the fight eager to grab their share of any plunder. The Germans and Danes fought gallantly, retreating deeper and deeper into the wood, but they were losing the battle. The need for self preservation took over and those that were left attempted to flee with the bloodshed in the wood continuing for over two hours. Even after the battle ended the slaughter did not cease; the clansmen of Ross-shire and

Sutherland for many days after continued pursuing and killing those who had escaped the battle. Hurry and some of the Danish and German musketeers attempted to make a stand, but the Orcadians crumbled in panic. Two hundred of them were drowned trying to escape across the waters of the Kyle of Sutherland. In a matter of minutes the whole affair was over. Carbisdale was not a battle: it was a rout. The defeated soldiers were hunted over the slopes of Creag a' Choineachan by Strachan's troopers and local hostile clansmen for two hours. Four hundred were killed and over four hundred and fifty taken prisoner including Sir John Hurry, whose amazing career as a soldier was shortly to come to an end.

3.9.2.6 Death and Transfiguration

Despite his wounds Montrose,[109/5], managed to escape from the debacle at Carbisdale with help from Major Sinclair. For some days he managed to avoid capture, disguised as a shepherd, until he finally fell captive to Neil Macleod of Assyant,[283/3] at Ardvreck Castle.[297/2] MacLeod was an ally of the Earl of Sutherland. Already condemned to death in absentia, he was taken to Edinburgh where he heard his fate read out by Archibald Johnston at Parliament House. He was to be hanged at the town cross with a copy of *De Rebus*, Bishop George Wishart's laudatory history of the marquess' life and exploits round his neck. He was to swing on the scaffold for three hours after which time he would be taken down, his head cut off and his body divided in four quarters. His head would be displayed on a spike at the Tollbooth Prison while his arms and legs would be sent for similar display at Glasgow, Perth, Stirling and Aberdeen. Only his trunk was to be shown any mercy: for if he repented his crimes, it would be buried in consecrated ground at Greyfriars otherwise it would be deposited in a common grave outside the city on the nearby Burgh Muir. Needless to say he would concede nothing to his enemies. Sentence was carried out on 21st May. He accepted his fate with courage and like the king before him, was transfigured in death. Hurry followed soon after. With all options now exhausted Charles took the Covenants,[298/2] against his conscience and judgement. He arrived in Scotland that summer. Unfortunately for him so did Cromwell.[299/2]

3.9.3 The Battle of Dunbar

Sir William Sinclair of Rosslyn,[23/3] was killed leading the Clan Sinclair.[Ch. 3] He was the last Knight to be buried in full armour below Rosslyn Chapel.

[5.3] General Monck,[312/1], sacked Rosslyn Castle,[5.2] but the Chapel was spared although used for stabling horses. Sir John Sinclair of Rosslyn sent to Tynemouth Castle.[313] The Battle (3rd September 1650) was a battle of The Third English Civil war.[314] The English Parliamentarian forces under Oliver Cromwell,[298/3] defeated a Scottish army commanded by David Leslie,[302/1] which is loyal to King Charles II, who had been proclaimed King of Scots on 5th February 1649.

"Cromwell at Dunbar", by Andrew Carrick Gow

3.9.3.1 Background

The English Parliament had long suspected the true intentions of the Scots. Their worst fears were realised when the Engagers invaded England in 1648, however the Duke of Hamilton was proved to be a poor commander and was easily defeated at The Battle of Preston.[315] On June 23rd 1650 Charles II landed in Scotland at Garmouth in Moray. On his arrival he signed the 1638 Covenant and the 1643 Solemn League and Covenant,[298/2] and was proclaimed King of Scots. This infuriated the English authorities and they decided to invade Scotland. Sir Thomas Fairfax, the Army's commander, disagreed with this strategy and resigned. Oliver Cromwell was made General in his place. John Lambert was appointed Sergeant Major General and the Army's second-in-command. As Cromwell led his army over the border at Berwick-upon-Tweed in July 1650, the Scottish general Sir David Leslie, decided that his best strategy was to avoid a direct conflict with the enemy. His army were not the battle hardend veterans of The Thirty Years War,[316] who had taken the field for the Scots at Newburn and Marston Moor. Many of them had perished during the Civil War and the ill fated 1648 invasion of England. Far more had left active service after the former event. This meant that a new army had to be raised and trained by the remaining veteran soldiers. Eventually the army comprised some 12,000 soldiers, outnumbering the English army of 11,000 men. Though the Scots soldiers were well armed, the lack of time meant they were poorly trained compared to their English counterparts all of whom had served with Oliver Cromwell for years. Leslie chose therefore to shelter his troops behind strong fortifications around Edinburgh and refused to be drawn

out to meet the English in battle. Furthermore between Edinburgh and the border, Leslie adopted a scorched earth policy thus forcing Cromwell,[299/5] to obtain all of his supplies from England, most arriving by sea through the port at Dunbar. Whether in a genuine attempt to avoid prolonging the conflict or whether because of the difficult circumstances he found himself in, Cromwell sought to persuade the Scots to accept the English point of view. Claiming that it was the King who was his enemy rather than the Scottish people, he wrote to his opponents on 3rd August famously stating *I beseech you, in the bowels of Christ, think it possible you may be mistaken.* This plea, however, was unsuccessful.

3.9.3.2 The Battle

By early September the English army, weakened by illness and demoralised by lack of success, began to withdraw towards its supply base at Dunbar. Leslie,[303/2] believing that the English army was retreating, ordered his army to advance in pursuit. The Scots army reached Dunbar first and Leslie positioned his troops overlooking the town and the Berwick Road, which was Cromwell's land route back to England. However, the Scots army was funded by the Church of Scotland.[317] Eager not to waste funds, the church officials put Leslie under great pressure to finish the battle quickly. On 2nd September 1650, Leslie brought his army down from Doon Hill and approached the town. Witnessing this manoeuvre Cromwell quickly realised that here was an opportunity for him to turn the tables on the Scots. That night under cover of darkness, Cromwell secretly re-deployed a large number of his troops to a position opposite the Scottish right flank. Just before dawn on 3rd September shouting their battle cry '*The Lord of Hosts!*', the English launched a surprise attack. Soldiers in the centre and on the left flank caught Leslie's

Unidentified blue and white Scots flag, captured at Dunbar 1650 (BM Harl. 1460/5), probably belonged to Campbell of Lawer's Regiment

Third Captain's Colour, Steward's Edinburgh Regiment (BM Harl. 1460/98), captured at Dunbar

men unawares but were held by the greater number of Scottish opponents. On the right flank however, the Scots soldiers were pushed back under the weight of superior English numbers until their lines started to disintegrate. Observing this disaster the rest of the Scottish army lost heart, broke ranks and fled. In the rout that followed, the English cavalry drove the Scots army from the field in disorder. Cromwell claimed that 3,000 Scots were killed. On the other hand Sir James Balfour a senior officer with the Scottish army, noted in his journal that there were *"8 or 900 killed"*. There is similar disagreement about the number of Scottish prisoners taken:- Cromwell claimed that there were 10,000 while the English Royalist leader, Sir Edward Walker put the number at 6,000, of which 1,000 sick and wounded men were quickly released. The more conservative estimates of the Scottish casualties areborne out by the fact that, the day after the battle, Leslie,[303/3] retreated to Stirling with some 4,000-5,000 of his remaining troops.

3.9.3.3 The aftermath

As a result of the destruction of the Scottish army, Cromwell was able to march unopposed to Edinburgh. He quickly captured the Scottish capital although Edinburgh Castle,[204/4] held out until the end of December. The prisoners were then force- marched south towards England in order to prevent any attempt to rescue them. The conditions on the march were so appalling that many of the prisoners died of starvation illness or exhaustion. By 11th September when the remnants arrived at Durham Cathedral where they were to be imprisoned, only 3,000 Scottish soldiers were still alive. If Sir Edward Walker's statement that 6,000 prisoners were taken and 5,000 of them were marched south was correct, then 2,000 captives perished on the way to Durham. Of the estimated 5,000 Scottish soldiers that began the march southwards from Dunbar over 3,500 died either on the march or during imprisonment in Durham Cathedral, more than the total number killed on the battlefield. Of the 1,400 survivors the majority were eventually transported as slave labour to English colonies in the New World and the Caribbean· After formally accepting the Solemn Oath and Covenant,[298/3] Charles, was finally crowned King in Scotland on 1st January 1651.

3.9.3.4 Footnotes

1. Although Durham Cathedral offered a degree of shelter the English failed to provide their prisoners with adequate food or fuel. For a

time, the prisoners kept warm by burning all of the woodwork in the Cathedral with the notable exception of Prior Castell's Clock in the South Transept.[318] It is thought that they left the clockalone because it carries a thistle, the emblem of Scotland on it. The prisoners did take the opportunity to revenge themselves on the tombs of the Neville family however, beheading their effigies and most of the statuary in the Cathedral. Lord Ralph had commanded part of the English army which had defeated the Scots at The Battle of Neville's Cross,[Ch 3] in 1346 on the outskirts of Durham City.

2. By the end of October, cold, malnutrition and disease had resulted in the deaths of another 1,600 of the Scots soldiers. The bodies of many of those who had died were buried in a mass grave in the form of a trench running northwards from the Cathedral. The location of their remains was then forgotten for almost three centuries until rediscovered by workmen in 1946. There is no permanent memorial to these soldiers and it is suggested that they had received neither Christian burial nor blessing, although their story is briefly told in the Cathedral guidebook. In 1933 the Cathedral approved in principle a request by the Scottish Covenanter's,[107/4] Memorials Association to erect a suitable memorial or plaque but progress seems to have stalled at this stage. A campaign properly to respect and remember the "Dunbar Martyrs" was launched at the end of 2007, aiming at least to gain a Christian blessing for the dead and an adequate memorial at the Cathedral burial site or even possible exhumation of the remains and reburial in Scotland (Dunbar Martyrs site).

3.9.4 The Battle of Worcester

The Clan Sinclair led by John, 9th Lord Sinclair, fought for King Charles II. John Sinclair was captured by Oliver Cromwell's,[299/3] forces, imprisoned in The Tower of London,[200/2] and then at Windsor Castle,[319/1] until 1660, when he was liberated by General Monck.[312/2] The Battle took place on 3rd September 1651 at Worcester England and was the final battle of The English Civil War.[320/1] Oliver Cromwell and the Parliamentarians defeated the Royalist, predominantly Scottish, forces of King Charles II. The 16,000 Royalist forces were overwhelmed by the 28,000 strong "New Model Army" of Cromwell.[321/1]

3.9.4.1 Invasion of England

Oliver Cromwell in the Battle of Worcester

The king was aided by Scottish allies and was attempting to regain the throne that had been lost when his father Charles I, was executed. The commander of the Scots Sir David Leslie,[303/2] supported the plan of fighting in Scotland, where royal support was strongest. Charles however, insisted on making war in England. He calculated that Cromwell's,[299/5] campaign north of the River Forth would allow the main Scottish Royalist army which was south of the Forth to steal the march on the Roundhead,[322] New Model Army,[321/2] in a race to London. He hoped to rally not merely the old faithful Royalists, but also the overwhelming numerical strength of the English Presbyterians,[114/3] to his standard. He calculated that his alliance with the Scottish Presbyterian Covenanters,[107/3] and his signing of the Solemn League and Covenant,[298/2] would encourage English Presbyterians to support him against the English Independent faction which had grown in power over the last few years. The Royalist army was kept well in hand, no excesses were allowed, and in a week the Royalists covered 150 miles in marked contrast to the Duke of Hamilton's ill fated expedition of 1648.

On 8th August the troops were given a well-earned rest between Penrith and Kendal. But the Royalists were mistaken in supposing that the enemy was taken aback by their new move. Everything had been foreseen both by Cromwell and by the Council of State in Westminster. The latter had called out the greater part of the militia on 7th August. Lieutenant-General Charles Fleetwood began to draw together the midland contingents at Banbury. The London-trained bands turned out for field service no more than 14,000 strong. Every suspected Royalist was closely watched and the magazines of arms in the country-houses of the gentry were for the most part removed into the strong places. On his part Cromwell had quietly made his preparations. Perth passed into his hands on 22nd August and he brought back his army to Leith by 5th August. Thence he dispatched Lieutenant-General John Lambert with a cavalry corps to harass the invaders. Major-General Thomas Harrison was already at Newcastle picking thebest of the county mounted-troops to add to his own regulars. On 9th August, Charles II, was at Kendal, Lambert hovering in his rear and Harrison marching swiftly to bar his way at the Mersey. Thomas Fairfax emerged for a moment from his retirement to organize the Yorkshire levies, and the best of these as well as of the Lancashire, Cheshire and Staffordshire militias were directed upon Warrington, which Harrison reached on 15th August, a few hours in front of Charles's advanced guard. Lambert too, slipping round the left flank of the enemy, joined Harrison, and the English fell back (16th August), slowly and without letting themselves be drawn into a fight, along the London road.

3.9.4.2 Worcester campaign

Cromwell [299/8] meanwhile, leaving George Monck,[312/4] with the least efficient regiments to carry on the war in Scotland had reached the river Tyne in seven days and thence, marching 20 miles a day in extreme heat with the country people carrying their arms and equipment the regulars entered Ferrybridge on 19th August, at which date Lambert, Harrison and the north-western militia were about Congleton. It seemed probable that a great battle would take place between Lichfield and Coventry on or just after 25th August and that Cromwell, Harrison, Lambert and Fleetwood would all take part in it. But the scene and the date of the denouement,[323] were changed by the enemy's movements. Shortly after leaving Warrington the young king had resolved to abandon the direct march on London and to make for the Severn valley, where his father had found the most constant and the most numerous adherents in the first war and which had been the centre of gravity of the English Royalist movement of 1648. Sir Edward Massey formerly the Parliamentary governor of Gloucester, was now with Charles II,[Ch 4] and it was hoped that he would induce his fellow Presbyterians,[114/3] to take arms. The military quality of the Welsh Royalists was well proved,

A young Charles II, painted two years after the Battle of Worcester

Oliver Cromwell

that of the Gloucestershire Presbyterians not less so and based on Gloucester and Worcester as his father had been based on Oxford, Charles II hoped, naturally, to deal with an independent minority more effectually than Charles I, had done with a Parliamentary majority of the people of England. But even the pure Royalism which now ruled in the invading army could not alter the fact that it was a Scottish army and it was not an independent faction but all England that took arms against.

Charles arrived at Worcester on 22nd August and sent five days in resting the troops preparing for further operations and fathering and arming the few recruits who came in. The delay was to prove fatal; it was a necessity of the case foreseen and accepted when the march to Worcester had been decided upon. Had the other course, that of marching on London via Lichfield, been taken the battle would have been fought three days earlier with the same result. Cromwell the Lord General, had during his march south thrown out successively two flying columns under Colonel Robert Lilburne to deal with the Lancashire detachment ofthe enemy on their way to join the main Royalist army at The Battle of Wigan Lane [324/1] on 25th August and as affairs turned out Cromwell [299/10] merely shifted the area of his concentration to marches to the south-west, to Evesham.

Early on 28th August, Lambert surprised the passage of the Severn at Upton, 6 miles below Worcester, and in the action which followed Massey [p103] was severly wounded. Fleetwood followed Lambert. [p102]. The enemy was now only 16,000 strong and disheartened by the apathy with which they had been received in districts formely all their own. Cromwell, for the only time in his military career had a two-to-one numberical superiority. On 30th August, Cromwell delayed the start of the battle to give time for two pontoon bridges to be constructed, one over the Severn and the other over the River Teme close to their confluence. The delay allowed Cromwell to launch his attach on 3rd September, on year to the day since his victory at The Battle of Dunbar [325/1] in 1650.

3.9.4.3 The Battle

Cromwell,[299/6] took his measures deliberately. Lilburne from Lancashire and Major Mercer with the Worcestershire horse were to secure Bewdley Bridge, 20 miles north of Worcester and on the enemy's line of retreat. Fleetwood was to force his way across the Teme and attack St John's, the western suburb of Worcester. While Lambert commanded the Eastern

Flank of the Army which would advance and encircle the Eastern walls of Worcester, Cromwell would lead the attack on the southern ramparts of the city. The assault started on the morning of 3rd September and initially the initiative lay with the Parliamentarians. Fleetwood forced passage of the Teme over the pontoon bridges against Royalists under the command of Major General Montgomery. Colonel Richard Dean's initial attempts to cross the Powick Bridge (where Prince Rupert of the Rhine had won The Battle of Powick Bridge,[326/1] his first victory in 1642) failed against stubborn resistance by the Royalists (many of whom were battle-hardened Scottish Highlanders) commanded by Colonel Keith. By force of arms and numbers the Royalist army was pushed backward by the New Model Army,[321/2] with Cromwell on the eastern bank of the Severn and Fleetwood on the western sweeping in a semicircle four miles long up toward Worcester. The Royalists contested every hedgerow around Powick meadows. This stubborn resistance on the west bank of the Severn north of the Teme was becoming a serious problem for the Parliamentarians, so Cromwell led Parliamentary reinforcements from the eastern side of the town over the Severn pontoon bridge to aid Fleetwood.

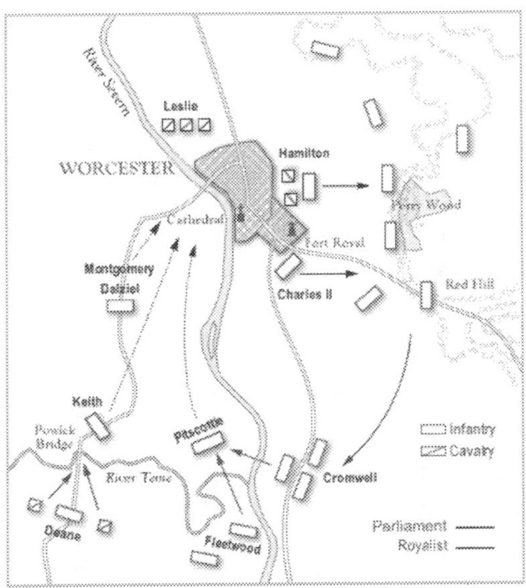

Map Battle of Worcester

Charles II,[A1.2.8.2] from his vantage point on top of Worcester cathedral's tower realised that an opportunity existed to attack the now-exposed eastern flank of the Parliamentary army. As the defenders on the Western side of the city retreated in good order into the city (although during this manoeuver Keith was captured and Montgomery was badly wounded), Charles ordered two sorties to attack the Parliamentary forces east of the city. The north-eastern sortie through St. Martin's Gate was commanded by the Duke of Hamilton and attacked the Parliamentary lines at Perry Wood. The south-eastern one through Sidbury Gate was led by Charles II,[A1.2.8.2] and attacked Red Hill. The Royalist cavalry under the command of David Leslie,[305/3] that was gathered on Pitchcroft meadow on the northern side of the city did not receive orders to aid the sorties and Leslie chose not to do so under his own initiative. Cromwell,[299/7] seeing the difficulty that his east flank was under rushed back over the Severn pontoon bridge with three brigades of troops to reinforce the flank. Although they were pushed back, the Parliamentarians under Lambert were too numerous and experienced to be defeated by such a move. After an hour in which the Parliamentarians initially retreated under the unexpected attack when reinforced by Cromwell's three brigades, they in turn forced the Royalists to retreat back toward the city. The Royalist retreat turned into a rout in which Parliamentarian and Royalist forces intermingled and skirmished up to and into the city. The Royalist position became untenable when the Essex militia stormed and captured Fort Royal, (a redoubt,[327] on a small hill to the south-east of Worcester overlooking the Sidbury gate), turning the Royalist guns to fire on Worcester. Once in the city Charles II removed his armour and found a freshmount, he attempted to rally his troops but it was to no avail. A desperate Royalist cavalry charge down Sidbury Street and High Street led by the Earl of Cleveland and Major William Careless amongst others, allowed King Charles to escape the city by St. Martin's Gate. The defences of the city were stormed from three different directions as darkness came on, regulars and militia fighting with equal gallantry. Most of the few thousands of the Royalists who escaped during the night were easily captured by Lilburne and Mercer, or by the militia which watched every road in Yorkshire and Lancashire. Even the country people brought in scores of prisoners, for officers and men alike, stunned by the suddenness of the disaster, offered no resistance.

3.9.4.4 Aftermath

About 3,000 men were killed during the battle and a further 10,000 were taken prisoner at Worcester or soon afterward. The Earl of Derby was executed, while the other English prisoners were conscripted into the New Model Army,[321/3] and sent to Ireland. Around 8,000 Scottish prisoners were deported to New England, Bermuda and the West Indies to work for landowners as indentured labourers. Parliamentary casualties numbered in the low hundreds. Charles II escaped after many adventures including one famous incident where he hid from a Parliamentarian patrol in an oak tree in the grounds of Boscobel House. After the battle Cromwell,[301/4] returned to Aylesbury Buckinghamshire, one of the parliamentarian strongholds and close to the seat of his late cousin the civil war hero John Hampden. He stayed at the aptly named King's Head Inn Aylesbury and it was here that he received the thanks of Parliament for his final defeat of the Royalists. The result of the battle was in brief, one of those rare victories in which a pursuit is superfluous. Cromwell thought the victory was the greatest of all the favours, or mercies, given to him by God. He famously wrote to William Lenthall, the Speaker of the House of Commons "*The dimensions of this mercy are above my thoughts. It is, for aught I know, a crowning mercy*". The phase "*Crowning Mercy*" is frequently linked to the battle, descriptive of the complete destruction of the last Royalist army and the end of The English Civil Wars.[320/2] The Parliamentary militia were sent home within a week. Cromwell, who had ridiculed "such stuff" six months ago knew them better now. "*Your new raised forces,*" he wrote to the Rump Parliament, "*did perform singular good service, for which they deserve a very high estimation and acknowledgement*". The New England preacher Hugh Peters gave the militia a rousing farewell sermon "*when their wives and children should ask them where they had been and what news, they should say they had been at Worcester, where England's sorrows began, and where they were happily ended*", referring to the first clash of the Royalist and Parliamentarian Armies at The Battle of Powick Bridge,[326/2] on 23rd September 1642 almost exactly nine years before. Before the battle King Charles II, contracted the Worcester Clothiers to outfit his army with uniforms but was unable to pay the £453.3s bill. In June 2008 Charles Prince of Wales paid off the 357 year old debt.

3.9.4.5 Legacy

In early April 1786 John Adams and Thomas Jefferson visited Fort Royal Hill at the battlefield at Worcester. David McCullough wrote in his definitive biography John Adamsthat Adams was "*deeply moved*" but disappointed at the locals' lack of knowledge of the battle, giving the townspeople an "*impromptu lecture*":-

> *"The people in the neighborhood appeared so ignorant and careless at Worcester that I was provoked and asked 'And do Englishmen so soon forget theground where liberty was fought for? Tell your neighbors and your children that this is holy ground, much holier than that on which your churches stand. All England should come in pilgrimage to this hill, once a year."*

3.9.5 The Battle of Altimarlach - Scotland's last Clan Battle

king's troops, and they marched north to Wick from Perth. They arrived on the 18th of May and camped at Braemore near Morven. This was part of the Berriedale estate which Campbell,[148/2] laid claim to as Earl of Caithness. The army believed to be 800 strong, marched on the 12th of July and reached the Hill of Yarrows which was known for a long time as *Torran nan Gael* – the Highlanders Hill. From there Campbell and his men had a great view of the surrounding area. Whilst on the hill a thick mist descended and Campbell decided to take this opportunity to advance on Wick. However, the mist lifted as he was heading down, and the alarm was promptly raised by the Sinclair forces in the town. When Campbell and his men reached the bottom of the hill they headed for Stirkoke and Altimarlach where he split his army in two; deploying one lot on the haugh,[328] and the rest were hidden in a gully. Sinclair moved his men estimated to be around the same size as Campbells, out of the town and headed along Wick River to meet the enemy army.

The Arms of the Earl of Caithness

As they reached the haugh just at the point where a burn met the river, the Campbells launched a surprise attack followed shortly by an ambush by the men in the gully. The Sinclairs were in a tight position, pressed against the river bank. At this point the Wick River is rather deep and as the Campbells pushed forward many of the Sinclairs fell into the water and drowned. For those who fell in to the flowing river but managed to make it across to the opposite bank on the Moss of Bronsie, awaiting for them there were reserves from Campbells army who summarily continued the fighting, killing many who made it across. The battle ended in a decisive victory for Sir John Campbell of Glenorchy, and it is generally viewed as a humiliating defeat for the Sinclairs. It is estimated that Sinclair lost around 300 men in the battle whilst Campbell saw few from his side killed and those that did die were buried where a commemorative cross now stands. Peace was made however the following day when a truce was signed in the old Wick Town Hall just east of present day Market Square. Afterwards, Campbell,[148/5] split up part of his army around Caithness where he levied the rents and taxes and ruled over the people in an oppressive manner. It is said that on Campbell's march to Caithness to claim the estates, his piper, Finlay Ban MacIvor, composed two famous pipe tunes: *Breadalbane Gathering* and *The Campbells are Coming*. The former was said to have been played spontaneous in the middle of the battle not long before the Sinclairs began to give way. Until relatively recently it was considered a gross insult to play either piece in Wick.[155/4] Campbell remained Earl of Caithness only until 1681. It is thought that George Sinclair had some influential and powerful friends because he took his case to the Council, and by act of parliament George was granted the Earldom, making him the 7th Earl,[Ch 4] and putting the title back into the Sinclair family where it has remained ever since.

The monument to the battle of Altimarlach

3.9.6 Other events (1601–1698)

21st October 1601	Henry 5th Lord Sinclair died and was succeeded by grandson Henry.
Storming of Kirkwall castle,[272/2] (1614)	Henry Sinclair Wadsetter (1570–1614), died leading 100 men to besiege The Kirkwall Castle. He became paralyzed and died at night. Kirkwall Castle, was an Orkney waterfront stronghold built by Prince Henry in 1390.
Chief Magistrate appointment (1657)	George Sinclair, 6th Earl of Caithness,[4.3.10] was present when Oliver Cromwell,[299/5] was proclaimed Chief Magistrate of Three Three Nations in Edinburgh.
Succession (1698)	George Sinclair, 7th Earl of Caithness,[Ch 4] died. He was succeeded by John Sinclair of Murchill,[329/1] (Murkle), 8th Earl, his cousin.

3.10 18th century and Jacobite Risings

Portrait of King James II by Sir Godfrey Kneller

The Jacobite,[113/1] risings were a series of uprisings, rebellions and wars in Britain and Ireland occurring between 1688 and 1746. The uprisings were aimed at returning. James VII of Scotland and II of England, and later his descendants of the House of Stuart, to the throne after he was deposed by Parliament during the Glorious Revolution. The major Jacobite Risings were called the Jacobite Rebellions by the ruling governments. The "First Jacobite Rebellion" and "Second Jacobite Rebellion" were known respectively as "The Fifteen" and "The Forty-Five" after the years in which they occurred (1715 and 1745). Although each Jacobite Rising had unique features, they were part of a larger series of military campaigns by Jacobites attempting to restore the Stuart Kings to the thrones of Scotland and England (and after 1707, Great Britain). James VII of Scotland, and II of England was deposed in 1688 and the thrones were claimed by his daughter Mary II, jointly with her husband the Dutch-born William of Orange. After the House of Hanover,[330/2] succeeded to the British throne in 1714, the risings continued and intensified. They continued until the last Jacobite Rebellion ("the Forty-Five"), led by Charles Edward Stuart,(The Young Pretender), who was soundly defeated at The Battle of Culloden,[Ch 3] in 1746. This ended any realistic hope of a Stuart restoration. During the 1715 Jacobite Risings, the Clan Sinclair,[Ch.3] supported the Jacobite cause, however, by the time of The 1745 Jacobite Rising, the Clan Sinclair supported The British Hanovarian Government.

3.10.1 1715 Jacobite Uprisings

3.10.1.1 The Battle of Sheriffmuir

David Sinclair of Brabsterdorran,[331] fights for Jacobite cause, as did John, Master of Sinclair, who fled to Orkney and then to Europe. The Battle of Sheriffmuir was an engagement in 1715 at the height of the Jacobite rebellion in England and Scotland, John Erskine 6th Earl of Mar, standard-bearer for the Jacobite,[113/3] cause in Scotland mustered Highland chiefs, and on 6th September 1715 declared James Francis Edward Stuart,(The "Old Pretender") as King of Scots.

Battle of Sheriffmuir

3.10.1.1.1 History

With an army of about 12,000 men Mar proceeded to take Perth and commanded much of the northern Highlands. Following unsuccessful skirmishes against John Campbell, 2nd Duke of Argyll (based at Stirling), Mar was eventually persuaded to lead his full army south on 10th November. Spies informed Argyll of Mar's actions, and he moved his army of about 4,000 to Sheriffmuir, near Dunblane. The two armies met on the battlefield on 13th November. Argyll was seriously outnumbered by the Jacobite army (which was somewhat diminished from its previous numbers) and his left wing, commanded by General Whetham was far shorter than the Jacobites' opposing right. Argyll's right wing attacked, and /managed to drive the Highlanders back, but Whetham's soldiers were overpowered by a much larger force. Argyll came to the aid of Whetham's men. By evening, both armies were seriously reduced and although Mar had a great advantage in numbers, he refused to risk the entirety of his army allowing Argyll to withdraw. The battle was inconclusive with both sides claiming victory. However in strategic terms Argyll had halted the Jacobite advance. Those government regiments present that were titled 'King's' were awarded the White Horse of Hanover as a badge of battle honor. The engagement only served to demoralize the Jacobite army who with their superior numbers, felt they should have decisively won. Mar's French and Spanish supporters in particular withdrew their forces. On 23rd December, the Old Pretender, who had been exiled in France, landed at Peterhead, his cause largely lost. He met with Mar at Perth, but was unable to rouse the disheartened army. Argyll, reinforced and invigorated, soon advanced north while the Jacobite,[113/6] army fled to Montrose and The Pretender returned to France. The Army moved to Ruthven and dispersed. The period was fatal in the extreme to the Jacobite Pretender. The whole body of his adherents in the south had fallen into the hands of generals Willis and Carpenter at Preston, and Inverness, while all the adjacent country had been recovered to the government, through the exertions of pro-government clans including the Earl of Sutherland, Fraser Lord Lovat, the Rosses, the Munros and the Forbeses. The number of the slain on the side of the rebels has been stated to have been eight hundred among whom were the John Lyon, 5th Earl of Strathmore and Kinghorne and the chief of Clan MacDonald of Clan Ranald and several others of distinction. Panmure and Drummond of Logie were among the wounded. It meant that the Jacobite army had to withdraw to Perth. Argyll considered himself the victor and struck a medal to commemorate his feat. Of the government army there were killed and wounded, upwards of six hundred. Lord Forfar was the only person of eminence killed on that side. A popular Jacobite song, *"Will Ye Go to Sheriffmuir"*, was written about the battle. As with many such songs, the battle is presented as a noble victory for the Jacobite army. The song was collected by and perhaps written by James Hogg in 1819.

3.10.1.1.2 Robert Burns and "The Battle of Sherramuir"

The Battle was the subject of "The Battle of Sherramuir", one of the most famous songs written by Robert Burns. The song was written when Burns toured the Highlands in 1787 and was first published in The Scots Musical Museum, appearing in Volume III, 1790. It was written to be sung to the

"Cameronian Rant". Burns knew that the battle ended so inconclusively that it was unclear which side had won and the poem is the account of the battle by two shepherds taking contrary views. One of the shepherds believes that *"the red-coat lads wi' black cockades"* routed the rebels, painting a fearful picture of how they managed to *"hough the Clans like nine-pin kyles"*. The other shepherd is just as convinced that the Jacobites,[113/7] *"did pursue / The horsemen back to Forth, man"* with the eventual result that *"... mony a huntit, poor Red-coat / For fear amaist did swarf, man."* Dissatisfied with the first published version of the poem, Burns re-wrote it sometime after 1790. The revised version was published after Burns' death by his editor James Currie MD in *The Complete Poetical Works of Robert Burns:* With Explanatory and Glossarial Notes; And a Life of the Author (1800).

3.10.2 1745 Jacobite Rising

3.10.2.1 The Battle of Culloden

Sir James Sinclair of Rosslyn commanded The Royal Scots,[332/1] on the British Hanoverian Government,[331/3] side. About 500 Caithness Sinclairs were ready to join the *Jacobites* but instead followed their chief, James Sinclair, who supported the British Hanoverians.[330/5] The Battle of Culloden,[Ch 3] (Scottish Gaelic: Blàr Chùil Lodair) was the final confrontation of the 1745 Jacobite Rising. Taking place on 16th April1746, the battle pitted the Jacobite forces of Charles Edward Stuart, against an army commanded by William Augustus Duke of Cumberland,[333/1] loyal to the British government. The Jacobite cause to overthrow the reigning House of Hanover and restore the House of Stuart, to the British throne was dealt a decisive defeat at Culloden; Charles Stuart never mounted any further attempts to challenge Hanoverian power in Britain. The conflict was the last pitched battle fought on British soil, occurring near Inverness in the Scottish Highlands. Charles Stuart's army consisted largely of Scottish Highlanders as well as a number of Lowland Scots and a small detachment of Englishmen from Manchester. The Jacobites were supported and supplied by the Kingdom of

An incident in the rebellion of 1745, by David Morier

France; French Irish units loyal to France were part of the Jacobite army. The Government force was mostly Lowlanders but also included a few Highlanders, a significant number of English, a battalion of Ulstermen and a small number of Hessians,[334] and Austrians. Meeting on Culloden Moor the battle was both quick and bloody, taking place within an hour. Following an unsuccessful Highland charge against the Government lines the Jacobites were routed and driven from the field. Between 1,500 and 2,000 Jacobites we killed or wounded in the brief time, while Government losses were lighter with 50 dead and 259 wounded. The aftermath of the battle and subsequent crackdown on Jacobitism was brutal earning Cumberland,[334/2] the sobriquet *"Butcher"*. Efforts were taken to further integrate Scotland into Great Britain; civil penalties were introduced to weaken Gaelic,[15/6] culture and attack the Scottish clan system.

3.10.3 Colonial Wars

3.10.3.1 The Battle of the Plains of Abraham

Lt. A. Sinclair carried the colours for General Wolfe.[335/1] He later became a Major General. The Battle was also known as the Battle of Quebec, (Bataille des Plaines d'Abraham or Première bataille de Québec in French) was a pivotal battle in The Seven Years' War,[336] (referred to as the French and Indian War in the United States). The confrontation, which began on 13th September 1759 was fought between the British Army and Navy and the French Army, on a plateau just outside the walls of Quebec City on land that was originally owned by a farmer named Abraham Martin, hence the name of the battle. The battle involved fewer than 10,000 troops between both sides but proved to be a deciding moment in the conflict between France and Britain over the fate of New France, influencing the later creation of Canada. The culmination of a three-month siege by the British the battle lasted about 15 minutes.

British troops commanded by General James Wolfe successfully resisted the column advance of French troops and Canadian military under Louis-Joseph Marquis de Montcalm, using new tactics that proved extremely effective against standard military formations used in most large European conflicts. Both generals were mortally wounded during the battle; Wolfe received a blow that would end his life within only a few minutes of engagement and Montcalm died the next morning after receiving a bullet wound just below his ribs. In the wake of the battle France's remaining military force in Canada and the rest of North America came under increasing pressure from British forces. While the French forces continued to fight and prevailed in several battles after Quebec was captured the British did not relinquish their hold on the fortress. That tenacity carried over to other areas in North America; within four years, nearly all of France's possessions in eastern North America would be ceded to Great Britain.

3.10.3.2 The Battle of Charlestown

John Sinclair, son and heir of William, a Major in 76th Foot, wounded in the groin by a musket ball when reconnoitring with Sir Henry Clinton.[337] The battle was a small engagement between Confederate cavalry forces under Brigadier John D. Imboden and and the Union forces under Col. Benjamin L. Simpson on October 18th, 1863, at Charlestown, West Virginia, as part of the Bristoe and Mine Run Campaigns, resulting in a Confederate victory.

3.10.3.2.1 Background

As the Confederate Army of Northern Virginia and the Union Army of the Potomac dueled it out in central Virginia during the Bristoe campaign, General Robert E. Lee,[338] dispatched cavalry under Brigadier General John Imboden to raid in the Shenandoah Valley and attack the vulnerable Union garrison at Charlestown, West Vir-ginia, in an effort to draw Union forces away from his front. By October 17th, Imboden's force had reached Berryville, where they skirmished with a company of the 1st New York Cavalry before driving them back to Charlestown. The presence of the Confederates was reported to Col. Benjamin Simpson, commander of the Charlestown garrison. The inexperienced Simpson, having been mustered into service only 17 days earlier, dismissed recommendations to fall back on the much more strongly defended Harpers Ferry, believing Charlestown was not the target of the Confederate raid.

3.10.3.2.2 Battle

At dawn on the 18th, Union pickets south of Charlestown were driven back by Imboden's advance. Simpson's 9th Maryland Infantry, numbering some 375 men, took up position in the Jefferson County Courthouse (in which John Brown,[339] was tried and hanged) and ordered the cavalry, consisting of one company each of the Loudoun Rangers and 6th Michigan Cavalry, to "take care of themselves". Upon entering town, Imboden sent a flag of truce to negotiate surrender, to which Simpson refused. The cavalry, seeing the hopelessness of the situation, decided to fight their way out and unite with the Harpers Ferry garrison. On the northeast outskirts of town, the Union cavalry encountered the 18th Virginia Cavalry and 62nd Virginia Mounted Infantry, who unleashed a volley at the column, sending several troopers and their horses to the ground. Those troopers who were still mounted broke left around their felled comrades and serendipitously rode into the Confederate right, which was proved to be its weak spot. The Union cavalry cut its way out, taking heavy losses: 17 captured, 2 killed and several wounded and nearly every horse shot, several killed. Meanwhile, back in Charlestown, Imboden brought up his artillery, and again demanded the garrison's surrender, which was rebuked for a second time, whereupon Imboden began to shell the town. Under the artillery fire, Simpson was forcedto abandon the courthouse and marched his men to a field northwest of town, not far from the earlier cavalry engagement. Imboden massed his forces in a woods facing the field and unleashed a deadly volley. After several minutes and only a few shots fired in return, Simpson finally surrendered his force, now totaling some 365 men. The artillery fire had not gone unnoticed in nearby Harpers Ferry; the 17th Indiana battery, Cole's Maryland Cavalry, and the remainder of the Loudoun Rangers and 6th Michigan, totaling 300 men in all, were dispatched to reinforce the besieged garrison. Within 15 minutes they had engaged Imboden's force and a fierce firefight ensued that lasted the entirety of the afternoon. The reinforcements, however, were not strong enough to drive off Imboden and liberate the prisoners. At around 5 p.m. the 34th Massachusetts Infantry, 400 strong, arrived, having been marched 18 miles from their camp at Berrysville to the sound of the artillery fire. As the sun set, the Bay Staters attacked Imboden, who with the cover of darkness elected to withdraw while still in possession of his prisoners and plunder from the town.

3.10.3.2.3 Aftermath

Imboden successfully attacked and defeated the Union garrison at Charlestown, exposing the weaknesses of Union forces in the Shanandoah Valley, taking only losses. While his raid was successful, it had little overall impact on the fall campaigns, which ended shortly thereafter as the two armies went into winter quarters. For the Union's part, at considerable loss, they saved Charlestown from being sacked and burned and turned back Imboden's raid, which if had been allowed to continue may have had a larger strategic impact on the campaign in central Virginia.

3.10.4 Other events (1708–1761)

Sinclair duels (1708)	Chief John, Master of Sinclair, (Son of Henry Lord Sinclair) kills Ensign Schaw and Captain Alexander Schaw in duels. He was exiled to Prussia but later pardoned by Queen Anne of Great Britain.[340]
Arms capture (1715)	John, Master of Sinclair, captured a vessel with 420 stand of arms bound for The Earl of Sutherland.
Rosslyn Chapel	 *Interior of Rosslyn Chapel* Sir James Sinclair glazed the windows of Rosslyn Chapel for the first time, relaid the floor with flagstones and repaired the roof of the chapel
Resignation (1736)	Sir James Sinclair of Rosslyn,[23/5] resigned his office as hereditary Grand Master Mason of Scotland,[341/1] to The Scottish Lodges,[342] on their foundation. He was later re-appointed for his life.
Assassination (1739)	Major Malcolm Sinclair, *'A good and faithful servant of* Sweden,' was charged with affairs of State. He was ass assissinated at Grunberg in Siesia,[343] by agents of Czarina Anna of Russia.

Commander (4th June 1745)	Sir James Sinclair of Rosslyn,[23/6] a Lieutenant general with The Royal Scots,[332/2] was appointed the Commander of the British Forces in Flanders
General (10th Mar. 1761)	Sir James Sinclair M.P., who should have been 11th Lord Sinclair, was gazetted,[344] a General.

4. The Sinclair Barony and Earldoms

The family are descended from:-

- Rognvald 'the mighty',[345/1] Jarl,[129/2] or Chief of the Orkneys and Earl of Moere,[130/2] and Romsdahal, [346] in Norway. Born in 835 AD.

- Rollo,[7/2] 1st Duke of Normandy,[10/2] The son of Rognvald 'the mighty' who first fought and then, in 912, made peace with King Charles 'the Simple' [347] of France. At the treaty they signed at St Clair-sur-Epte [18/2] whence the family takes its name, Rollo was created 1st Duke of Normandy and he later married Gizelle, one of Charles' daughters.

4.1 The Barony of Roslyn

4.1.1 William "The Seemly" Sinclair 1st Baron of Roslin (b. 1028–d. 1093)

William "The seemly" St. Clair" came to England with his first cousin, William the Conqueror,[4/2] and fought with him at The Battle of Hastings,[348] in 1066. Before that, in 1047, he had fought with his father William Walderne,[20/2] against William Duke of Normandy,[4/2]/[10/2] at The Battle of Val es Dunes.[349] He arrived in Scotland with the Saxon[A5.1.5] princess Margaret,[125/2] from the court of Hungary, where she was brought up. She was the daughter of Edward the Confessor,[350/2] of England and married Malcolm III Canmore,of Scotland, and became Queen Margaret. William was called in allusion to his 'fair deportment' 'the Seemly St Clair' and was made cup-bearer,[351] to Queen Margaret. and granted the Barony of

Rosslyn,[23/12] in 1070. He was also made Warden of the Southern Marches. [259/3] with responsibility for defending Scotland's border against the frequent attacks of the English, and died fighting William the Conqueror when he later invaded Scotland. His descendants became possessors besides Roslin, of Cousland,[352/1] Pentland,[29/2] Catticune, and other lands. They later also obtained the Earldom of Orkney,[A4.2] From the same stock sprung the Earls of Caithness.

4.1.2 Henry Sinclair 2nd Baron of Roslin (b. 1060–d. 1110)

Succeeded 1093. He was the first who was born in Scotland and was known as Henri *"the Holy"* de St Clair. He was called *"the Holy"* because he was a Crusader; and many of his descendants were also Crusaders. He accompanied Edgar Atheling, brother of Scotland's Queen Margaret,[125/3] on The First Crusade (1096 -1099),[353/1] and took part in The Siege of Antioch,[354] in 1098. Knighted by King Malcolm III who confirmed the Barony of Rosslyn,[23/2] and also awarded Henry the Barony of Pentland,[29/3] following a number of military successes against the English. He was with King Malcolm III, when he was killed in 1093 during The Battle of Alnwick,[24/3] in Northumberland.

4.1.3 Sir Henry St Clair 3rd Baron of Rosslyn (d. 1214)

Succeeded c.1153. The first St Clair to live at Rosslyn. Knighted by King David I, and made a Privy councillor,[58/2] he was sent by King William the Lion as ambassador to Henry II,[355] of England, to reclaim from the English king the disputed territory of Northumberland. He fought at The Battle of Northallerton,[356] in 1138 and was rewarded with the gift of Cardian,[?] in 1153, thereafter being known as Cardain Saint clair.

4.1.4 Sir William St Clair, 4th Baron of Rosslyn (d. 1243)

Succeeded 1214.

4.1.5 Sir Henry St Clair, 5th Baron of Rosslyn (d. 1270)

Succeeded 1243. Assisted King Alexander III in the capture of the Western Isles.

4.1.6 Sir William St Clair, 6th Baron of Rosslyn (d. 1297)

Succeeded c.1270. Appointed as ambassador to France, he was captured at the Battle of Dunbar in 1296,[Ch 3] and died in the Tower of London,[200/3] in the following year.

4.1.7 Henry Sinclair (1275–1331) 7th Baron of Roslin

Succeeded 1297. Fought with his two sons John and William at Bannockburn. The king, Robert the Bruce, rewarded him for his bravery with the gift of Pentland Moor.[29/4] He was one of the Scottish nobles who in 1320 signed The Declaration of Arbroath which proclaimed to the Pope Scottish Independence from England. Henry's brother William was made Bishop of Dunkeld and displayed great valour in 1317 when he repelled an invasion of the English who had landed on the Fife coast while the King was in Ireland. Thereafter the King referred to William as 'the fighting Bishop'. After the death of Robert the Bruce,[A2.3] Sir Henry's two sons, William and John, were chosen along with Sir James Douglas,[143/2]/[A2.3] and Sir Robert Logan of Restalrig,[246/2] to carry the King's heart to Jerusalem and deposit it in The Church of the Holy Sepulchre.[357] They never reached their destination; during a fierce battle with the Moors,[30/2] at Teba,[Ch 3] in Spain in 1330, William, his brother John, and Douglas were killed. The Moors were so impressed by the courage of the Scottish Knights that they allowed the survivors to take their dead - and Bruce's heart - for burial back home.

4.1.8 William Sinclair 8th Baron of Roslin (d. 1358)

Succeeded 1331. Married Isabella de Strathern, daughter of Malise, (Maol-Ísa,[132/2]) Earl of Caithness,[Ch 4] Strathearn, and Orkney.[Ch 4] Malise had no male heirs and after William's death, his and Isabella's son Henry was recognised as 42nd Earl of Orkney in 1369 and ten years later as the first St Clair Prince of Orkney. In addition to the titles inherited from his father, Henry also became Lord Shetland, Lord Sinclair, Lord Chief Justice of Scotland, Admiral of the Seas, Great Protector, and Keeper and Defender of the Prince of Scotland.

4.1.9 Henry I 9th Baron of Roslin (b. 1345–d. 1400)

Lord of Shetland (c.1345–c.1400), was a Scottish explore. He is sometimes identified by the alternative spelling, Henry St Clair. He was the grandfather of William Sinclair, the builder of Rosslyn Chapel.[Ch 5] He is also noted for being the subject of legend that he undertook early explorations of Greenland and North America in about the year 1398. He was the son and heir of William Sinclair, Lord of Roslin,[23/9] and his wife Isobel of Strathearn, a daughter of Maol Ísa, Earl of Orkney.[Ch 5] Henry Sinclair's maternal grandfather had been deprived of much of his lands (the Earldom of Strathearn being completely lost to the King of Scots). Sometime after 13th September 1358, Henry's father died, at which point Henry Sinclair succeeded as Baron of Roslin, Pentland,[29/4] and Cousland,[352/3] a group of minor properties in Lothian. The Sinclair Diploma, written or at least commissioned by his grandson states he married Joneta (or Joan, ou Jean) Haliburton, daughter of Walter de Haliburton, 1st Lord Haliburton of Dirleton,[358/1] and that they had a son Henry, who became the next Earl of Orkney.[4.2] Also they apparently had a daughter Elizabeth Sinclair, who married the justiary John Drummond of Cargill. Three cousins - Alexander de L'Arde, Lord of Caithness Malise Sparre, Lord of Skaldale,[?] and Henry Sinclair - were rivals for the succession to the Earldom of Orkney. On August 2nd 1379 at Marstrand, near Tønsberg, Norway, King Haakon VI of Norway,[31/2] invested and confirmed Sinclair as the Norwegian Earl of Orkney, over a rival claim by his cousin Malise Sparre. In 1389, Sinclair attended the coronation of King Eric of Pomerania,[359] in Norway, pledging his oath of Fealty.[360] Historians have speculated that in 1391, Sinclair and his troops slew Malise Sparre near Scalloway Tingwall parish, Shetland. It is unclear when Henry Sinclair died. *The Sinclair Diploma*, states: "*...he retirit to the parts of Orchadie and josit them to the latter tyme of his life, and deit Erile of Orchadie, and for the defence of the country was slain there cruellie by his enemiis...*" We also know that sometime in 1401: "*The English invaded, burnt and spoiled certain islands of Orkney.*" This was part of an English retaliation for a Scottish attack on an English fleet near Aberdeen. The assumption is that Henry either died opposing this invasion, or was already dead.

4.1.10 Sir Henry St Clair 10th Baron of Rosslyn (d. 1420)

Succeeded 1400. Married Egida, daughter of Sir William Douglas, thus acquiring the Lordship of Nithsdale,[361/1] The Wardenship of The Three Marches,[259/4] and six further baronies. He was guardian to James I of Scotland,during his minority. In 1406 the 12-year-old Prince was sent to the French court for education and safety and was accompanied by Sir Henry. Captured by the English off Flamborough Head,[362/1] both were taken to the Tower of London.[200/4] The heir to the Scottish throne remained in captivity for eighteen years, returning home to Scotland in 1424 and then only in exchange for £40,000, a sum described as a bill for the upkeep and education of the young prince. Sir Henry obtained his own freedom in 1407 by payment of a ransom. Succeeded 1420, Founder of Rosslyn Chapel.[5.3] 1st Earl of Caithness.

4.1.11 William Sinclair 11th Baron of Roslin (b.1420–d.1484)

(1455–1476),[Ch 4] 3rd Earl of Orkney (1455–1470),[Ch 4] and 1st Lord Sinclair. He was Chief of Clan Sinclair,[Ch 3] and Admiral of Scotland,[32/2] in 1436 and High Chancellor,[363] from 1454-1456. He was the grandson of the explorer Henry Sinclair, 1st Earl of Orkney,[Ch 4] and son of Henry Sinclair, 2nd Earl of Orkney,[Ch 4] for a time protector of the young James Stuart, the later James I of Scotland He first married Margaret Douglas, daughter of Archibald, 4th Earl of Douglas,[364] and 1st Duke of Touraine,[365] and widow of the Earl of Buchan.[366] By this marriage he had one son William and four daughters. Margaret died in 1452 and he married secondly Marjory, daughter of Alexander Sutherland of Dunbeath,[133/2] by who he had five sons, Oliver, William, David, Robert, and John. The founder of the Chapel held vast territories and influence. His power was seen by King James II,as a threat, the more so since Sir William's sister Catherine was married to the King's brother, the Duke of Albany.[367/1] Relationships between the King and his brother were difficult and at one stage James imprisoned Albany in Edinburg Castle.[204/2]

In 1445 James II gave Sir William the Earldom of Caithness in exchange for that of Nithsdale,[361/2] and in 1471 Ravenscraig for the earldom of Orkney. James II had acquired Orkney by his marriage to Queen Margaret of Denmark,[139/2] and it was formally annexed to the Scottish Crown by Act of Parliament in 1471. During his lifetime Sir William divided his estates between his three eldest sons: William, from his first marriage, and Oliver and William, from his second. By far the best portions of the estate went to Oliver and thus his eldest son, known as 'William the Waster' was effectively disinherited. He received from his father only the barony of Newburgh in Aberdeenshire. Rosslyn,[23/12] Pentland,[29/2] and the more prestigious land went to Oliver. William the Waster disputed his brother's claim to Rosslyn and a subsequent contract between them was agreed, which confirmed Oliver's right to the estates at Rosslyn. But Oliver ceded to William other lands in Midlothian, together with the castles of Ravensheugh,[140/2] and Dysart,[368] in Fife. William was also afterwards declared by Act of Parliament chief of the St Clairs with the title of Baron Sinclair. To the second son of his second marriage, also called William, Sir William had given in 1476 the Earldom of Caithness after resigning the post. (It was around this point that the spelling "Sinclair" came into general use although the Earls of Roslin still prefer to use the older form of "St. Clair"). Thus by the time of the founder's death in 1484, his vast possessions had been divided amongst three branches of his family: the Lords St Clair of Dysart,[138/2] the St Clairs of Rosslyn,[23/13] and the Sinclairs of Caithness.[Ch 4] All in all, the Sinclair ancestry is well and thoroughly represented in Scottish and British high nobility, thanks to marriages of his daughters and other descendants. William's daughter of his second marriage, Lady Eleanor Sinclair, married John Stewart, 1st Earl of Atholl,[187/2] a relative of the Kings. Lord Henry Darnley,[146/2] and his son James I of England, descend from Eleanor and through them, quite a many royal house of Europe. His other daughter by this marriage, Catherine Sinclair, married Alexander Stewart, 1st Duke of Albany,[367/2] a nephew of the said Atholl.

4.1.12 Sir Oliver St Clair 12th Baron of Rosslyn (d. 1525)

Succeeded 1484, The Barony of Rosslyn passed to Oliver who married a daughter of Lord Borthwick and had four sons, George, Oliver, William, and John. The last became Bishop of Brechin and performed the marriage ceremony between Mary Queen of Scots,[145/2] and Henry Stuart, Lord Darnley, at Holyrood on July 29th, 1565.

4.1.13 Sir William St Clair 13th Baron of Rosslyn (d.1554)

Succeeded 1525. Further endowed the Chapel with land for dwelling houses and gardens.

4.1.14 Sir William St Clair 14th Baron of Rosslyn (d. 1602)

Succeeded c.1554. Appointed Lord Chief Justice,[369] of Scotland by Queen Mary, in 1559.

4.1.15 Sir William St Clair 15th Baron of Rosslyn (d. 1610)

Succeeded c.1602. Brother of the former Baron who made significant additions to Rosslyn Castle.[Ch 5] He built the vaults, the great hall and the clock-tower, as well as the great turnpike,[370] - the large stone staircase, four feet wide, leading up from the basement to the top floor of the Castle. Heriditary Patron of Masons in 1st St. Clair Charter,[371] in 1602.

4.1.16 Sir William St Clair 16th Baron of Rosslyn (d. 1650)

Succeeded c.1610. Was granted the charters of 1630 from the Masons of Scotland, recognising that the position of Grand Master Mason of Scotland,[341/2] had been hereditary in the St Clair family since it was granted by James II in 1441. The original charters had been destroyed in a fire. William continued his father's work to Rosslyn Castle,[Ch 5] building over the vaults up to the level of the courtyard. He died in 1650. Confirmed Heriditary Patron of Masons in 2nd St. Clair Charter,[372] in 1628

4.1.17 Sir John St Clair 17th Baron of Rosslyn (d. 1690)

Succeeded 1650. Held out for a time when the Castle was besieged in 1650 by Cromwell's.[299/3] troops under General Monk.[312/2] but was eventually captured and sent to Tynemouth Castle,[313/2] only returning to Rosslyn,[23/13] shortly before his death in 1690.

4.1.18 Sir James St Clair, 18th Baron of Rosslyn (d.1706)

Succeeded 1690. Brother of the previous Baron. He had two sons, the eldest of which, James, was killed at the Battle of the Boyne in 1690, leaving the son of his younger brother Alexander to succeed.

4.1.19 Sir William St Clair, 19th Baron of Rosslyn (d. 1778)

Succeeded 1706. The last male heir of the Rosslyn branch of the St Clairs. Was considered by Sir Walter Scott,who knew him well, to be a Scottish laird of the old school and he described him thus:'*The last Rosslyn was a man considerably over six feet, with dark grey locks, erect and graceful, broad shouldered, athletic, for the business of war or chase, a noble eye of chastened pride and undoubted authority, and features handsome and striking in their general effect though somewhat harsh and exaggerated when considered in detail. His complexion was dark and grizzled and we schoolboys crowded to see him perform feats of strength and skill in the old Scottish games of Golf and Archery, used to think and say amongst ourselves, the whole figure resembled the famous founder of the Douglas race. In all the manly sports which require strength and dexterity, Rosslyn was unrivalled, but his particular delight was in archery'.* He was four times Captain of the Honourable Company of Edinburgh Golfers and on three occasions, the last at the age of 68, won the Silver Club, which from 1744 was awarded in open competition by the town of Edinburgh. He was also a brigadier of the Royal Company of Archers, the Queen's Body Guard for Scotland. Having no male heir, he resigned his office as hereditary Grand Master Mason of Scotland,[341/3] to the Scottish Lodges,[342/2] at their foundation in 1736. The Lodges then appointed him as the first non-hereditary Grand Master Mason of at their meeting on St Andrew's day of the same year. In his funeral oration in 1778 it was said that:*'Descended from an illustrious house, whose heroes have often bled in their country's cause, he inherited their intrepid spirit, united with the milder virtue of humanity and polished manners of a gentleman non sibi sed societati vixit (he did not live for himself but for his community).* He had married Cordelia, daughter of Sir George Wishart, baronet of Clifton Hall, by whom he had three sons and five daughters. But all died young except his daughter Sarah, through whom the succession then passed.

4.1.20 Subsequent title holders (Non-Sinclair)

4.1.20.1 Alexander Wedderburn St Clair 1st Earl of Rosslyn (d. 1805)

Succeeded 1778. Sarah married Sir Peter Wedderburn of Chester Hall and they had a son Alexander and a daughter Janet. Janet was married to Sir Henry Erskine, 5th Baronet of Alva.[373] Alexander Wedderburn St Clair did much towards the preservation of the Chapel.[5.3] He became Solicitor General in 1771, Attorney General in 1778, Lord Chief Justice in 1780, and Lord Chancellor in Pitt's government of 1793, a post he held until 1801.

In 1801 he was created 1st Earl of Rosslyn,[23/13] in the county of Midlothian, with a provision for the succession. When he died in 1805 he was succeeded by his nephew, his sister Sarah's son, Sir James St Clair-Erskine.

4.1.20.2 Sir James St Clair-Erskine 2nd Earl of Rosslyn (d. 1837)

Succeeded 1805. At various times Member of Parliament for Castle Rising, Morpeth, and Kirkcaldy, Director General of Chancery in Scotland, Lord President of the Council, and Grand Master Mason of Scotland. He married Henrietta Bouverie, daughter of the Hon. Edward Bouverie. When he died in 1837, he was succeeded by his son James Alexander.

4.1.20.3 James Alexander St Clair-Erskine 3rd Earl of Rosslyn (d. 1866)

Succeeded 1837. Master of the Buckhounds,[374] and under-Secretary of State for War in 1859. He married Frances Wemyss, daughter of Lt. General William Wemyss of Wemyss Castle in Fife. He instructed the architect David Bryce to carry out restoration work at the Chapel.[5.3] The carvings in the Lady Chapel were attended to and stones were relaid in the sacristy,[375/1] and an altar established there. The Chapel was rededicated on Tuesday April 22nd 1862, by the Bishop of Edinburgh.

4.1.20.4 Francis Robert St Clair-Erskine 4th Earl of Rosslyn (d. 1890)

Succeeded 1866, died 1890. Together with his title, he inherited from his father an estate in Fife of more than three thousand acres, worth over nine thousand pounds in rents and coal-mining royalties. He was High Commissioner to The General Assembly of the Church of Scotland,[376] on four occasions and captain of The Corps of Gentleman at Arms.[377] In 1870 he held a Grand Masonic Fette at Rosslyn attended by over one thousand freemasons,[341/3]/[172/2] and the following year he was elected 69th Grand Master Mason of Scotland.[341/4] When he indicated in the summer of 1871 that he did not wish to be considered for re-election, a petition of seven thousand signatures raised by the Lodges persuaded him to reconsider. He married Blanche Adeliza in 1866, second daughter of Henry Fitzroy and widow of the Hon. Charles Maynard. The 4th Earl was a poet of some substance and there is reason to believe the tradition that he would have been made Poet Laureate,[378] in succession to Tennyson,[379] but for his death in 1890. He added an apse,[380] to the Chapel to serve as a baptistery with an organ loft above. The work is by Andrew Kerr. The Earl also filled the baptistery,[381] arch with the handsome oak tracer which you see today, decorated with his crest.

4.1.20.5 James Francis Harry St Clair-Erskine 5th Earl of Rosslyn (d. 1939)

Succeeded 1890, died 1939. Married in 1890 Violet, daughter of Robert Charles de Grey Vyner. At their wedding the Prince of Wales, later Edward VII,[382] proposed the health of bride and groom. Harry was a close friend of the prince who later became godfather to his son. Like the 4th Earl, he was a keen racehorse owner. A particular favourite was Buccaneer, who won the Gold Cup at Ascot. But he was also a gambler, and on one occasion bet £15,000 on Buccaneer to win the Manchester Cup. The horse lost. He gambled at the roulette tables of Cannes and Monte Carlo and recounted his exploits in his autobiography *My Gamble With Life*. Six years after inheriting title, properties, estate, colleries at Dysart,[141/3] assets of £50,000, and a steam yacht of great splendour, he had lost everything and was declared bankrupt. The family silver, gold and silver plate was sold at a three-day auction in Edinburgh. His Marriage to Violet ended when he was discovered by his father-in-law to have presented a £2000 turquoise tiara to a lady friend. He was succeeded by his grandson.

4.1.20.6 Anthony Hugh Francis Harry St Clair-Erskine, 6th Earl of Rosslyn (d.1977)

Succeeded 1939. Instructed significant programme of work to the Chapel,[A5.3] in the 1950s when the sacristy,[375/2] roof was repaired and the interior carvings cleaned by hand over a period of years.

4.1.20.7 Peter St Clair-Erskine, 7th and current Earl of Rosslyn

Married 1982 Helen, Countess of Rosslyn. Two sons, two daughters: Jamie, Lord Loughborough, Born 1986. Lady Alice St Clair-Erskine, Born 1988 Lady Lucia St Clair-Erskine, Born 1993 and The Honourable Harry St Clair-Erskine. Born 1995.

4.2 The Earldom of Orkney

The Earl of Orkney was originally a Jarl,[129/4] ruling Orkney, Shetland and parts of Caithness and Sutherland. The Earls were periodically subject to the Kings of Norway for the Northern Isles and later also to the Kings of Alba,[52//4] for those parts of their territory in mainland Scotland (i.e. Caithness and Sutherland). The Earl's status as a Norwegian vassal,[174/3] was formalised in 1195. In 1232, a Scottish dynasty descended from The Mormaers of Angus,[383] replaced the previous family descended from The Mormaers of Atholl,[187/3] although it remained formally subject to Norway. This family was in turn replaced by the descendants of The Mormaers of Strathearn,[384/1] and later still by the Sinclair family,[Ch.3] during whose time, Orkney passed to Scots control. The first known Earl of Orkney was Rognvald Eysteinsson,[Ch 4] (Rognvald, Earl of Møre,[130/2]), who died around 890. Subsequent Earls, with one exception, were descended from Rognvald or his brother Sigurd,[Ch 4] until 1232.

4.2.1 Norse Earls of Orkney (9th century–1231)

The Norse Earldom was frequently under joint rule. The possessions of the Earldom included the Mormaerdom of Caithness,[Ch 4] and, until 1194, the Shetland Islands.

Ragnvald Eysteinsson	Earl of Møre	9th century
Sigurd Eysteinsson (Sigurd the Mighty)	Brother of Ragnvald	9th century
Guthorm Sigurdsson		c. 890
Hallad Rognvaldsson		c. 891–c. 893
Turf-Einar Rognvaldsson /.. (Turf-Einar)		c. 893–c. 946
Arnkel Turf-Einarsson		946–954 (died at the same battle as Eric /..................... Bloodaxe.[385])
Erlend Turf-Einarsson		(d. 954) (died at the same battle as Eric Bloodaxe)

Thorfinn Turf-Einarsson /... (Thorfinn Skull-Splitter)		c. 963–c. 976
Arnfinn Thorfinnsson	With Havard, Ljot and Hlodvir	c. 976–c. 991
Havard Thorfinnsson	With Arnfinn, Ljot and Hlodvir	c. 976–c. 991
Ljot Thorfinnsson	With Arnfinn, Havard and Hlodvir	c. 976–c. 991
Hlodvir Thorfinnsson	With Arnfinn, Havard and Ljot	c. 980–c. 991
Sigurd Hlodvirsson (Sigurd the Stout)		991–1014
Brusi Sigurdsson	With Einar, Sumarlidi and Thorfinn	1014–1030
Einar Sigurdsson (Einar Wry-mouth)	With Brusi and Sumarlidi	1014–1020
Sumarlidi Sigurdsson	With Brusi and Einar	1014–1015
Thorfinn Sigurdsson (Thorfinn the Mighty)	With Brusi and Rögnvald	1020–1064
Rögnvald Brusason	With Thorfinn	c. 1037–c. 1045
Paul and Erlend Thorfinnsson		1064–1098
Sigurd Magnusson (Sigurd the Jerusalem-farer)	Later King of Norway, son of King Magnus Bareleg	1098–1103

Haakon Paulsson	Son of Paul Thorfinsson with Magnus	1103-1123
Magnus Erlendsson /...	With Haakon	1108-1117
Harald Haakansson	With Paul	1122-1127
Paul Haakonsson	With Harald	1122-1137
Rögnvald Kali Kolsson (Saint Rögnvald)	With Harald Maddadsson and Erlend	1136-1158
Harald Maddadsson	With Rögnvald, Erlend and Harald Eiriksson	1134–1206
Erlend Haraldsson	Son of Harald Haakonsson, with Harald Maddadsson	1151–1154
Harald Eiriksson	In Caithness, grand-son of Rögnvald Kali, with Harald	1191–1194
David Haraldsson	With Heinrik and Jon	1206–1214
Heinrik Haraldsson	In Caithness, with David and Jon	1206–before 1231
Jon Haraldsson	With David and Heinrik	1206–1231

4.2.2 Scottish Earls under the Norwegian Crown

Magnus	son of Gille Brigte, /....... Mormaer of Angus,[383/2] was granted the Earldom of Orkney by King Haakon /................. Haakonsson.	1206–1231
Magnus	Son of Gille Brigte	c. 1236–1239
Gille Brigte	Son of Magnus	1239–?
Gille Brigte	Son of Gille Brigte, /....... perhaps the same as the previous Gille Brigte	?–1256
Magnus	Son of Gille Brigte	1256–1273
Magnus Magnusson		1273–1284
Jón Magnússon		1284–c. 1300
Magnús Jónsson		c. 1300–1321

4.2.3 The Strathearn and Sinclair Earls

Some time after Magnus Jonsson's death, around 1331, the Earldom was granted to Maol Íosa V,[132/3] (Malise), Mormaer of Strathearn,[384/2] a distant relative of the first Earl Earl Gille Brigte. Maol Íosa ruled Orkney and Caithness from 1331 to 1350. He left several daughters, but no sons. Orkney passed to his son-in-law, the Swedish councillor Erengisle Suneson.[Ch 4] Another son-in-law, Alexander de l'Ard,[Ch 4] ruled as Earl of Caithness from 1350 until 1375, when the Earldom passed to the King of the Scots. In 1379, the Earldom of Orkney, without Caithness, was granted to another son-in-law of Maol Íosa, Henry Sinclair,[Ch 4] by King Haakon VI Magnusson.[386] Earl Henry ruled until his death in 1401, and was succeeded by a son named Henry,[Ch 4] who was followed by his son Earl William, to whom the Earldom of Caithness was granted by the King of Scots in 1455.

However, Orkney and Shetland were pledged to James III,[A1.2.8.1] in place of a dowry for his bride Margaret of Denmark,[139/2] by Christian I.[387]

James took the Earldom of Orkney for the Crown in 1470, and William was thereafter Earl of Caithness alone until he resigned the Earldom in favour of his son William in 1476, dying in 1484.

4.2.3.1 Maol Íosa (Strathearn 1330–1334; Caithness 1331–1334) 1331–1350

Maol Íosa V,[132/4] of Strathearn (also Maol Íosa of Orkney) was the last of the native Gaelic,[15/7] family of Strathearn mormaers.[384/3] He ruled Strathearn as mormaer/earl between 1330 and 1334, and was Earl of Orkney between 1331 and 1350. His career began promisingly. On the death of his father Maol Íosa IV in 1329, he inherited Strathearn. In 1330, he inherited the title Earldom of Orkney (with the Mormaerdom of Caithness) through his great-grandmother, Earl Gilbert (Gille Brighde)'s,[Ch 4] daughter Maud, who had married Maol Íosa II. Maol Íosa's downfall came as a result of a renewed Balliol onslaught which followed the death of King Robert I Maol Íosa sided with Edward Balliol,[144/2] and the English, and fought for the Balliol side at the Battle of Halidon Hill.[388] However, the Anglo-Balliol alliance turned its back on Maol Íosa, and awarded the Mormaerdom to John de Warenne, 7th Earl of Surrey.[202/2]

On the return to power of King David II,[A1.2.7] Maol Íosa was forgiven, but his Mormaerdom was not restored, instead going to Sir Maurice de Moravia. Maol Íosa spent the rest of his days vainly trying to regain it. Maol Íosa married twice, the second time to Marjory, daughter of Aodh, Earl of Ross. He had four daughters, but no sons Maol Íosa died in 1350. Strathearn was never returned to his heirs, who divided or competed over his more northern inheritance. A grandson named Alexander de l'Arde,[Ch 4] took seat in Caithness, whilst Erengisle Sunesson,[Ch 4] the husband of one of his daughters (possibly named Agnes), received the earl's title of Orkney. Ultimately, lands in both of these and the Norse earldom (that by decision of Haakon VI of Norway,[386/2] in 1379) passed to his grandson Henry Sinclair I, Earl of Orkney,[Ch 4] son of William Sinclair, Lord of Rosslyn,[23/14] and Maol Iosa's (youngest) daughter Isobel of Strathearn.

4.2.3.2 Erengisle Suneson (Orkney only) 1353–1357 (d. 26th Dec. 1392)

Erengisle Sunesson of Hultboda, Earl of Orkney was an important Swedish magnate in 14th century. In his later life, he was known as Jarl *Erengisle* in

Sweden. He was knight, high councillor and titular earl.[389] He was usually a supporter of his king, Magnus VII of Norway,[390] and Sweden, although in some instances he was in alliance with king's rivals. The king's Norwegian tasks for him led to his marriage with an unnamed daughter (possibly Agnes) of Maol Íosa, Earl of Orkney,[Ch 4] Caithness and Strathearn. Because Maol Íosa did not have sons, families of his daughters divided or competed over his inheritance. Erengisle became the Earl of Orkney, although there is little evidence that he ever treated it as anything other than a high title, bringing him prestige over the then titleless Scandinavian nobility, or that he ever stayed in the earldom. In 1357 Earl Erengisle was among magnates who proclaimed Eric, the eldest son of king Magnus, as king in place of the father. He then led negotiations which resulted in reconciliation between father and son and them sharing the kingship. In 1379, when his Strathearn wife already was (long) deceased, King Haakon VI of Norway,[386/4] granted the earldom of Orkney to Maol Iosa's (youngest) grandson, Henry Sinclair, Earl of Orkney. The widowed earl Erengisle however continued to use the title until his death (as evidenced by e.g. his appellation,[391] in the text of his last will and testament).

4.2.3.3 Alexander de l'Ard, (Caithness only) 1350–1375

4.2.3.4 Henry I Sinclair 1s Earl of Orkney (b. 1345 –d. 1400)

Henry I Sinclair, Earl of Orkney and feudal,[42/4] baron of Roslin,[Ch 4] (c. 1345–c. 1400) was a Scottish nobleman. He is sometimes identified by another spelling of his surname, St. Clair. He was the grandfather of William Sinclair, 1st Earl of Caithness, [Ch 4] the builder of Rosslyn Chapel.[Ch 5] He is best known today because of a modern legend that he took part in explorations of Greenland and North America almost 100 years before Christopher Columbus. William Thomson, in his book *The New History of Orkney*, wrote: "It has been Earl Henry's singular fate to enjoy an ever-expanding posthumous reputation which has very little to do with anything he achieved in his lifetime."

4.2.3.5 Henry II Sinclair 2nd Earl of Orkney (1375–1420)

Henry II, 10th Baron of Roslin,[4.1.10] 2nd Earl of Orkney, inherited 1400, was a Scottish nobleman and Pantler,[392] of Scotland. He was son of Henry Sinclair, 1st Earl of Orkney by his wife Jean, daughter of John Haliburton of Dirleton,[358/2] and succeeded his father in 1404. In about 1407, he married Egidia Douglas, daughter of Sir William Douglas of Nithsdale,[361/2] and maternal granddaughter of King Robert II of Scotland, they were the parents of William Sinclair, 3rd Earl of Orkney and Beatrix Sinclair, who married James Douglas, 7th Earl of Douglas. He was taken prisoner leading his tenants and associates against the English at The Battle of Homildon Hill,[393] in 1402, but was soon released. In 1406, he escorted Prince James to France aboard the ship *Maryenknight* but the ship was captured by English pirates off Flamborough head.[362/2] Both were imprisoned in the Tower of London.[200/3] In 1407, he escaped or was released on payment of a ransom from the Tower. He died of Influenza c1420.

4.2.3.6 Wiliiam Sinclair 3rd Earl of Orkney (1404–1484)

4.3 The Earldom of Caithness

4.3.1 1st Creation (1334)

Earl of Caithness is a title that has been created several times in the Peerage of Scotland,[394/2] and has a very complex history. Its first grant, in the modern sense as to have been counted in strict lists of peerages, is now generally held to have taken place in favor of Maol Íosa V,[132/2] Earl of Strathearn,[384/3] in 1334, although in the true circumstances of 14th century, this presumably was just a recognition of his hereditary right to the ancient Earldom/Mormaership of Caithness. The next year however, all of his titles were declared forfeit for treason. Earlier, Caithness had been intermittently held, presumably always as Fief,[395] of Scotland, by the Norse Earls of Orkney,[Ch 4] at least since the days of the childhood of Thorfinn Sigurdsson,[Ch 4] in c,1020 but possibly already several decades before. The modern reconstruction of holders of Peerage Earldoms, do not usually include those of Mormaerdom of Caithness, although there is no essential difference between them and for example, those of Mormaers of Lennox,[188/2] Mormaers of Strathearn and Mormaers of Angus.[383/2] The next grant after Maol Íosa was to David Stewart,[Ch 4] a younger son of Robert II of Scotland. His heiress, Euphemia, resigned the title in 1390 in favour of her uncle Walter, 1st Earl of Atholl.[187/2] Walter himself resigned the title in 1428 in favour of his son Allan, but he retained the Earldom of Atholl for himself. Upon Allan's death, Walter again came to hold both

Earldoms. However, both were lost when he was executed for high treason in 1437, his titles being forfeit.

4.3.2 2nd Creation (1335)

The 2nd creation was for David Stewart, Prince of Scotland, was a 14th century Scottish magnate. He was the eldest son of the second marriage of King Robert II of Scotland with Euphemia de Ross. King Robert, on the day of his coronation, is given the title of Earl of Strathearn and on the following day his son David does homage to him under the title of Earl of Strathearn. The same year, David obtained a charter of the Barony of Urguhart. He received the Castle of Braal in Caithness and given the title Earl of Caithness. In 1377 he was given the titles Earl Palatine of Strathearn and Caithness. He was involved in a major dispute with his older half-brother, Alexander Stewart, Earl of Buchan who by 1385 had occupied his Castle at Urquhart. It is uncertain, but it is highly likely that he died in March 1386, and no later than 1389. His wife appears to have been a daughter of Sir Alexander Lindsay of Glenesk, and sister of David Lindsay 1st Earl of Crawford. They had a daughter, Euphemia, who succeeded to the earldom.

4.3.3 3rd Creation (1452)

The third creation of the title was for Sir George Crichton,[396] in 1452, but he surrendered the title in the same year.

4.3.4 Final creation (1455)

The final creation of the Earldom was made in 1455, by King James II of Scotland, (1437-1460) for William Sinclair, (b. 1404-d.1484) 3rd Earl of Orkney,[Ch 4] He was the grandson of Henry Sinclair, 1st Earl of Orkney,[Ch 4] the first of the name. He reluctantly surrendered the Orkney title with his encompassing Island estates including Kirkwall Castle,[272/2] to James III, (1460-1488) in 1470, in return for The incomplete Castle of Ravenscraig,[140/3] on the Fifeshire coast and other token lands. James III had, in 1469, received the rights of the King of Norway to Orkney territories, as pledge of dowry of his wife Margaret of Denmark.[139/2] In this way, the Scottish crown tightened its grip to Orkney and Shetland, a hitherto Norwegian territory, by moving all other important holders away. In effect Orkney became a Stewart interest much to the dismay of the disinherited Sinclairs, who continued to interfere in the Orkney estates. Notably in 1529 at The Battle of Summerdale,[Ch 3] north of Kirkwall when George 3rd Earl of Caithness,[Ch 4] was slain along with all of his men while fighting his own distant kin the Sinclairs of Orkney on behalf of King James V of Scots (1513-1542) and again during the reign of King James VI of Scots (1567-1603) when George 5th Earl of Caithness,[Ch 4] sent another Sinclair army which successfully routed the Stewart, rebels led by Patrick Stewart Earl of Orkney.[397] William as 1st Earl of Caithness and Earl or 'Jarl',[129/4] of Orkney is most noted in history for the construction of Roslin castle,[Ch 5] and the ornate Rosslyn chapel,[Ch 5] in Mid Lothian in the 1440's. His son, also William, 2nd Earl of Caithness,[Ch 4] built Girnigoe,[Ch 5] and the castle of Knockinnan,[398/1] near Dunbeath,[Ch 5] some time after 1470 and before his death at The Battle of Flodden,[Ch 3] in 1513 along with King James IV, of Scots (1488-1513). His son John then became 3rd Earl of Caithness,[Ch 4] and he too, as already noted, was slain in battle in 1529, leaving his son George to inherit Girnigoe as 4th Earl of Caithness.[Ch 4]

Anciently a third of the lands of Caithness, including the future site of Girnigoe were held by the Cheyne,[A4] family. Around 1350 (some accounts claim 1354) Reginald Cheyne, the Clan head, died ending the male line of descent, leaving two daughters to inherit the Cheyne estates. One of his daughters married on to the Keiths,while the other is alleged to have married on to the Sinclairs,[Ch.3] dividing the estate into two, which would explain why the Keith tower of Ackergill,[Ch 5] is only one mile away from the Sinclair fortalice,[399] of Girnigoe. However this alleged marriage appears false since the Sinclair claim to Caithness was based on the original Jarldom,[129/4] of Orkney and Caithness so in theory they also held rights to the lands of Ackergill. The two castles of Ackergill and Girnigoe held by two rival families so close together was bound to lead to violence. Not only between the Keiths and Sinclairs but with the Sunderelands, Oliphants and Mackays,who also held lands around Caithness. In fact these feuds got so out of hand that even the Campbells from further afield got involved. It is also stated that Reginald Cheyne's second daughter in actual fact married Nicholas Sutherland since this was how the Sutherlands obtained the Cheyne castles of Old Wick,[Ch 5] and Berriedale,[402/1] which then passed to the Oliphants and Forse castle,[403] which passed to the Keiths. Interestingly both Old Wick and Berriedale were later annexed by the belligerent Sinclairs in their attempts to rule the whole of Caithness. In 1544 George 4th Earl of Caithness,[Ch 4] seized the Episcopal fortress of Scrabster castle,[404] north of

Thurso, from Alexander Gordon, a son of the Earl of Sunderland who had been installed as a temporary Bishop while the Bishop of Caithness was banished. Later when the Earl of Sunderland was made hereditary keeper of Scrabster castle it was described as being "situated among the wild and uncivilised Scots". This phrase though directed at the Caithness area in general surely sums up the lifestyle of the Sinclairs of Caithness. In 1547 George sallied forth from Girnigoe to attack and seize Ackergill castle,[Ch 5] taking Alexander Keith, said captain and his servant John Skarlet hostage. Detaining them not only at Girnigoe,[Ch 5] but at the moated oblong tower house of Braal,[Ch 5] near the River Thurso, which had only recently passed to the Sinclairs,[Ch. 3] from the Crichton family. Why Keith and Skarlet were moved between these two strong castles and other unspecified locations is unclear. Likely it was in case the Keiths mounted a rescue attempt. Or it may be that any assault on Ackergill by the Keiths would result in the deaths of the hostages. So Keith and Skarlet were bargaining chips.

Despite his high handed behaviour George was given remission for his actions by Queen Mary the Regent (Mary Queen of Scots,[145/2] mother). By 1549 Queen Mary installed Lord Oliphant, as keeper of Ackergill possibly to separate the feuding Keiths and Sinclairs until a more permanent solution regarding ownership of Ackergill could be arranged. Also in 1549 George was distracted from this feud, for a time, while be began building the long Z-plan tower house of Barrogill castle near John O' Groats, known today as Castle Mey,[Ch 5] held by Elizabeth The Queen Mother. In 1556 George again besieged Ackergill when it was in the hands of William Keith Earl Marischal.[405/2] This time though he appears to have stormed the barmkin,[406] wall but been unable to secure the tower house. Yet again he was given remission for his actions which angered the Keiths.

George's attacks were not only confined to local rival Clans but on his own kin Sinclair of Dunbeath,[133/2] descended from a younger brother of the 3rd Earl of Caithness,[Ch 4] noted in possession of Dunbeath castle,[Ch 5] in 1529,who built the L-plan tower house of Dounreay,[407] in the 1560's. As the dispute escalated Dounreay castle was besieged by a Sinclair army from Girnigoe. The outcome of the siege appears to be unrecorded.

In 1567 at Helmsdale castle,[408] during a banquet, George arranged for John 11th Earl of Sunderland, his wife Helen and family to be poisoned by Isobel Sinclair the Earl of Sunderland's aunt. The plan was that Isobel's son would inherit the Earldom of Sunderland. So these estates could be seized by the Sinclairs. However, her son was accidentally poisoned and died along with the other guests aside from the true heir who was able to escape and inherit as 12th Earl of Sunderland. As time progressed George became so extreme in his activities that by 1571 he, it is alleged, even arrested his own son and heir, John, Master of Caithness, imprisoning him in one of the cells of Girnigoe,[Ch 5] on suspicion of rebelling against his rule as Justiciary of Caithness. Certainly in 1569 John had clashed with the Oliphants in the village of Wick,[155/2] resulting in him besieging Lord Oliphant in the oblong keep of Old Wick castle,[Ch 5] for eight days, until Lord Oliphant was obliged to surrender due to lack of food and water as noted in the report sent to the Privy Council.[58/2] It appears the Sinclairs then continued to occupy Old Wick. And in 1570 John had burnt down Dornoch Cathedral and sacked the town. But there was no suggestion of him trying to seize Girnigoe or Knockkinnan.[406/2] Surprisingly other historians have unearthed another reason for John's imprisonment. On one hand George as Justiciary of Caithness as an official had to be seen to rebuke his son. But apparently behind the scenes he was furious at his son's "lenity towards the town folk of Dornoch". John simply wasn't as ruthless and efficient as his father leaving witnesses behind to complain to the Privy Council. Because John took too long to die (seven years) his father had him fed on nothing but "salted beef, and then, with holding all drink from him, left him to die of a raging thirst". Although other accounts claim John died at Knockinnan.

In 1582 John's son George inherited as 5th Earl of Caithness.[Ch 4] One of his first actions as Earl was to kill the two jailers responsible for his father's murder, for which he received a remission from the Privy Council as such action was justifiable. He then started a raiding campaign against the Earl of Sunderland which was unacceptable to the Council and he was bound over to keep the peace. In 1588 he resisted a 12 day siege at Girnigoe,[Ch 5] by the Earl of Sunderland who failed to make any real impression so the surrounding lands were sacked and Keiss castle,[Ch 5] across the bay from Girnigoe,[Ch 5] was damaged before the raiders withdrew. George then repaired Girnigoe adding the ornate oriel window.[409] Around the same time the Sinclair family as a whole undertook a great building work. In 1592 they added a new wing to Cadholl castle.[410] In 1600 a cadet branch of the Dunbeath,[133/2] Sinclairs built the L-plan tower of Brims castle,[5.11] at the same time as George rebuilt Keiss as a Z-plan tower. Also to keep up with his kin George began building the new cluster of towers in front of Girnigoe known as Sinclair castle as a symbol of his wealth and power. In 1606 he acquired Berriedale castle,[411] adding it to the long list of Sinclair strongholds throughout Caithness. With his empire expanding George quickly ran short of funds so he resorted to minting his own forged coinage at Girnigoe castle to circulate throughout the North of Scotland to try and cover his many debts. He like his ancestors before him also interfered in local feuds when he sent Clan Gunn disguised as Clan MacKay of Dirlot castle,[412] (which originally belonged to the Gunns) to burn Lord Forbes corn. When the MacKays, sent witnesses to prove they were innocent George had them drowned so no links could be traced back to him. In 1623 Girnigoe/Sinclair castle,[Ch 5] and Ackergill,[Ch 5] (which had recently passed legally to the Sinclairs) were stormed and sacked by Sir Robert Gordon of Sutherland.[413] The Gordons also appear to have assaulted Braal,[5.6] but were unsuccessful in taking this tower but damaged the new Manor house which was under construction nearby.

In 1643 George died, as he was predeceased by his son, Lord Berriedale and grandson, the Master of Berriedale, his title and debts passed to his great grandson also George 6th Earl of Caithness.[Ch 4] In 1651 Oliver Cromwell's,[299/3] troops seized and damaged Dunbeath,[5.8] Dounreay,[407/2] and Ackergill.[Ch 5] Cromwell also sent a garrison of 70 foot and 15 horse to hold Girnigoe/Sinclair castle. Despite family debts George started building Thurso castle,[Ch 5] and married a daughter of Campbell, Marquis of Argyll perhaps in an effort to cover his great grandfather's debts as the Campbells were major creditors. But when he died without issue in 1676. his widow married her own kinsman, Sir John Campbell of Glenorchy,[148/2] who then claimed Girnigoe/Sinclair castle and estates including the title Earl of Caithness. This resulted in the rightful heir, George Sinclair of Keiss,[142/3] castle storming Girnigoe/Sinclair,[Ch 5] and Old Wick,[Ch 5] castles by force of arms in 1679 to contest his right as Earl of Caithness which had been denied him by law. In reply in 1680 the Campbells marched north in an attempt to seize Old Wick castle under cover of any early morning mist. Suddenly the fog cleared and the castle garrison raised the alarm sending riders to Girnigoe/Sinclair castle. The Campbells appeared to withdraw but split their forces into two to ambush and rout the Sinclair army from Girnigoe/Sinclair at The battle of Altimarlach,[Ch 3] some four miles from Wick. Girnigoe/Sinclair,[Ch 5] was then stormed by the Campbells and Keiss castle damaged (today there are still musket holes above the doorway of Keiss,[142/5] from this assault). In 1690 George Sinclair of Keiss again besieged Girnigoe/Sinclair castle this time with heavy cannon ironically destroying his inheritance. The castle though back in Sinclair hands with

George as 7th Earl of Caithness,[Ch 4] was abandoned as a residence leaving the sad shell that remains today.

4.3.5 Disturbance to normal succession

George, 6th Earl of the Sinclair line,[Ch 4] was the last Earl to cause a disturbance in the normal succession of the title. In 1672, he agreed that at his death, all of his lands and titles would pass to Sir John Campbell,[148/3] who was his creditor. In 1677, the 6th Earl died and King Charles II granted him a patent, creating him Earl of Caithness. Later however, the 6th Earl's heir, also named George,[Ch 4] was confirmed in his titles by the law. Therefore, in order to compensate for the loss of the Earldom, Charles II created Sir John Campbell Earl of Breadalbane,[414] and Holland.[Ch 4] Thereafter, the Earldom of Caithness has passed solely within the Sinclair family without any further resignations other irregularities. The Earl of Caithness also holds the title of Lord Berriedale,[415/1] which was created in the Peerage of Scotland,[404/3] in 1455. That title is used as a courtesy title for the Earl's eldest son and heir.

4.3.6 William Sinclair 2nd Earl of Caithness (b. 9th Sept. 1459–d. 1513)

In 1476, William, 1st Earl of Caithness wished to disinherit his eldest son who was known as "the waster". Therefore, so that the Earldom would not pass to him, he resigned the title in favour of his younger son, another William. He was a Scottish nobleman born in Ravenscraig Castle, Kirkcaldy, Scotland,[140/2] to William Sinclair, 1st Earl of Caithness,[Ch 4] and Marjory Sutherland. He married Margaret Keith, daughter of Sir Gilbert Keith. He fought and died in The Battle of Flodden Field.[Ch 3] William and Margaret had two children:-

- John Sinclair, 3rd Earl of Caithness (d. 1529),[Ch 4] married Elizabeth Sutherland (d.1527).
- Alexander Sinclair.

William Sinclair was the person reputed to have brought Enochian Magick,[415] to Scotland. He may have had a third child Margaret, according to some sources. Dame Margaret Sinclair, according to these sources married Sir Thomas Kirkpatrick. They had no children.

4.3.7 John Sinclair 3rd Earl (d. 1529)

Succeeded 1513 John was killed at The Battle of Summerdale,[Ch 3] in Orkney in the year 1529 and was succeeded by his son George.

4.3.8 George Sinclair 4th Earl (d. 1582)

Succeeded 1529 Resigned 1545. Son of John 3rd Earl

4.3.9 George Sinclair 5th Earl (b. 1566–d. 1643)

Grandson of George 4th Earl, son of John, Master of Caithness, who died in prison at Girnigoe,[Ch 5] in 1576. George having survived both his son and Grandson was succeeded by his great Grandson George

4.3.10 George Sinclair 6th Earl (d. 1677)

Succeeded 1643. Resigned 1672. This George, being encumbered with debt and having no male issue, sold his title and estates to John John Campbell of Glenorchy.[155/3] He died in 1677. The title was disputed by George Sinclair of Keiss,[149/3] a descendent of the 5th earl by his second son, who ultimately obtained the Earldom.

4.3.11 John Campbell 1st Earl of Breadalbane and Holland (b. 1613–d. 1717)

4.3.12 George Sinclair 7th Earl (d. 1698)

George of Keiss, now Earl of Caithness, died unmarried and was succeeded by his second cousin,Sir John Sinclair of Murkle,[330] (The lands of Murkle appear to have been the first bestowed on James Sinclair, 2nd son of John, Master of Caithness. His son Sir James was created a baronet of Scotland and Nova Scotia in 1636. Sir James' eldest son John (afterwords Earl of Caithness) left four sons-Alexander (who succeeded him, John, Francis and Archibald. John studied law and became a judge at the Court of Session,[416] with the title of Lord Murkle. The first James Sinclair married Elizabeth Stewart, daughter of The Earl of Orkney, and their son James, the baronet, married Jean, daughter of Stewartof Mains and Burray also in Orkney.

4.3.13 John Sinclair 8th Earl (d. 1705)

4.3.14 Alexander Sinclair 9th Earl (b. 1685–d. 1765)

Died without male heir and was succeeded by his William Sinclair of Rattan,[471], who was lineally descended from Sir John Sinclair of Greenland and Rattan,2nd brother of the 5th Earl.[Ch 4]

4.3.15 William Sinclair 10th Earl (b. 1727–d. 1765)

William of Rattan was succeeded by his son John, Lord of Berriedale,[414/2] a major in the army.

4.3.16 John Sinclair 11th Earl (b. 1757–d. 1789)

Was unmarried and succeeded by Sir James Sinclair of Mey,[289/2] youngest son of the 4th Earl.

4.3.17 James Sinclair 12th Earl (b. 1766–d. 1823)

4.3.18 Alexander Campbell Sinclair 13th Earl (b. 1790–d. 1855)

4.3.19 James Sinclair 14th Earl of Caithness (16th Aug. 1821 – 28th Mar. 1881)

Styled Lord Berriedale from 1823 to 1855. He was a Scottish Liberal politician, scientist and inventor. He was the son of Alexander Sinclair, 13th Earl of Caithness and his wife Frances Harriet, daughter of the Very Reverend William Leigh, Dean of Hereford. He inherited the title in 1855 on the death of his father and his wife Frances Harriet, daughter of the Very Reverend William Leigh, Dean of Hereford. He inherited the title in 1855 on the death of his father.

4.3.20 George Sinclair 15th Earl of Caithness (1858–1889)

He was the eldest son of James Sinclair, 14th Earl of Caithness and his first wife Louisa Georgiana Philips. He was educated privately and at Magdalene College Cam-bridge. On 28th Mar. 1881, he succeeded his father as Earl of Caithness and 2nd Baron Barrogill.[420] He served as Lord Lieutenant of Caithness,[421] from 1881 until his death in 1889. Suffering from epilepsy throughout his short life, his illness killed him at the age of 31. He died following an epileptic seizure at the Palace Hotel in Edinburgh. He never married and so did not have any children. By his will, the 15th Earl bequeathed The Castle of Mey,[5.4] and its lands and estates out of the hands of the Sinclairs, leaving the future Earls of Caithness without a family seat. He left it all to his friend, Mr. F. G. Heathcote on the condition that he took the name of Sinclair (which he did) and that he lived in the Castle for at least 3 months of each year (which he also did).

4.3.21 James Augustus Sinclair
16th Earl of Caithness (b. 1827–d. 1891)

Inherited 1889.

4.3.22 John Sutherland Sinclair
17th Earl of Caithness (b.1857–d. 1914)

4.3.23 Norman Macleod Sinclair
18th Earl of Caithness (b. 1862–d. 1947)

Inherited1914

4.3.24 Brigadier James Sinclair
19th Earl of Caithness (1906–1965)

He was a distinguished British Army officer during World War II,[422] and was also Chief of Clan Sinclair. He joined The Gordon Highlanders,[428] (now amalgamated with the Highlanders (Seaforth,[423] Gordons and Camerons,[424]) and rose to the rank of Brigadier and as such led his regiment (part of the 51st Highland Division) through France, Belgium and Holland into Germany during World War II and was decorated with the Distinguished Service Order. In 1949, he was appointed the first Commander of the Ceylon Army, and played a major role in establishing it as a regular army from the volunteer Ceylon Defence Force till 1952. After leaving the army, he was appointed the Regiment's Colonel of his old Regiment The Gordon Highlanders. He succeeded his sonless paternal uncle as 19th Earl of Caithness. His first wife, by whom he had three daughters (Jean, Margaret and Fiona), died during the war and after it, in 1946, he married a widow Gabrielle Ormerod whose husband had been killed on active service in Africa, leaving her with a daughter (Susie). In 1947, while posted to Germany another daughter (Bridget) was born and the next year in Burma Malcolm, Lord Berriedale,[421/3] was born. In 1955 he was appointted factor (land agent and manager) of Her Majesty The Queen's Private Estate at Balmoral Aberdeenshire, where he lived until his death in 1965. His son Lord Berriedale, then became the 20th Earl of Caithness and Chief of Clan Sinclair.

4.3.25 Malcolm Ian Sinclair 20th Earl of Caithness (b. 3rd Nov. 1948)

He is a British Conservative politician and member of the House of Lords, as one of the remaining hereditary peers. He is also chief of Clan Sinclair. He is the Chief Executive of The Clan Sinclair Trust.[2/2] The Earl was educated at Marlborough College and Royal Agricultural College, Cirencester. Lord Caithness served as a House of Lords government whip under Margaret Thatcher, from 1984 to 1985. He then moved to the Department of Transport as a Parliamentary Under Secretary of State, serving until 1986, when he became a Minister of State at the Home Office. In 1988 he was once again moved, this time to be Minister of State at the Department of Environment. In 1989, he became Paymaster-General. In 1990, Lord Caithness was again shuffled to the Foreign Office as a Minister of State and then in 1992 back to the Department of Transport. He married Diana Caroline Coke (1953–1994) in 1975. In January 1994, Lord Caithness resigned from the Government following the suicide of his wife Diana, Countess of Caithness, who according to the BBC "shot herself in despair at his relationship with another woman." In 2004, he married Leila C. Jenkins in Rosslyn Chapel. [5.3] The Earl filed for divorce a year later. With the passage of The House of Lords Act 1999,[425] Lord Caithness, along with most other hereditary peers, lost his automatic right to sit in the House of Lords. He was however elected as one of the 90 representative peers to remain in the House of Lords under the provisions of the Act. He was made a Privy Counsellor,[58/2] in 1990. He is an opponent of Fractional-reserve banking.[426]

In 2009 the Earl said "*...I do not believe there is an obligation towards the clan in any formal sense. For many years I took no interest in the Clan because I was too busy earning a living and bringing up the family...If a chief can give the time, particularly to the Diaspora,*[427] *then there are huge rewards for everyone and I would hope that most chiefs can do that.*" In 2010, The Chief of the Clan Sinclair was advertised on the internet as the host for a £7,588 UK trip, including a tour of Westminster and the chance to meet "various colleagues" including the Speaker. The House of Lords Commissioner for Standards, Paul Kernaghan, said the Earl had clearly breached the rules on use of Westminster facilities. The Earl apologised and promised not to do it again. The heir apparent is the present holder's son, Alexander James Richard Sinclair, Lord Berriedale,[421/4] born in 1981.

5. Sinclair castles

Castles that were either built by the *Sinclairs* or came into their possession include:-

5.1 Castle Sinclair Girnigoe

Perhaps the best-known Sinclair Castle. It was dramatically situated on the cliffs just outside Wick. [155/2] and is considered to be one of the earliest seats of Clan Sinclair. [Ch. 3] Although now ruined, it is well worth a visit and it still contains both a secret chamber in the vaulting of the kitchen ceiling and a grim dungeon where, it is said, in 1577 George Sinclair, the 4th Earl of Caithness,[Ch 4] imprisoned his own son John, Master of Caithness (heir apparent) in Castle Sinclair Girnigoe, on suspicion of rebelling against his rule. He was held there for seven years, after which his father fed him a diet of salted beef with nothing to drink, so that he eventually died insane from thirst.

Castle Sinclair Girnigoe in Caithness

5.1.1 History

In its earliest incarnation, Castle Sinclair Girnigoe was known only as Castle Girnigoe. It was built by William Sinclair, the 2nd Earl of Caithness,[Ch 4] probably sometime between 1476 and 1496, but before his death at The

Castle Sinclair Girnigoe from Sinclair's Bay

Battle of Flodden.[Ch 3] in 1513. There are some indications that the castle was built upon the foundations of an earlier fortalice.[179/2] The castle was extended in 1606 with new structures consisting of a gatehouse and other buildings surrounded by a curtain wall, these connected to rest of the castle by a drawbridge over a rock-cut ravine.

At this time, the Earl of Caithness obtained official permission in an Act of Parliament, to change the name from Castle Girnigoe to Castle Sinclair. However, both names remained in use. Girnigoe was an adapted 5 story L-plan crow-stepped gabled tower house, which sat upon a rocky promontory jutting out into Sinclair Bay. This tower was adjoined to various outbuildings within a surrounding wall which encompassed the entire promontory. There is some evidence to suggest that the tower house of Girnigoe is a 17th century addition. Girnigoe has a number of special architectural details, including a small secret chamber in the vaulted ceiling of the kitchen, a rock-cut stairway down to the sea, and a well (now filled-in) in the lowest level of the tower. Castle Sinclair Girnigoe was continuously inhabited by the Sinclair Earls of Caithness,[Ch 4] until George Sinclair the 6th Earl of Caithness,[Ch 4] died without issue in 1676, after which John Campbell of Glen Orchy,[148/3] who married George Sinclair's widow, claimed the title of Earl of Caithness as well as Castle Sinclair Girnigoe. George Sinclair of Keiss,[142/2] who was considered the rightful heir stormed the castle in 1679, an action which led to The Battle of Altimarlech,[Ch 3] in 1680, in which the Campbells were victorious. In 1690 George Sinclair of Keiss once again besieged the castle, but this time destroyed it with heavy cannon fire, though recent investigations seem to discount the cannon fire story. Although he reclaimed the title of Earl of Caithness for Clan Sinclair,[Ch. 3] Castle Sinclair Girnigoe was now a ruined shell. Until recently it had been allowed to fall into decay.

Castle Sinclair Girnigoe today.

Castles Sinclair & Girnigo, Caithness

Castle Sinclair Girnigoe drawn in 1821

It is the most spectacular ruin in the North of Scotland, and was erected in the late 14th century as an enclosure Castle with the main Tower at the West end. It was completely impregnable until it became a ruin in the mid 1600s. The promontory on which it stands had been cut away from the mainland both at its base and half way along by great ditches dividing the Castle into two baileys.[428] The Castle was constantly altered over time to take account of changes in weaponry and social conditions. The main access was through the west Barbican,[429] on the west side of the moat, over a drawbridge, past a portcullis,[430] and through the long vaulted pend of the Gatehouse Tower. This remains, but the chimney above is late 16th-early 17th century. The buildings that surround the outer bailey,[428/2] courtyard are also of that period but built on earlier foundations and the curtain walling on the south side is mid 15th century. A second drawbridge gave access to the inner bailey and on the edge of the second trench the Tower House built in 16th century, again on earlier foundations, and which rises to three storeys, with one wing behind on the sea side. Behind that again was the inner bailey of a courtyard with buildings dating from the late 14th-late 15th century. One of the two rooms forming the basement of this Tower House probably contained a deep well (now infilled) and was vaulted, as was the entire ground storey. By contrast, the upper floors were constructed of timber. A stone stair descended to a sally port,[431] at sea level at the East end of the peninsular. The Castle was the stronghold of the Sinclair family who were made Earls of Caithness,[4.3] in 1455 and remained the seat until besieged by cannon (for the first time in Caithness) in 1680. Since that time it has been allowed to fall into decay. In 1606 the Earl of Caithness obtained an Act of Parliament to change the name of the Castle from Castle Girnigoe to Castle Sinclair but both names remained in use which led to the confusion and error that there were 2 Castles on the site. The Castle is the official seat of the Earldom and is now owned by the Clan Sinclair Trust,[2/2] which is seeking to preserve it and the first phase of work started in August 2004.

5.1.2 The Castle today

Recently, the Clan Sinclair Trust has begun restoration work on the Castle in an attempt to preserve the archeological and historical importance of the structure. Once restored, it will be one of the few castles open to the public which are accessible to handicapped people.

5.2 Roslin Castle

The approach to Roslin Castle over the bridge, and showing the east range behind the ruined gatehouse

Roslin Castle (sometimes spelt Rosslyn) is a partially ruined castle near the village of Roslin in Midlothian, Scotland. It is located around 9 miles south of Edinburgh, on the north bank of the North Esk, only a few hundred metres from the famous Rosslyn Chapel.[Ch 5] There has been a castle on the site since the early 14th century,when the Sinclair family, Earls of Caithness,[Ch 4] and Barons of Roslin,[Ch 4] fortified the site although the present ruins are of slightly later date. Following destruction during the War of The Rough Wooing,[432/1] of 1544 the castle was rebuilt. This structure built into the cliffs of Roslin Glen,[210/2] has remained at least partially habitable ever since. The castle is accessed via a high bridge which replaced an earlier drawbridge. Roslin was renovated in the 1980s and now serves as holiday accommodation.

5.2.1 History

The first castle at Roslin was built in the 1330s for Henry Sinclair, Earl of Orkney.[Ch 4] The Sinclair, or St Clair, family (also anciently spelt *Sanctclare*), were of Norman,[5/4] origin, and had held land in The Lothians,[433] since 1162. It was built on a rocky promontory near the site of the Battle of Roslin,[Ch 3] where the Scots defeated the English in 1303. In the late 14th or early 15th century, Henry's son Henry, 2nd Earl of Orkney,[4.2.04] built a new rectangular round-cornered keep,[440/1] at the south-west corner. The courtyard was entered via a drawbridge over an artificial ditch, giving access to a pend in the small north range. The castle was damaged by a domestic fire in1452. It was a scriptorium,[434] during the middle ages, and five St Clair manuscripts, dating back

The bridge giving access to Roslin Castle

to1488, are in the National Library of Scotland. These include the Rosslyn-Hay manuscript believed to be the earliest extant work in Scots prose. Legend has it that during the domestic fire the Earl was in consternation because of his valuable manuscripts but they were lowered to safety from a window by his chaplain. Roslin was more severely damaged by the Earl of Hertford who burned the castle during The War of the Rough Wooing,[432/2] in 1544. The keep,[435/2] was almost totally destroyed, although its one remaining ruined wall can still be seen. The castle was rebuilt in the late 16th century. A new five-storey east range was built into the side of the rock, and the gatehouse was rebuilt, this time with a permanent stone bridge. The upper part of the east range was renovated in 1622 with renaissance details and carving to door and window surrounds. Roslin suffered again from the artillery of Cromwell's,[299/2] commander in Scotland General Monck,[312/2] in 1650. It was further damaged by a Reforming mob in 1688. By the 18th century the structure was dilapidated, though part of the east range has always remained habitable. From 1982 to 1988 the east range was restored by architects Simpson and Brown. The current owner, the Earl of Rosslyn,[Ch 4] a descendant of the Sinclairs, leases the castle as holiday accommodation via the Landmark Trust. The castle is a Scheduled Ancient Monument and a Category A listed building.

5.2.2 Architecture

The castle stands precipitously above a loop of the River North Esk, which protects it on three sides. This rocky promontory was breached on the north side to form a ditch giving further protection. The castle is approached from Roslin,[23/6] across this ditch, via a precipitous bridge and through the ruined gatehouse.

5.2.3 Ruins

The remains of the gatehouse and north range comprise only fragments of walls and one side of the entrance arch, with the remains of a bartizan,[436] above. Along the west side of the castle, the 15th-century curtain wall remains standing to a considerable height. This section of wall has six openings at the base, one of which served as a postern,[437] gate.

The west curtain wall, with the ruined keep beyond.

On the outer face, the six bays are divided by rounded buttresses.[438] Old sketches of Roslin show bartizans,[437] above each of these buttresses with a wall-walk connecting them. To the south of this wall is the remaining wall of the keep. The mound beneath is formed from the collapsed remnants of the other three walls. The ruin suggests that the keep was around 16m by 12m, with walls 2.9m thick rising to a machicolated,[439] parapet.

5.2.4 East Range

The restored east range measures around 31m by 10m with a pitched roof and crow-step gables.,[1/3] It is entered through a richly carved doorway, dated 1622 and initialled SWS for Sir William Sinclair, which gives access to the third floor. The three lower floors are cut into the rock and each has four vaulted rooms, with a fifth in the south-east tower. These lower levels were used for service rooms, with the principal rooms in the two upper floors. At the lowest level was a kitchen with a bakehouse above. On the exterior, gunloops,[440] are found on the south wall, with several shot-holes on the east. All five floors are connected by a central scale-and-platt,[438] staircase, added in the early 17th century to replace a turnpike,[441] stair in the south-west. The rooms of the upper floors have impressive panelling and decorated ceilings. The main hall in the south part of the block has been divided, but retains a large fireplace with the carved initials WS and JE, for William Sinclair and his wife Jean Edmonstone and the date 1597.

East facade of the east range, showing the large windows to the principal rooms above, with smaller windows to the service areas below.

5.3 Rosslyn Chapel

Properly named the Collegiate Chapel of St. Matthew, was founded on a small hill above Roslin Glen,[210/2] as a Roman Catholic collegiate church (with between 4 and 6 ordained canons and two boy choristers) in the mid-15th century. Rosslyn Chapel and the nearby Roslin Castle,[Ch 5] are located at the village of Roslin,[23/7] Midlothian,Scotland. The chapel was founded by William Sinclair, 1st Earl of Caithness,[Ch 4] (also spelled "Sainteclaire/

Saintclair/ Sinclair/ St. Clair") of the Sinclair family, a noble family descended from Norman,[5/4] knights, using the standard designs the mediaeval architects made available to him. Rosslyn Chapel is the third Sinclair place of worship at Roslin - the first being in Roslin Castle,[Ch 5] and the second (whose crumbling buttresses,[438/2] can still be seen today) in what is now Roslin Cemetery. The purpose of the college was to celebrate the Divine Office throughout the day and night and also to celebrate Holy Mass for all the faithful departed including the deceased mem bers of the Sinclair family. During this period the rich heritage of plainsong (a single melodic line) or polyphony (vocal harmony) would be used to enrich the singing of the liturgy.[442] An endowment was made that would pay for the upkeep of the priests and choristers in perpetuity and they also had parochial responsibilities. After the Scottish Reformation (1560) Roman Catholic worship in the Chapel was brought to an end, although the Sinclair family continued to be Roman Catholics until the early 18th century. From that time the Chapel was closed to public worship until 1861 when it was opened again as a place of worship according to the rites of the Scottish Episcopal,[112/2] Church. In later years the Chapel has featured in speculative theories regarding Freemasonry,[341/2] and The Knights Templar.[247/2] The Chapel is currently undergoing an extensive programme of conservation. This includes work to the roof, the stone, the carvings, the stained glass and the organ. A steel canopy was erected over the chapel roof for 14 years. This was to prevent further rain damage to the church and also to give it a chance to dry out properly Major stonework repairs are due for completion by the end of 2011. The last major scaffolding was removed in August 2010.

Rosslyn Chapel

Interior of the chapel.

5.4 The Castle of Mey

Castle of Mey

Another former Sinclair property which, although was originally known as the Castle of Mey, its name was changed for a time to Barrogill Castle. It was built by George Sinclair, 4th Earl of Caithness.[Ch 4] In 1952, the castle was purchased by HM The Queen Mother, who changed its name back to Castle of Mey. It is located in Caithness, on the north coast of Scotland, about 6 miles west of John o' Groats. In fine weather there are views from the castle north to the Orkney Islands.

5.4.1 History

The lands of Mey,[289/2] belonged to the Bishops of Caithness. The Castle of Mey was built between 1566 and 1572, possibly on the site of an earlier fortification by George Sinclair 4th Earl of Caithness. Originally a Z-plan tower house of three storeys, it had a projecting wing at the south-east and a square tower at the north-west. The Castle passed to George Sinclair's younger son William founder of the Sinclairs of Mey, although it later became the seat of the Earls. The Castle's name was changed to Barrogill and it was extended several times, in the 17th and 18th centuries and again in 1821 when Tudor Gothic,[443] style alterations were made, to designs by William Burn. Barrogill passed out of the Sinclair family in 1889, on the death of the 15th Earl,[Ch 4] and in 1928 it was purchased by Captain Imbert-Terry. The Castle was used as an officers' rest home during the Second World War and in 1950 the estate farms were sold off.

5.4.2 Royal residence

The castle was in a semi-derelict state when in 1952, it and its policies (attached lands) were purchased by Queen Elizabeth The Queen Mother, the widow of King George VI,[444] who had died earlier in the year. The Queen Mother set about restoring the castle for use as a holiday home, removing some of the 19th century additions and reinstating the Castle's original name. She regularly visited it in August and October from 1955 until her death in March 2002, the last visit being in October 2001. In July 1996 The Queen Mother made the property the policies and the farm over to the Queen Elizabeth Castle of Mey Trust, which has opened the castle and garden to the public regularly since her death. It is now open seven days a week from 1st May until 30th September each year with a closed period of ten days at the end of July and the beginning of August, when Their Royal Highnesses The Duke and Duchess of Rothesay,[445] usually stay at Mey. The Trust opened a new Visitors Centre in early 2007 and the visitor numbers for that year topped 29,000.

5.4.3 Ghost

The castle is reputedly haunted by The Green Lady, ghost of the daughter of George, 5th Earl of Caithness,[4.3.07] Elizabeth Sinclair. Having fallen in love with a local ploughman, the unhappy girl was imprisoned in the castle attic by her angry father and in a fit of despair, she threw herself from a window.

5.5 Ackergill Tower

Ackergill Tower (or Ackergill Castle) is a Scottish castle located north of Wick,[162/2] Caithness. It is a category A listed building. It was built in the late 15th or early 16th century by an unknown member of the clan Keith. Its construction material is stone cladding. It is still in use and is open to the public.

Ackergill Tower

5.5.1 Early history

The Clan Keith under John Keith, inherited the lands of Ackergill,[453] in 1354 from the Cheynes family. Ackergill Tower may have been built by his son, but was first mentioned in 1538. A legend relates the tale of a young woman by the name of Helen Gunn who was abducted by John Keith for her beauty. She flung herself or fell, from the highest tower to escape her abductor's advances. Supposedly her ghost is still seen, wearing a long red rustling ball gown and a tall head of black hair. This was in the late 14th or early 15th century and is said to have been the true beginning for all feuding between the Gunns and Keiths. It led to The Battle of Champions,[446] in either 1478 or 1464, a judicial combat which led to a massacre of the Gunns by the Keiths at the chapel of St Tear (or Tayre) just east of the village.

5.5.2 The Keiths and Sinclairs

In 1547, the Sinclairs of Castle Sinclair Girnigoe,[Ch 5] attacked and seized the castle. Mary of Guise, [447] then Regent of Scotland, granted the Sinclairs remission for this and returned Ackergill Tower to the Keiths. She later installed Laurence Oliphant, 4th Lord Oliphant as keeper of Ackergill, in 1549. The Sinclairs again captured the castle in 1556 for which they were again granted remission. In 1593 Robert Keith, brother to the William Keith 6th Earl Marischal,[403/1] (who rightfully owned the tower), seized Ackergill by force for which he was declared a rebel, and the castle was returned to the Earl. In 1598 another Keith, one John Keith of Subster, attacked the tower in the dead of night, taking its occupants by surprise and capturing the place. In 1612 the Sinclairs acquired Ackergill Tower once again, but through legal means, when it was sold to the Earl of Caithness by the Earl Marischal. However, by 1623 it was under assault once more when it was besieged by Sir Robert Gordon during his feud with George Sinclair, 5th Earl of Caithness, [Ch 4] but the Sinclairs surrendered the castle before any assault took place. In 1651 Oliver Cromwell,[299/4] may have used Ackergill Castle to garrison his troops during his siege of the Keith's Dunnottar Castle,[448] as he was hunting for the Honours of Scotland. In 1676, John Campbell, 2nd Earl of Breadalbane and Holland,[Ch 4] took possession of Ackergill Tower in repayment of debts owed to him by the Sinclairs.

5.5.3 The Dunbars Cont

John Campbell put Ackergill Tower up for sale in 1699 and it was bought by Sir William Dunbar,of Hempriggs.[449/1] The Dunbars began extensive renovations, including the addition of a lean-to-shaped extension to the tower. In the mid 19th century further additions including a cap house,[450] were made by the architect David Bryce on behalf of George Sutherland Dunbar 7th Lord Duffus. It remained in the hands of the Dunbars of Hempriggs,[449/2] until 1986, when it was sold. The castle underwent a two-year period of restoration work before opening as an exclusive hotel and business venue. The tower was sold on in 2009 although the new owners have maintained the existing business.

5.5.4 The castle

Ackergill Tower is a five-story oblong tower house. The four-storey wing to the rear was added in the early 18th century.

5.6 Braal Castle

Braal Castle is located by the River Thurso north of the village of Halkirk in Caithness, northern Scotland. The ruined castle which dates back to the mid-14th century, was originally known as the Castle of Brathwell. Its construction material is stone. It is currently privately owned and in a ruined condition. It is not open to the public. It was controlled by the Earl of Caithness,[Ch 4] from the 14th to the 18th century.

5.6.1 History

The site may have been occupied by Harold II of Orkney,[Ch 4] Mormaer of Caithness (d. 1206), although the present building is of the 14th century. The "Castle of Brathwell" was granted by King Robert II of Scotland to his son, David Stewart, Earl of Caithness.[Ch 4] His descendant Walter Stewart, forfeited his estates in 1437 when he was executed for his role in the murder of King James I. In 1450 the castle was bestowed by James II upon Sir George Crichton,[452] Lord High Admiral of Scotland,[32/2] who was briefly created Earl of Caithness in 1452. In 1455 the earldom and castle were granted by James II to William Sinclair, Baron of Roslin,[Ch 4] and Lord Chancellor of Scotland. [453] The castle passed to the Sinclairs of Ulbster, [153/2] a branch of the Sinclair Earls of Caithness,[4.3] in the 18th century. Building of an adjacent mansion was begun, although construction was abandoned. In 1856 a hotel was built over these foundations. The building was requisitioned by the Armed Forces during the Second World War,[454] and was converted into flats in the 1970s.

5.6.2 The castle

The castle is located on a defensive site, above the River Thurso. It comprises a tower house, around (39 by 36 feet, with walls 8-10 ft thick. The entrance is at first-floor level, leading into a large hall. A stair in the wall led up to an upper floor and a parapet walk, although the upper parts of the castle have not survived. It has now been made into attractive apartment accommodation.

5.7 Dunbeath Castle

Dunbeath Castle is located on the east coast of Caithness 1.2mls. south of Dunbeath, in northern Scotland. Although a castle has stood here since the 15th century, the present building is of mainly 17th century origin, with 19th century extensions.

5.7.1 History

A castle is first recorded on the rocky peninsula at Dunbeath,[133/2] in 1428, when the lands belonged to the Earl of Caithness.[Ch 4] The first recorded laird,[462] was Alexander Sutherland. It later became the property of the Clan Sinclair,[Ch. 3] through the marriage of the daughter of Alexander Sutherland to William Sinclair (1410–1484), the first Sinclair Earl of Caithness.[Ch 4] The Sinclairs replaced the earlier structure with a four-storey tower house in 1620. In March 1650, Dunbeath was attacked by the Royalist forces of James Graham, 1st Marquess of Montrose,[109/1] during the Wars of the Three Kingdoms.[106/2] Sir John Sinclair rode to Edinburgh to warn of Montrose's arrival leaving his wife to defend Dunbeath against Sir John Hurry. She soon surrendered, and a Royalist garrison was installed. Montrose was defeated in April at the Battle of Carbisdale,[Ch 3] and the opposition forces, under David Leslie, recaptured the castle. The castle was extensively remodelled in the 17th century by Sir William Sinclair, and again in 1853 and 1881 when David Bryce was the architect. From 1894 to 1945 the castle was owned by Vice-Admiral Sir Edwyn Alexander-Sinclair. In that year after 325 years of occupation by the Sinclair Family, the castle was sold to Bertram Currie. In 1967 it was sold again to Harry Blythe and Helen (Sinclaire) Blythe. The castle remained in their possession until 1976 when it was sold to Ray Stanton Avery. In 1997 the castle was sold to the current owner, Stuart Wyndham Murray-Threipland. The castle remains a private residence today and is not open to the public.

5.7.2 The castle

The oldest part of the castle lies at the south-west corner and dates largely from the 17th century. More modern additions have been made to the north and east, in a Scots Baronial style[453] to match the earlier building. The interiors are much altered. The defensive site was enhanced by a dry ditch on the landward side, which cuts across the narrow promontory on which the castle stands.

5.8 Keiss Castle

Keiss (Scottish Gaelic: *Cèis*) is a fishing village at the northern end of Sinclairs Bay on the east coast of Scotland. Keiss Castle, which is now partially ruined, is located less than 1 mile north of the village centre, on sheer cliffs overlooking the bay, and has been a major tourist attraction for many years. Keiss House replaced Keiss Castle around 1755.

New and old castles, Keiss

5.9 Castle of Old Wick

The Castle of Old Wick known also as the Old Man of Wick was built in the 12th century when the Norwegian earldom of Orkney included Caithness and was united under Harald Maddadsson.[Ch 4] The castle is thought to have been his stronghold on the mainland of Britain. There is evidence that the site was occupied before the present castle was built. All that remains today is a tall tower sitting on the very edge of the cliffs, about half a mile south of Wick Bay and of the modern town of Wick,[155/2] but originally the castle had at least 4 stories as well as extra buildings containing workshops and other quarters. supporter of Edward,[28/4] I during his attempt to establish John Balliol as King of Scotland, although there is no evidence of a battle having taken place there. It was abandoned in the18th century. The castle was built to the same plan as Brough Castle, which is about 29 kilometres to the north/northwest, on the Pentland Firth coast of Caithness.

The Castle of Old Wick

5.10 Thurso castle

Thurso Castle stands as a gallant ruined reminder of its former Gothic glory. Thurso means Thor's River, named by the Vikings,[8/3] who inhabited Thurso in the 900's. The structure looks out over the River Thurso like a bold Viking watchman standing guard opposite the Orkney

Thurso castle

Isles. The castle was actually home to the old Earls of Caithness, the present mansion having been built in 1660 by George, Earl of Caithness.[Ch 4] John Sinclair built grand rooms at the back of the building which demonstrates a fine example of Scottish mansion building. Unfortunately there was a fire, and in 1952 parts of the castle had to be demolished leaving it roofless. The former fortress is perched literally a stone's throw away from the jagged cliffs, the tide of the river lapping at its feet. This building is as beautiful as the harsh, stunning and dramatic scenery which it inhabits.

5.11 Braal castle

Braal Castle is located by the River Thurso north of the village of Halkirk, in Caithness, northern Scotland. The ruined castle, which dates back to the mid-14th century, was originally known as the Castle of Brathwell.

5.11.1 History

The site may have been occupied by Harold II of Orkney,[454] Mormaer of Caithness,[455] (d. 1206), although the present building is of the 14th century. The "Castle of Brathwell" was granted by King Robert II of Scotland to his son, David Stewart, Earl of Caithness. His descendant, Walter Stewart,[456] forfeited his estates in 1437 when he was executed for his role in the murder of King James I. In 1450, the castle was bestowed by James II upon Sir George Crichton,[457] Lord High Admiral of Scotland, who was briefly created Earl of Caithness in 1452. In 1455, the earldom and castle were granted by James II to William Sinclair, Baron of Roslin and Lord Chancellor of Scotland. The castle passed to the Sinclairs of Ulbster,[35/2] a branch of the Sinclair Earls of Caithness, in the 18th century. Building of an adjacent mansion was begun, although construction was abandoned. In 1856 a hotel was built over these foundations. The building was requisitioned by the Armed Forces during the Second World War,[458] and was converted into flats in the 1970s.

5.11.2 The castle

The castle is located on a defensive site, above the River Thurso. It comprises a tower house, around 39 by 36 feet, with walls 8-10 ft thick. The entrance is at first-floor level, leading into a large hall. A stair in the wall led up to an upper floor and a parapet walk, although the upper parts of the castle have not survived. It has now been made into attractive apartment accommodation.

5.12 Brims castle

Brims castle

The remains of Brims Castle, a late 16th-century rubble-built tower house on the L-plan consisting of a crow-step gabled main block, three storeys and an attic in height, lying East-West with a projecting stair wing in the north-east. An open wall-head turret commands the entrance at first floor level in the East of the stair wing. A courtyard to the north has been filled with later subsidiary buildings on the east, but on the west there remains part of the high curtain wall, containing a round-arched and mouled gateway, surmounted by an empty heraldic panel space. Still partly occupied as part of the adjoining farm, Brims Castle belonged to the Sinclair family. It is located about four miles west of Thurso, Caithness, Scotland. There is also a small harbour, or port,(Port of Brims) a headland or spit (Brims Ness) and a small burial ground about half a mile away. It is the second most northerly castle on the British Mainland, with the Castle of Mey, a few miles to the east just beating it as the most northerly.

INDEX

1.	Crow-stepped gable	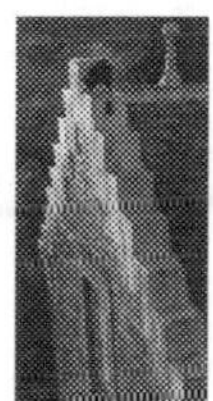 Crow-steps on a Scottish baronial builing
2.	The Clan Sinclair Trust	The Sinclair and Girnigoe Castle Trust now called The Clan Sinclair Trust was formed in 1999 and it now controls the castles.
3.	The World Monuments Fund	WMF's mission is to preserve the world's architectural heritage.
4.	William the Conqueror	 William I (circa 1028 – 9th Sept. 1087), (Guillaume le Conquérant), was the first Norman King of England from Christmas 1066
5	Norman	The Normans were the people who gave their name to Normandy, a region in northern France. They were descended from Norse Viking conquerors.
6.	Norman invasion	The Norman conquest of England began on 28th September 1066 with the invasion of England by William the Conqueror. He became known as this after his victory at the Battle of Hastings 14th October 1066. By early 1071, he had secured control of most of England.
7.	Rollo	Rollo (Rolf) the first Duke of Normandy was a Viking warlord from Norway who, with his followers, settled the western portion of France. Rollo was William the Conqueror's grathfather.

8.	Viking	The term Viking (from Old Norse víkingr) is customarily used to refer to the Norse (Scandinavian) explorers, warriors, merchants, and pirates.
9	Normandy	The Normandy region of France combines a 360-mile dramatic coastline, including the dramatically evocative World War II landing beaches, with a verdant interior of lush farmland, bustling market towns, and historic landmarks.
10.	The Dukes of Normandy	The Duke of Normandy is the title of the reigning monarch of the British Crown Dependencies of the Bailiwick of Guernsey and the Bailiwick of Jersey.
11.	The Birth of Scotland	In 843 Kenneth Macalpine, King of the Scots, achieved a union between Scots and Picts, becoming king of the territory north of the Forth and Clyde. This became known as Scotia. Malcolm II defeated the Angles in 1018, and brought Lothian, into the kingdom. Duncan I, his grandson succeeded him in 1034. Duncan already ruled the Britons, and so now the four kingdoms were united into one Scotland.
12.	Henry VIII	Henry VIII (28th June 1491 – 28th January 1547) was King of England from 21st April 1509 until his death. Besides his six marriages, Henry VIII is known for his role in the separation of the Church of England from the Roman Catholic Church.
13.	Patronymics	A component of a personal name based on the name of one's father, grandfather or an even earlier male ancestor.
14.	Matronymics	A component of a name based on the name of one's mother or a female ancestor.
15.	Gaelic	Scottish Gaelic is a Celtic language native to Scotland. A member of the Goidelic branch of the Celtic languages, Scottish Gaelic, like Modern Irish and Manx, developed out of Middle Irish.
16.	Saint-Clair-sur-epte	Saint-Clair-sur-Epte is a little village located north central of France.

17.	Giverny	Giverny sits on the "right bank" of the River Seine where the river Epte meets the Seine.
18.	Treaty of Saint-Clair- sur-epte	The Treaty of Saint-Clair-sur-Epte was signed in the autumn of 911 between Charles III of France and Rollo, the leader of the Vikings, to settle the Normans in Neustria and to protect Charles' kingdom from any new invasions.
19.	William de Sancto Claro	William de Sancto Claro, whose father had come over with William the Conqueror in 1066, came to Scotland with his wife.
20.	Waldernus Compte de. St Claro	Father of William de Sancto Claro.
21.	Margaret, daughter of Richard Duke of /....... Normandy.	Saint Margaret (c. 1045 – 16th November 1093), also known as Queen Margaret consort of Malcolm III King of Scots. She was the sister of Edgar Ætheling the short-ruling Anglo-Saxon King of England.
22.	Progenitor	An originator of a line of descent.
23.	Rosslyn	Sometimes spelt "Roslin" is a village in Midlothian, Scotland.
24.	The Battle of Alnwick / (1093)	The Battle of Alnwick (1093) is one of two battles fought near the town of Alnwick, in Northumberland, England. In the battle, which occurred on 13th November 1093.
25.	Herdmanston	An area in East Lothian.
26.	Yolande de Dreux	Yolande belonged to the Capetian dynasty and had close ties to other prominent noble families. Her father was a descendant of King Louis VI of France. She was the second wife of Alexander III, King of Scots.
27.	Ragman Rolls	Refers to the collection of instruments by which the nobility and gentry of Scotland subscribed allegiance to King Edward I of England
28.	King Edward I of /...... England (1239-1307)	King Edward I of England Also known as Edward Longshanks and the Hammer of the Scots, was King of England from 1272 to 1307.
29.	The Pentlands	The Pentland Hills are a range of hills to the south-west of Edinburgh, Scotland. The range is around 20 miles in length.

30.	Moorish warriors	The description *Moors* has referred to several historic and modern populations of Berber, Black African and Arab descent from Northern Africa, some of whom came to conquer and occupy the Iberian Peninsula for nearly 800 years.
31.	King Haco of Norway	King Haco of Norway was a master whom his servants loved. For nearly half a century he had sat upon the throne of the ancient kings.
32.	Admiral of Scotland	The Lord High Admiral of Scotland was one of the Great Offices of State of the Kingdom of Scotland before the Union with England in 1707. The office was one of considerable power.
33.	Novadamus	A charter of novodamus, in Scottish feudal land law, is a fresh grant of lands to the grantee.
34.	Mey	Mey is a remote village, located on the north coast of Scotland in Caithness.
35.	Ulbster	Ulbster is a scattered crofting township, located on the east coast of the former county of Caithness.
36.	Progeny	A genetic descendant or offspring.
37.	Scotland	The Kingdom of Scotland emerged as an independent sovereign state in the Early Middle Ages and continued to exist until 1707. On May 1st 1707, Scotland entered into a political union with England to create The United Kingdom of Great Britain. It resulted from the Treaty of Union agreed in 1706 and enacted by the twin Acts of Union passed by the Parliaments of both countries.

38.	Clan Chief	 *A romantic depiction of a clan chief illustrated by R. R. McIan, from James Logan's The Clans of the Scottish Highlands, 1845.* The Scottish Gaelic word clann means children. In early times, and possibly even today, clan members believed themselves to descend from a common ancestor, the founder of the Scottish clan. From its perceived founder a clan takes its name. The clan chief is the representative of this founder.
39.	The Lord Lyon King of Arms	 *The arms of office of the Lord Lyon King of Arms* The head of Lyon Court, is the most junior of the Great Officers of State in Scotland and is the Scottish official with responsibility for regulating heraldry in that country.
40.	Heraldry	Heraldry is the practice of designing, displaying, describing, and recording coats of arms and heraldic badges.
41.	Coat of Arms	The main meaning of a coat of arms is, the design is a symbol unique to a person, family, corporation, or state.
42.	Tanist	The heir apparent to an ancient Celtic chief, elected during the chief's lifetime.
43.	Septs	A sept is an English word for a division of a family, especially a division of a clan.
44.	Sir Thomas Innes of Learney	Sir Thomas Innes of Learney, GCVO, WS (1893–1971) was Lord Lyon from 1945 to 1969, after having been Carrick Pursuivant and Albany Herald in the 1930s.
45.	Undifferenced arms	Undifferenced arms (or plain arms) are coats of arms which have no marks distinguishing the bearer by birth order or family position.

46.	Chiefs seal of arms	The Chiefs seal of arms, incorporated by the Lord Lyon's letters Patent, is the seal of the corporation, like a company seal, but only the chief is empowered by law to seal important documents on behalf of his clan.
47.	Highlands	The Scottish Highlands (Scottish Gaelic: *A' Ghàidheal- tachd* meaning *Land of the Gaels*) is a historice region and distinguishable from the Scottish Lowlands where English replaced Scottish Gaelic. Traditionally, from a Gaelic-speaking point of view, it includes both the Western Isles and the Highlands.
48.	Celtic/Norse	The Celts were a diverse group of tribal societies in Iron Age and Roman-era Europe who spoke Celtic languages. Norsemen were a group of people who spoke what is now called the Old Norse language belonging to a North Germanic branch of languages.
49.	Norman Fuedal /......... Society	Feudalism was a set of political and military customs in medieval Europe that flourished between the 9th and 15th centuries. Broadly defined as a system of holding land in exchange for service or labour.
50.	Suzerainty	A suzerain can refer to a feudal lord, to whom vassals must pay tribute.
51.	High King	A high king is a king who holds a position of seniority over a group of other kings, without the title of Emperor.
52.	Alba	The Scottish Gaelic name for Scotland.
53.	Primogeniture	Primogeniture is the right by law or custom, of the firstborn to inherit the entire estate, to the exclusion of younger siblings. Historically, the term implied males heirs only
54.	Medieval	The Middle Ages (adjectival form: medieval) was a period of European history from the 5th to the 15th century.
55.	Tacksmen	A tacksman meaning was a land-holder of intermediate legal and social status in Scottish Highland society.

56.	Run-rig	Run-rig, or runrig, was a system of land occupation practised, especially in Scotland. The name refers to the ridge and furrow pattern characteristic of this system (and some others), with alternating "runs" (furrows) and "rigs" (ridges).
57.	The Fine	The Gaelic term for clan.
58.	Scottish Privy Council	Was a body that advised the King.
59.	Irish Gaels	The Irish Gaels are an ethnic linguistic group which originated in Ireland and then spread to Scotland and the Isle of Man.
60.	Tudor English	*The Tudor Rose* The Tudor dynasty or House of Tudor was a European royal house of Welsh origin that ruled the Kingdom of England and its realms, including Ireland. Its monarch was Henry Tudor, a descendant of the English royal House of Lancaster.
61.	Buannachan	A military caste if mercenaries evolved called the buannachan, meaning hired soldier
62.	Irish Plantations	The Irish Plantations in 16th and 17th century Ireland were confiscated land by the British crown and the subsequent colonisation of this land with settlers from England and Scotland.
63.	The Battle of Mulroy in Lochaber	The Battle of Maol Ruadh (Mulroy or Maoile Ruaidh) was fought in August 1688 in the Lochaber district of Scotland between the Chattan Confederation led by the Clan Mackintosh against the Clan MacDonald of Keppoch och and the Clan Cameron. It is sometimes described as the last of the private battles between clans.
64.	Reiving	Border Reivers were raiders along the Anglo–Scottish border from the late 13th century to the end of the 16th century. Their ranks consisted of both Scottish and English families.

65.	Cateran	The term cateran (from the Gaelic *ceathairne*, referred to a band of fighting men of a Scottish Highland clan; hence the term applied to the Highland, and later to any, marauders or cattle-lifters.
66.	Lairds	A Laird is a member of the gentry and is a heritable title in Scotland.
67.	Lowland pipes	The Lowland pipes (also known as border pipes) are a type of bagpipe related to the Scottish Great Highland Bagpipe.
68.	Brythonic Celtic	An insular Celtic language known as British or Brythonic.
69.	Anglian	Is a modern English word for a Germanic-speaking people who took their name from the ancestral cultural region of Angeln, a district located in Schleswig-Holstein, Germany.
70.	Galloway	An area in south western Scotland. It usually refers to the former counties of Wigtownshire (or historically West Galloway) and Kirkcudbrightshire (or historically East Galloway). It is part of the Dumfries and Galloway council area of Scotland.
71.	Norse/Gaelic	These were a people of Gaelic and Scandinavian origin who dominated much of the Irish Sea region and western Scotland for a part of the Middle Ages.
72.	Gaelic/Celtic	The Celtic language family is divided into (Irish, Scots and Manx Gaelic) as well as a Welsh, Breton, Cornish branch.
73.	Burghs	A burgh was an autonomous corporate entity in Scotland and Northern England, usually a town. This type of administrative division existed from the 12th century, when King David I created the first royal burghs.
74.	Demesne	Demesne of the crown, or royal demesne, was that part of the crown lands not granted to feudal tenants but managed by crown stewards.
75.	Carrick	The word Carrick comes from the Gaelic word *Carraig*, meaning rock or rocky place. The county of Carrick was eventually combined into Ayrshire.

76.	Galwegian Gaelic	An extinct branch of Celtic language dialect formerly spoken in South West Scotland.
77.	Rosehaugh	A private landed estate on the south of the Black Isle.
78.	Agricutural Revolution	British Agricultural Revolution describes a period of development in Britain between the 17th century and the end of the 19th century, which saw increase in agricultural productivity. This in turn supported unprecedented population growth, and helped drive the Industrial Revolution.
79.	Lowland clearances	The Lowland Clearances (Scottish Gaelic: *Fuadaich nan Galltachd*) in Scotland were one of the results of the British Agricultural Revolution, where thousands of cottars and tenant farmers from the southern counties of Scotland migrated from farms and small holdings to the new industrial centres of Glasgow Edinburgh and northern England or emigrated abroad.
80.	King George IV	(George Augustus Frederick; 1762-1830 was the King of the United Kingdom of Great Britain and Ireland and also of Hanover from the death of his father, George III, in 1820.
81.	The Senchus Fer n-Alban	The Senchus Fer n-Alban (The History of the men of Scotland) is an Old Irish medieval text. It provides genea-logies for kings of Dál Riata and a census of the kingdoms.
82.	Dál Riata	Dál Riata (also Dalriada or Dalriata) was a Gaelic overkingdom on the western coast of Scotland with some territory on the northeast coast of Ireland. It encompassed roughly today's Argyll and Bute, Lochaber and County Antrim.
83.	The Cenél nGabraín	This was a kingroup which dominated the kingship of Dál Riata until the late 7th century and contin-ued to provide kings thereafter.
84.	Kintyre	Kintyre (Scottish Gaelic: *Cinn Tìre*, is a peninsula in western Scotland, in the southwest of Argyll and Bute. The region stretches approximately 30 miles, from the Mull of Kintyre to East Loch Tarbert in the north.

85.	Gabrán mac Doman-/... gairt	A King of Dál Riata in the middle of the 6th century. He is the eponymous ancestor of the Cenél nGabraín.
86.	The Cenel nOengusa	A kin group who ruled the island of Islay, and perhaps nearby Colonsay, off the western coast of Scotland in the early Middle Ages.
87.	Islay	Islay Scottish Gaelic: *Ìle*a Scottish island, known as "The Queen of the Hebrides" (*Banrìgh nan Eilean*), is the southernmost island of the Inner Hebrides. It lies in Argyll just west of Jura.
88.	Jura	The Isle of Jura can be found off the west coast of Scotland, and more specifically a few miles north-east from Islay.
89.	Óengus Mór mac Eirc	The Senchus fer n-Alban, a census and genealogy of the kingdom of Dál Riata, lists the Cenél nÓengusa as one of the three kin groups making up the kingdom in Argyll.
90.	The Cenél Loairn	The Cenél Loairn controlled parts of northern Argyll around the Firth of Lorne, but perhaps including the Isle of Mull, Morvern and Ardnamurchan. The chief place of the kingdom appears to have been at Dun Ollaigh, near Oban.
91.	Lorne	Lorne (Scottish Gaelic: *Latharn*) is an ancient district in the west of Scotland, now part of the Argyll and Bute council area.
92.	Mull	The Isle of Mull or simply Mull (Scottish Gaelic *Muile*), is the second largest island of the Inner Hebrides, off the west coast of Scotland in the council area of Argyll and Bute.
93.	Ardnamurchan	Ardnamurchan (Scottish Gaelic: *Àird nam Murchan*: headland of the great seas) is a 50 square miles peninsula in Lochaber, Highland, Scotland, noted for being very unspoilt and undisturbed.
94.	Loarn mac Eirc	Loarn mac Eirc was a legendary King of Dál Riata who may have lived in the 5th century.

95.	The Cenél Comgaill	Spoken of rarely recent interpretation suggest however, that the kindred may have been important in the Gaelicisation of the Picts. They are thought to have been centred in Cowal, which is plausibly derived from Comgall or Comgaill, and the isle of Bute.
96.	Cowal	Cowal (Scottish Gaelic: *Còmhghal*l) is a peninsula in Ar-gyll and Bute in the Scottish Highlands.
97.	Bute	Also known as the Isle of Bute, Scottish Gaelic: *Eilean Bhòid or Eilean Bhòdach*) is an island in the Firth of Clyde in Scotland. It now constitutes part of the council area of Argyll and Bute.
98.	Comgall mac Doman gairt	Comgall mac Domangairt was King of Dál Riata in the early 6th century. He was the son of Domangart Réti and grandson of Fergus Mór.
99.	Fenian	 *John O'Mahoney* Both the Fenian Brotherhood and Irish Republican Brotherhood (IRB) were fraternal organisations dedicated to the establishment of an independent Irish Republic in the 19th and early 20th century. The name was first applied by John O'Mahony, a Celtic scholar, to the members of the Irish republican group which he founded in the United States in 1858.
100.	Niall of the nine hostages	Niall *Noígíallach* (Old Irish "having nine hostages"), or in English, Niall of the Nine Hostages, son of Eochaid Mugmedón, was an Irish King, whose kindred (descendants) dominated Ireland from the 6th to the 10th century.
101.	Cenél nEóġain	Cenél nEóġain (Modern Irish: *Cenél nEoghain*) is the name of the kindred or descendants of Eógan mac /....... Néill, son of Niall Noígiallach founded the kingdom of Tír Eoghain in the 5th century. It comprises much of what is now County Tyrone.

102.	Ailech	 *Exterior view of Grianan of Aileach situated in County Donegal; the royal fort of the Kingdom of Aileach* Ailech (modern Irish Aileach or Oileach) was a medieval kingdom in Ireland, roughly centred on modern-day County Tyrone and the Inishowen peninsula in Ulster. The Kings of Ailech took their name from the Grianán of Ailech (Irish: *Grianán Ailigh*), a hillfort on top of Greenan Mountain in modern County Donegal.
103.	Macbeth	Mac Bethad mac Findlaích (Modern Gaelic: *MacBheatha mac Fhionnlaigh*, anglicised as Macbeth, and nicknamed Rí Deircc, "the Red King"; died 15th August 1057) was King of the Scots from 1040 until his death.
104.	Anglo-Norman	The Anglo-Normans were mainly the descendants of the Normans who ruled England following the Norman conquest by William the Conqueror in 1066.
105.	Flemish	Flemish is derived from the name of the County of Flanders, from Middle Dutch.
106.	The Civil Wars of the Three Kingdoms	The Wars of the Three Kingdoms formed an intertwined series of conflicts that took place in England, Ireland, and Scotland between 1639 and 1651 after these three countries had come under the "Personal Rule" of the same monarch. The English Civil War is the best-known of these conflicts.
107.	The Covenanters	The Covenanters were a Scottish Presbyterian movement that played an important part in the history of Scotland, during the 17th century. Two important covenants were *The National Covenant* and *The* Solemn League and Cove nant.

108. The Royalist House of Huntly

Huntly Castle

Huntly (Scottish Gaelic: *Srath Bhalgaidh* or *Hunndaidh*) is a town in Aberdeenshire, Scotland, formerly known as Milton of Strathbogie or simply Strathbogie. Huntly Castle, a beautiful castle overlooking The Gordon Schools. Both Huntly and the surrounding district of Gordon are named after a town and family that originated in the border country.

109. James Graham, 1st Marquess of Montrose

Marquess of Montrose

James Graham, 1st Marquess of Montrose (25th October 1612 – 21st May 1650) was a Scottish nobleman and soldier, who initially joined the Covenanters in the Wars of the Three Kingdoms, but subsequently supported King Charles I.

110. The wars of 1644- 77

Part of The Wars of the Three Kingdoms (see Index No. 106).

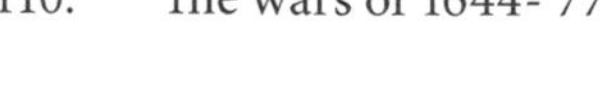

111. The Restoration of /.... Charles II

The Restoration of the monarchy began in 1660 when the English, Scottish and Irish monarchies were all restored under Charles II. following the Wars of The Three Kingdoms.

112. Episcopalianism

The theological doctrine of church government by bishops.

113. Jacobite

Culloden

Jacobite was the name given to supporters of King James VII of Scotland and II of Britain who fled from the country in 1689 to escape an invading army led William of Orange. The Jacobites took their name from Jacobus, the Latin name for James II.

114.	Presbyterianism	From the mid-16th century, Presbyterianism developed as a distinct branch of the Reformed church in Scotland, where the Kirk was reformed through Calvinism as interpreted in the works of John Knox.
115.	The Act of Procription	The Act of Proscription was an Act of the Parliament of Great Britain, which came into effect in Scotland on 1st August 1746. It was part of a series of efforts to assimilate the Scottish Highlands, ending their ability to revolt.
116.	The Heritable Durisdictions Act	The Heritable Jurisdictions (Scotland) Act, 1746 was an Act of Parliament passed by the Parliament of Great Britain in 1746. It abolished the traditional rights of jurisdiction afforded to a Scottish clan chief. The act implicitly repealed article XX of the Union with England Act, 1707, which had promised that all inheritable positions in Scotland would continue without change.
117.	The Dress Act	The Dress Act was part of the Act of Proscription which came into force on 1st August 1746 and made wearing /... *"the Highland Dress"* including tartan or a kilt illegal in Scotland as well as reiterating The Disarming Act.
118.	Armigorous clans	Clans entitled to have a coat of arms.
119.	The Advisory Committee on Tartan	Recommended a clan tartan to the Lord Lyon. Once approved by the Lord Lyon, the clan tartan is then recorded in the Lyon Court Books.
120.	Lyon Court Books	It is the prerogative of the Lord Lyon to record upon application, the thread count of a tartan in the Lyon Court Books. Precisely which tartans are recorded in the Lyon Court Book is entirely a matter of discretion for the Lord Lyon.

121.	Vestiarium Scoticum	The Vestiarium Scoticum (full title, *Vestiarium Scoti- /.... cum: from the Manuscript formerly in the Library of the Scots College at Douay. With an Introduction and Notes, by* John Sobieski Stuart) was first published by William Tait of Edinburgh in a limited edition in 1842. John Telfer Dunbar, in his seminal work *History of Highland Dress* referred to it as "probably the most controversial costume book ever written." After its publication, it was denounced as a forgery. Nevertheless, the role of the book in the history of Scottish tartans is immense, with many of the designs and patterns contained therein passing into the realm of "official" clan tartans.
122.	Sobieski Stuarts	John Sobieski Stuart and Charles Edward Stuart were names used by John Carter Allen and Charles Manning Allen, two 19th century as authors of a dubious book on Scottish tartans and clan dress, the Vestiarium Scoticum.
123.	Heraldic flags	In heraldry an heraldic flag is any of several types of flags, containing coats of arms, heraldic badges, or other devices.
124.	Gorse	 Gorse, furze, furse or whin, a yellow flowering spiny ever green. The most widely familiar species is Common Gorse, the only species native to much of western Europe, where it grows in sunny sites, usually on dry, sandy soils. Other species are characteristic of highly exposed Atlantic coastal heathland and mountain habitats.

125.	Saint Margaret of Scotland	Margaret, was born a Saxon in 1045 and raised in Hungary. She came to England in 1066 when her uncle, King Edward the Confessor, died and Margaret's brother, Edgar Atheling, decided to make a claim to the English throne (See also 21).
126.	Edward the Exile	Edward the Exile (1016 – Late August 1057), also called *Edward Ætheling*, son of King Edmund Ironside and of Ealdgyth. After the Danish conquest of England in 1016 Canute had him and his brother, Edmund, exiled to the Continent. It was at the instruction of their half brother and step brother that they be murdered, however they were secretly sent to Kiev
127.	King Stephen of England	Stephen (c. 1092/6 –1154), often referred to as Stephen of Blois, was a grandson of William the Conqueror. He was King of England from 1135 to his death, His reign was marked by the Anarchy, a civil war with his cousin and rival, the Empress Matilda.
128.	Sir Bernard Burke	Sir John Bernard Burke, CB (5th January 1814 – 12th December 1892) was a British officer of arms and genealogist.
129.	Jarl	A Scandinavian noble ranking immediately below the king.
130.	Moeri	A region in West Norway.
131.	King Harald Fairhair	King Harald Fairhair was the Viking king who defeated several petty kings in the Battle of Hafrsfjord and unified Norway into one kingdom in approx. AD 870.
132.	Malise V(Maol Íosa)	Maol Íosa V of Strathearn (also Maol Íosa of Orkney) was the last of the native Gaelic family of Strathearn mormaers. He ruled Strathearn as mormaer/earl between 1330 and 1334, and was Earl of Orkney between 1331 and 1350.
133.	Dunbeath	Dunbeath (Gaelic: *Dùn Beithe*) is a village in south-east Caithness.
134.	Sir Simon Fraser	Sir Simon Fraser of Oliver and Neidpath, Knight Banneret fought in the Wars of Scottish Independence.

135.	Neidpath Castle	Neidpath Castle is an L-plan rubble-built tower house, overlooking the River Tweed about 1 mile west of /......... Peebles in the Borders of Scotland. The castle is closed to the public.
136.	John Comyn	John Comyn (died 1308) was Earl of Buchan and an important member of Clan Comyn during the early 14th century. He was a chief opponent of Robert the Bruce in the civil war that paralleled the War of Scottish Independence.
137.	1st St Clair Prince of /. Orkney	Henry Sinclair as Earl of Orkney, was entitled to impose taxes and wear a crown if he chose to do so. Because of this, he is referred to as "Prince Henry Sinclair, Earl of Orkney", although it appears that he was never actually granted the title of Prince. Regardless, he was a vassal of the Kings of Scotland and Norway.
138.	The Earldom of Nithsdale	Earl of Nithsdale was a title in the Peerage of Scotland. It was created in 1620 for Robert Maxwell, 9th Lord /
139.	Princess Margaret of Denmark	Margaret of Denmark (23rd June 1456 – before 14th July 1486) was the Queen Consort of Scotland from 1469 to 1486 as the wife of King James III of Scotland. The future King James IV of Scotland was her eldest son.
140.	Ravenscraig Castle	 *Ravenscraig Castle, showing the large D-plan west tower, and the ruined east tower* Ravenscraig Castle is a ruined castle located in Kirkcaldy which dates from around 1460. The castle is an early example of artillery defence in Scotland.
141.	The Dysart Barony	 Dysart (Scottish Gaelic: Dìseart) is a former town and royal burgh located on the south-east coast between Kirkcaldy and West Wemyss in Fife. Dysart was once part of a wider estate owned by the St Clair or Sinclair family. They gainied burgh of barony status for the town towards the end of the 15th century.

142.	George Sinclair of Keiss	Keiss Castle was built by George the 5th Earl of Caithness who reigned between the years 1582-1643 a period of 61 years
143.	Sir James Douglas	Sir James Douglas (also known as Good Sir James and the Black Douglas), (circa 1286 – August 25th, 1330), was a Scottish soldier and knight who fought in the Scottish Wars of Independence.
144	Edward Balliol	Edward Balliol (c. 1283–1367) was a claimant to the Scottish throne (1314–1356). With English help, he briefly ruled the country from 1332 to 1336.
145.	Mary Queen of Scots	Mary, Queen of Scots (8th December 1542 – 8th February 1587), also known as Mary Stuart or Mary I of Scotland. Later Mary was tried and executed for treason by her first cousin Queen Elizabeth I
146.	Lord Darnley	Lord Henry Stewart Darnley, Earl of Ross and Duke of Albany, second husband of Mary, Queen of Scots, and through his mother Lady Margaret Douglas, was a great-grandson of the English King Henry VII.
147.	The Da Vinci Code	The Da Vinci Code is a 2003 mystery-detective novel written by Dan Brown. It follows symbologist Robert Langdon and Sophie Neveu as they investigate a murder in Paris's Louvre Museum and discover a battle between the Priory of Sion and Opus Dei over the possibility of Jesus having been married to Mary Magdalene.
148.	John Campbell of /..... Glenorchy	Sir John Campbell, 4th Baronet of Glenorchy in the /........ county of Perth.
149.	Burgess	Burgesses were merchants or craftsmen who owned pro- perty in burghs and were allowed to trade in burghs free of charge.
150.	Inverary	Inveraray (Scottish Gaelic: *Inbhir Aora;*) is a royal burgh in Argyll and Bute, Scotland. It is on the western shore of Loch Fyne,. It is the traditional county town of Argyll and ancestral home to the Duke of Argyll.

151.	Glen Aray	In the Parish of Inverary.
152.	The Kist	Journal/publication.
153.	Shira Glen	Glen Shira (*Gleann Siara* in Gaelic) is a glen within Argyll at the northern end of Loch Fyne, just to the north of Inveraray.
154.	Kenmore	In Perthshire on the banks of the River Tay.
155.	Wick	Wick (Scottish Gaelic: *Inbhir Ùige*) is an estuary town and a royal burgh in the north of the Highland council area of Scotland. The town straddles the River Wick and extends along both sides of Wick Bay.
156.	Edward Bruce	(Old French: *Edward de Brus*; Modern Scottish Gaelic: Eideard or Iomhair Bruis; c. 1280 – 14th October 1318), Edward of Bruce, was a younger brother of King Robert I of Scotland, who supported his brother in the struggle for the crown of Scotland, then pursued his own claim in Ireland.
157.	Finlaggan	 *Looking southwest down Loch Finlaggan showing Eilean Mòr with Eilean na Comhairle more distant.* Finlaggan, (Scottish Gaelic: *Port an Eilein*) is a historic site on Eilean Mòr in Loch Finlaggan. Loch, island, and castle lie around two km to the north-west of Ballygrant on Islay. Finlaggan was the seat of the Lords of the Isles and of Clan Donald
158.	The Exchequer Rolls of Scotland	The exchequer, one of the earliest government departments, developed out of the king's chamber, the branch of the royal household which oversaw the royal finances.
159.	Kilarrow	Kilarrow is the largest of the Islay parishes.
160.	The Stent Book	Acts of the Balliary of Islay 1718-1843, published in 1890.
161.	Trotternish	Trotternish or *Tròndairnis* (Scottish Gaelic) is the northernmost peninsula of the Isle of Skye, in Scotland
162.	Toftingall	In Caithness where there is a Loch Toftingall.

163.	Sennachie	The clan's tradition were upheld by the "sennachie", one of the most important members of the chief's household. Learned in the clan's history, he maintained its records and genealogy, organised the inauguration of each new chief and addressed the host at clan gatherings.
164.	The House of Sleat	Home of The Macdonald clan on Skye.
165.	Angus Og of Islay	Aonghas Óg mac Dhòmhnaill, Anglicized: Angus MacDonald the younger, Lord of Islay, (d. c. 1330) The chief of Clan Donald, he was a Hebridean nobleman.
166.	The Public Register of All Arms and Bearings in Scotland	Contains all recordings of Coats of Arms in Scotland from 1672 to the present day and it is added to daily. Coats of Arms cannot be used legally in Scotland unless they are recorded in that Register.
167.	Cathboll	In Tarbat of the Bishop of Moray.
168.	Tarbat	The whole of the parish of Tarbat belonged formerly to the county of Ross; but, in 1693, Cromarty and the property of the Earl was transferred to the erected county, barony of Tarbet. The parish is now almost equally divided between the shires of Ross and Cromarty.
169.	The Bishop of Moray	Ecclesiastical head of the Diocese of Moray in northern Scotland.
170.	Waldefgat	South of Scotland border country.
171.	Hypocoristic	A pet name or diminutive form of a name.
172.	Freemasonry	Freemasonry is a fraternal organisation that arose from obscure origins in the late 16th to early 17th century.
173.	King Haakon Haakonasson	Haakon Haakonarson (Early 1204 – 15th December 1263) (Old Norse: *Hákon Hákonarson*; Norwegian: *Håkon /...... Håkonsson*), also called Haakon the Old, was King of Norway from 1217 to 1263. Under his rule, medieval Norway reached its peak.
174.	Vassals	A vassal or feudatory is a person who has entered into a mutual obligation to a lord or monarch in the context of the feudal system in medieval Europe.

175.	Leidang fleet	The institution known as *leiðangr* (Old Norse), *leidang* (Norwegian), was a public levy of free farmers typical for medieval Scandinavians. It was a form of conscription.
176.	King Magnus III of /.. Mann	Magnus Barefoot or Magnus III Olafsson (1073 – 24 August 1103) was King of Norway from 1093 until 1103 and King of Mann and the Isles from 1099 until 1102.
177.	King Dubhghall mac / Ruaidhri	Dubhghall mac Ruaidhri, King of the Hebrides and Argyll, was the son of Ruaidhri mac Raghnaill and /........ brother of Ailean mac Ruaidhri. He fought on the side of Haakon IV of Norway for control of the Hebrides against other Scottish claimants.
178.	Isle of Arran	One of the most southerly Scottish islands and sits in the Firth of Clyde between Ayrshire and Kintyre.
179.	Island of Cumbrae	Great and Little (or Lesser) The islands of Cumbrae consist of Great Cumbrae Island and Little Cumbrae Island.
180.	Largs	On the Firth of Clyde in Ayrshire.
181.	Cunninghame	On the Isle of Arran.
182.	Longships	Were sea vessels made and used by the Vikings from the Nordic countries for trade, commerce, exploration, and warfare during the Viking Age. Designed with a shallow-draft hull designed for speed.
183.	Trading cog	A cog (or cog-built vessels) is a type of ship that first appeared in the 10th century, and was widely used from around the 12th century on. Cogs were generally built of oak.
184.	Lendmenn	Lendmann (plural *lendmenn*) was a title in medieval Norway. Lendmann was the highest rank attainable in the hird of the Norwegian king, and a lendmann stood beneath only earls and kings.
185.	Ogmund Crouchdance	Ogmund Crouchdance was a lendmann - a Norwegian noble in the 13th century and Governor of Orkdal under the Kings Håkon IV of Norway and Magnus VI of Norway. His nickname *Crouchdance* is probably derived from the name of a Norwegian medieval dance.

186.	High Steward of /....... Scotland	The title of High Steward or Great Steward was given in the 12th century to Walter Fitzalan, whose descendants became the House of Stewart.
187.	Atholl	Atholl or Athole (Scottish Gaelic: *Athall*; Old Gaelic *Athfhotla*) is a large historical division in the Scottish Highlands. Today it forms the northern part of Perth and Kinross, Scotland bordering Marr, Badenoch, Breadalbane, Strathearn, Perth and Lochaber.
188.	Lennox	Often referred to as "The Lennox", an historic mormaer- dom, earldom and then dukedom, in Stirling, Scotland.
189.	Merse	A territory located on the on the boundaries of Scotland and England on the east side; today part of Berwickshire.
190.	The Mearns	The County of Kincardine, also known as Kincardine- shire or The Mearns (from *A' Mhaoirne* meaning 'The /... Stewartry') was a local government county on the coast of north-east Scotland.
191.	Magnus the Lawmender	Magnus VI Lagabøte English: *Magnus the law-mender*) or Magnus Håkonsson (Old Norse: *Magnús /.................. Hákonarson*) (1st May 1238 – 9th May 1280), was King of Norway from 1263 until 1280.
192.	The Treaty of Perth	The Treaty of Perth, 1266, ended military conflict be- /... tween Norway, under King Magnus VI of Norway, and Scotland, under King Alexander III, over the sovereignty of the Hebrides and the Isle of Man.
193.	Simon de Montfort	Simon de Montfort, 6th Earl of Leicester, 1st Earl of Chester (23rd May 1208? – 4th Aug. 1265), sometimes referred to as Simon V de Montfort to distinguish him from other Simon de Montforts, was an Anglo- Norman nobleman. He led the barons' rebellion against King Henry III of England during the Second Barons' War of 1263-4, and subsequently became de facto ruler of England.

194.	The Provisions of /..... Oxford	The Provisions of Oxford are often regarded as one of England's first written constitution. Installed in 1258 by a group of barons led by Simon de Montfort, 6th Earl of Leicester, the provisions forced King Henry III of England to accept a new form of government in which power was placed in the hands of a council of twenty-four members.
195.	Henry III	Henry III (1 October 1207 – 16th November 1272) was the son and successor of John as King of England, reigning for 56 years from 1216 until his death. England prospered during his reign and his greatest monument is Westminster.
196.	Second Barons War	The Second Barons' War (1264–1267) was a civil war in England between the forces of a number of barons led by Prince Edward (later Edward I of England).
197.	Lewes Castle	Stands at the highest point of Lewes, East Sussex, England on an artificial mound constructed with chalk blocks. It was originally called Bray Castle.
198.	Mise of Lewes	The Mise of Lewes was a settlement made on 14th May 1264 between King Henry III of England and his /........... rebellious barons, led by Simon de Montfort. The settlement was made on the day of the Battle of Lewes, one of the two major battles of the Second Barons' War.
199.	The Battle of /............ Evesham	The Battle of Evesham was one of the two main battles of 13th century England's Second Barons' War. It marked the defeat rebellious barons by Prince Edward
200.	Tower of London	The Tower of London is a historic castle on the north bank of the River Thames in central London, England. It lies within the London Borough of Tower Hamlets. It was founded to wards the end of 1066 as part of the Norman Conquest of England
201.	St. Briavels Castle	St Briavels Castle is a moated Norman castle at St Briavels in the English county of Gloucestershire.

202.	John De Warren	John de Warenne, 6th Earl of Surrey (1231 – c. 29th /........ September 1304) was a prominent English nobleman and military commander during the reigns of Henry III of /.... England and Edward I of England. During the Second Barons' War he switched sides twice, ending up in /......... support of the king.
203.	Menteith	Menteith or Monteith (Scottish Gaelic: *Tèadhaich*), a /... district of south Perthshire, Scotland, roughly comprises the territory between the Teith and the Forth.
204.	Edinburgh castle	 *The castle dominates the Edinburgh skyline, as seen here from the Grassmarket to the south* Edinburgh Castle is a fortress in Edinburgh, Capital of Scotland, from its position atop the volcanic Castle Rock, Human habitation of the site is dated back as far as the 9th century BC, although the nature of early set tlement is unclear. There has been a royal castle here since at least the reign of David I in the 12th century, and the site continued to to be a royal residence until the Union of the Crowns in 1603. From the 15th century the Castle's residential role declined, and by the 17th century its principal role was as a military base with a large garrison. As one of the most important fortresses in the Kingdom of Scotland, Edinburgh Castle was involved in many historical conflicts, from the Wars of Scottish Independence in the 14th century, up to the Jacobite Rising of 1745, and has been besieged, both successfully and unsuccessfully, on several occasions.
205.	Siege engines	A siege engine is a device that is designed to break or circumvent city walls and other fortifications in siege warfare.

206.	Stirling castle	 *Stirling Castle, from the "King's Knot" gardens below the Castle Hill* The Castle is one of the largest and most important castles, both historically and architecturally, in Scotland. The castle sits atop Castle Hill, an intrusive crag, which forms part of the Stirling Sill geological formation. It is surrounded on three sides by steep cliffs, giving it a strong defensive position. Its strategic location, guarding what was, until the 1890s, the farthest downstream crossing of the River Forth, has made it an important fortification from the earliest times.
207.	The Stone of Scone	*Clach-na-cinneamhain*, (Scottish Gaelic: *An Lia Fàil*), also known as the Stone of Destiny and often referred to in England as The Coronation Stone, is an oblong block of red sandstone, used for centuries in the coronation of the monarchs of Scotland and later the monarchs of England, Great Britain and the United Kingdom. Historically, the artifact was kept at the now-ruined Scone Abbey in Scone, near Perth, Scotland.
208.	John Comyn III	John III Comyn, Lord of Badenoch and Lord of Lochaber or John "the Red", also known simply as the Red Comyn (died 10th February 1306) was a Scottish nobleman who was an important figure in the Wars of Scott- ish Independence, He is best known for having been stabbed to death by King Robert I of Scotland in Dumfries.
209.	Lord of Badenoch	was a magnate who ruled the lordship of Badenoch in the 13th century and early 14th century. is a traditional district which today forms part of Badenoch and Strathspey.
210.	Roslin Glen	Situated a short distance south of Roslin itself, Roslin Glen is an area of semi-natural ancient woodland including oak, ash, hazel, cherry and hawthorn.

211.	Sir John Seagrave	Sir John Seagrave, King Edward I's governor General to the "Province of Scotland".
212.	Ralph de Confrey	Led the second army of 10,000 at Bannockburn besieging nearby Dalhousie Castle.
213.	Castle of Dalhousie	Dalhousie Castle is in Midlothian, Scotland. It is situated near the town of Bonnyrigg, The castle was the seat of the Earls of Dalhousie, the chieftains of Clan Ramsay.
214.	Pikes	A pike is a pole weapon, a very long thrusting spear used extensively by infantry both for attacks on enemy foot soldiers and as a countermeasure against cavalry assaults. It is not intended to be thrown.
215.	Prior Abernethy	Prior Abernethy, was Cistercian prior of Mount Lothian, the western outpost or gate of Balentradoch, the Templar headquarters in Scotland.
216.	Cistercians	The Order of Cistercians is a Catholic religious order of enclosed monks and nuns.
217.	Scone Abbey	Scone Abbey (originally, Scone Priory) was a house of Augustinian canons based at Scone, Perthshire (Gowrie), Scotland, founded between 1114 and 1122.
218.	Borthwick castle	Borthwick Castle constructed in 1430 for Sir William Borthwick, is one of the largest and best-preserved surviving medieval Scottish fortifications. It is located east of the village of Borthwick.
219.	Aymer de Valence	2nd Earl of Pembroke (c. 1275 – 23 June 1324) was a Franco-English nobleman. One of the wealthiest and most powerful men of his age, he was a central player in the conflicts between Edward II of England and his nobility.
220.	The Battle of /............ Methven	The Battle of Methven took place at Methven in /........... Scotland in 1306, during the Wars of Scottish Indepen- dence.

221. The Battle of Dalrigh

The Battle of Dalrigh, also known as the Battle of Dail Righ, Battle of Dalry or Battle of Strathfillan, was fought in the summer of 1306 between the army of King Robert I of Scotland against the Clan MacDougall of Argyll. It took place at the hamlet of Dalrigh

222. Dunavery castle

Dunaverty Castle is located at the southern end of the Kintyre peninsula in western Scotland. The site was once a fort belonging to the Clan Donald (MacDonald).

223. Mull of Kintyre

Mull of Kintyre Lighthouse

The Mull of Kintyre (formerly *Cantyre*) is the south- westernmost tip of the Kintyre Peninsula in southwest

224. Dougal Macdougall

Ruled Lorne and the Isle of Mull in Argyll in the 13th century. During the Wars of Scottish Independence the MacDougalls were supporters of William Wallace but later fought in civil war in support of the powerful Clan Comyn, who were rivals to the throne of Scotland, against Robert the Bruce

225. Glen Trool

Glen Trool is a glen in the Southern Uplands, Galloway, Scotland. It contains Loch Trool. In April 1307 it was the site of the Battle of Glen Trool.

226. Sir Philip Mowbray

Sir Philip Mowbray or Philip de Mowbray was a Scottish gentleman and Governor of Stirling Castle in the 14th century. During the Wars of Scottish Independence, he made a deal with Edward Bruce, the King's younger brother, which led to The Battle of Bannockburn.

227. Bothwell castle

Bothwell Castle is a large medieval castle sited on a high, steep bank, above a bend in the River Clyde, in South Lanarkshire, Scotland. It is south-east of Glasgow. /...

228.	King Edward II of /..... England	Edward II (25th April 1284 – 21st September 1327), called Edward of Caernarfon, was King of England from 1307 until he was deposed by his wife Isabella in January 1327.. The reign of Edward II was considered by some to be disastrous for England, marked by alleged incompetence, political squabbling and military defeats. Notably his army was devastatingly defeated at Bannockburn,
229.	Piers Gaveston	Piers Gaveston, 1st Earl of Cornwall (c. 1284 – 19th June 1312) was an English nobleman of Gascon origin and was assigned to the household of Edward II's son, Edward of Carnarvon.
230.	Henry de Beaumont	Henry de Beaumont,4th Earl of Buchan and 1st Baron Beaumont (died 10th March 1340) was a key figure in the Anglo-Scots wars of Independence.
231.	Robert de Clifford	Robert de Clifford, 1st Baron de Clifford, also 1st Lord of Skipton (c. 1274–1314), was an English soldier who became first Lord Warden of the Marches, defending the English border with Scotland.
232.	Ingram de Umfraville	Sir Ingram de Umfraville was a Scottish noble who /........ played a particularly chequered role in the Wars of Scott- ish Independence.
233.	Guardian of Scotland	The Guardians of Scotland were the de facto heads of state of Scotland during the First Interregnum of 1290–1292, and the Second Interregnum of 1296–1306. During the many years of minority in Scotland's subsequent history, there were many guardians of Scotland and the post was a significant constitutional feature in the course of development for politics in the country.
234.	Red Comyn	John Comyn III Lord of Badenoch (see 208)
235.	Thomas Randolph,1st Earl of Moray	Thomas Randolph, 1st Earl of Moray (died 20th July 1332) was Regent of Scotland, an important figure in the Scottish Wars of Independence.

236.	Walter the Steward	Walter Stewart (c.1296 – 9th April 1327 at Bathgate Castle) was the 6th hereditary High Steward of Scotland. He was also the father of King Robert II of Scotland.
237.	Woad	Is a flowering plant. It is commonly called dyer's woad. Woad is also the name of a blue dye produced from the leaves of the plant.
238.	Henry de Bohun	Sir Henry de Bohun (died 23rd June 1314) was an English knight, the nephew of Humphrey de Bohun, Earl of Here- ford. He was killed on the first day of The Battle of Bannockburn by Robert the Bruce.
239.	Palfrey	A palfrey is a type (not a breed) of horse highly valued as a riding horse in the Middle Ages.
240.	Schiltron	A *sheltron* (also sceld-trome, schiltrom or shiltron) is a compact body of troops forming a battle array, shield wall or phalanx.
241.	Dunbar Castle	Dunbar Castle is the remnants of one of the most mighty fortresses in Scotland, situated over the harbour of the town of Dunbar, in East Lothian.
242.	Scots Wha Hae	*Scots Wha Hae* ("Scots, *Who Have*"; Scottish Gaelic: /..... *Brosnachadh Bhruis*) is a patriotic song of Scotland which served for centuries as an unofficial national /........ anthem of the country, but has lately been largely suplan- ted by Scotland the Brave and Flower of Scotland. The lyrics were written by Robert Burns in 1793, in the form of a speech given by Robert the Bruce before the Battle of Bannockburn.
243.	Flower of Scotland	Flower of Scotland (Scottish Gaelic: *Flùr na h-Alba,* Scots: Flouer o Scotland) is a Scottish song, used frequently at special occasions and sporting events. Although Scotland has no official national anthem, *Flower of Scotland* is one of a number of songs which unofficially fulfil this role.

244.	Edward III of England	Edward III (13th November 1312 – 21st June 1377) was King of England from 1327 and is noted for his military success, restoring royal authority after the disastrous reign of his father, Edward II. His reign saw vital developments and in particular the evolution of the English parliament
245.	Banneret	A knight banneret, was a Medieval knight ("a commoner of rank") who led a company of troops during time of war under his own banner
246.	Restalrig	Restalrig is a suburb of Edinburgh, Scotland.
247.	The Order of The /...... Knights Templar	The organization existed for nearly two centuries during the Middle Ages. Officially endorsed by the Catholic Church around 1129, the Order became a favored charity throughout Christendom,. Templar knights, in their distinctive white mantles with a red cross, were among the most skilled fighting units of the Crusades. Non-combatant members of the Order managed a large economicinfrasturcture.
248.	Berber	Berbers are the indigenous peoples of North Africa west of the Nile Valley.
249.	Col	Pass between two mountain peaks or a gap in a ridge.
250.	The Treaty of Male- stroit	The Treaty of Malestroit, was signed at the " Vestiges de la Madeleine " on the 19th of January 1343. This truce was between the English king Edward III and the French king Phillip VI.
251.	The Auld Alliance	The Auld Alliance (Scots) (French: *Vieille Alliance*) was an alliance between the kingdoms of Scotland and France. It played a significant role in the relations between Scotland, France and England from its beginning in 1295 until the 1560 Treaty of Edinburgh. The terms stipulated that if either country was attacked by England, the other country would invade English territory.
252.	Philip V1	Philip VI (1293 – 22nd August 1350), known as the Fortunate and of Valois, was the King of France from 1328 to his death.

253.	The Siege of Calais	The Siege of Calais began in 1346, towards the beginning of what would later be called the Hundred Years' War
254.	The Battle of Dupplin Moor	Was fought between supporters of the infant David II, the son of Robert the Bruce, and rebels supporting the Balliol claim in 1332.
255.	The Battle of Halidon Hill	The Battle of Halidon Hill (19th July 1333) was fought during the Second War of Scottish Independence. Scottish forces under Sir Archibald Douglas were heavily defeated while trying to relieve Berwick-upon-Tweed.
256.	The Anglo-Scottish Wars	The Anglo-Scottish Wars were a series of wars fought between England and Scotland during the 16th century. After the Wars of Scottish Independence, England and Scotland had fought several times during the 14th, 15th and 16th centuries
257.	Thomas Howard Earl of Surrey	Thomas Howard, 2nd Duke of Norfolk, KG, Earl Marshal (1443 – 21st May 1524), styled Earl of Surrey from 1483 to 1514, was the only son of John Howard, 1st Duke of Norfolk. He served four monarchs as a soldier and statesman.
258.	King Louis X11	Louis XII (27th June 1462 – 1st January 1515), called"the Father of the People". He reigned from 1498 to 1515 and pursued a very active foreign policy.
259.	Scottish East March	Scottish Marches was the term used for the Anglo-Scottish border during the late medieval and early modern eras. They were first conceived in a treaty be- /.... tween Henry III of England and Alexander III of Scot- /... land in 1249 as an attempt to control the Anglo-Scottish border by providing a buffer zone.
260.	Robert Lindsay of Pitscottie	Robert Lindsay of Pitscottie (also Lindesay or Lyndsay; c. 1532–1580) was a Scottish chronicler, author of *The Historie and Chronicles of Scotland, 1436–1565.*

261.	Culverins	Relatively a simple ancestor of the musket, and later a medieval cannon, adapted for use by the French in the 15th century, and later adapted for naval use by the English in the late 16th century.
262.	Sakers	A medium cannon slightly smaller than a culverin developed during the early 16th century.
263.	Rouge Croix pursuivan	A junior officer of arms.
264.	Bill	A polearm weapon used by infantry in medieval Europe.
265.	The Battle of /............ Marignano	The Battle of Marignano was fought during the phase of the Italian Wars (1494–1559), between France and the Old Swiss Confederacy.
266.	Halberdiers	A weapon of the 15th and 16th centuries having an axe-like blade and a steel spike mounted on the end of a long shaft.
267.	The Battle of Pinkie /.. Cleugh	The Battle of Pinkie Cleugh, on the banks of the River Esk near Musselburgh, Scotland on 10th September 1547, was part of the War of the Rough Wooing. It was the last pitched battle between Scottish and English armies. It was a catastrophic defeat for Scotland
268.	Richard III	Richard III (2nd October 1452 – 22nd August 1485) was King of England for two years, from 1483 until his death in 1485 during the Battle of Bosworth Field. His defeat at the Battle of Bosworth Field was the decisive battle of the Wars of the Roses and is sometimes regarded as the end of the Middle Ages in England.
269.	Royal Coat of Arms /.. of Scotland	The royal coat of arms of Scotland (commonly referred to as the Royal Arms of Scotland) was the official coat of arms of the monarchs of Scotland, and was used as the official coat of arms of the Kingdom of Scotland until the Acts of Union of 1707.
270.	Skats	A form of tax to the crown.

271.	Udallers	At the root of Udal law was the principle of the bonder – farmers who owned their properties outright and owed fealty to no superior. But although the udal system meant the bonder had no immediate superior, there were still obligations to the Norwegian Crown and a spat(tax) was paid.
272.	Kirkwall castle	Build in the 14th century by Henry Sinclair, Earl of Orkney, Kirkwall Castle, also known as King's Castle, was located in Kirkwall, the main settlement in the Orkney Islands of Scotland. It was located near Broad Street and Castle Street in the centre of Kirkwall. It was destroyed in 1614 and the last ruins were cleared in the 19th century.
273.	Scapa Flow	Scapa Flow (Old Norse: Skalpaflói—"bay of the long isthmus") is a body of water in the Orkney Islands
274.	Crone	A character in folklore of an old woman who is usually disagreeable, malicious, or sinister in manner, often with magical or supernatural associations that can make her either helpful or obstructing.
275.	Pitcairns	In Perth and Kinross.
276.	Pittendreich	A scattered settlement of Moray, it lies to a mile southwest of Elgin.
277.	Rough wooing	The War of the Rough Wooing (December 1543 – March 1550) was fought between Scotland and England. War was declared by Henry VIII of England, in an attempt to force the Scots to agree to a marriage between his son Edward and Mary, Queen of Scots. The term "Rough Wooing" was only coined many years later by Sir Walter Scott.
278.	Treaty of Greenwich	The Treaty of Greenwich contained two agreements both signed on 1st July 1543 in Greenwich between representatives of England and Scotland. The accord, overall, entailed a plan developed by Henry VIII of England to unite both kingdoms (i.e. Union of the Crowns)
279.	Cousin-german	A child of one's aunt or uncle; a first cousin

280.	George Gordon 1st /.... Marquis of Huntly	George Gordon, 1st Marquess of Huntly (1562 – 13th June 1636) was a Scottish nobleman who took a leading role in the political and military life of Scotland in the late 16th century.
281.	John Gordon 12th Earl of Sutherland	Earl of Sutherland is a title in the Peerage of Scotland. It was created circa 1230 for William de Moravia.
282.	Strathnaver	Strathnaver or (Scottish Gaelic: *Srath Nabhair*) is the fertile strath of the River Naver, famous salmon river that flows from Loch Naver to the north coast of Scotland.
283.	Assynt	Assynt (Scottish Gaelic: *Asainte*) is a parish in west Sutherland, Highland, Scotland – north of Ullapool.
284.	The Battle of Auldgown	The Gunns after discovering a secret plot during a temporary reconciliation between two pten tates of Sutherland and Caithness attchA temporary reconciliation having been patched up between the two potentates of Sutherland and Caithness, they at this time secretly laid a plan to attack Caithness at a place called Auldgown on the borders of Sutherland
285.	Eschew	To avoid habitually especially on moral or practical grounds: shun.
286.	The Battle of Leckmelm	The Battle of Leckmelm was a Scottish clan battle that took place in 1586, in the Scottish Highlands. It was fought between the Clan Gunn against the.Clan Sutherland, Clan Mackay and Clan MacLeod.
287.	Lochleven castle	Loch Leven Castle is a ruined castle on an island in Loch Leven, in the Perth and Kinross region of Scotland. Possibly built around 1300, the castle saw military action during the Wars of Scottish Independence (1296–1357).
288.	Earl of Bothwell	The title Earl of Bothwell has been created twice in the Peerage of Scotland. It was first created for Patrick Hepburn in 1488, and was forfeited in 1567. It was then created for Francis Stewart in 1587. And it was forfeited in 1612
289.	Mey	Mey, a hamlet in Canisbay parish, Caithness, on the coast road from Thurso to Huna and Wick.

290.	The Kalmar War	The Kalmar War (1611–1613) was a war between Denmark–Norway and Sweden.
291.	Colonel Alexander Ramsay	In 1612 Colonel Alexander Ramsay arrived in Gudbrandsdalen intent on reaching Sweden with a force of 550 Scots and a company of Caithness men lead by Colonel George Sinclair. It was thought the actual leader was Sinclair and Ramsay was more or less forgotten.
292.	Bedon Sejelstad	Colonel Sinclair was felled with a silver bullet from a /... single musket shot fired by militia-man Berdon Sejelstad.
293.	Scots Broadsword	From the mid 16th century to the turn of the 18th century the basket swords and similar forms were reaching their full pattern. After 1746 all basket hilt swords were of military pattern. These were the essential weapons for the Highlanders and the favourite fighting method was with the broadsword and target (shield) held on the other arm.
294.	Lochaber axe	The Lochaber axe was a halberd that came into use in Scotland around 1300. The name of the weapon derives from Lochaber, an area in the western Scottish Highlands, as the weapon was employed principally by the Scottish highlanders, who (generally without any cavalry of their own) required armament against cavalry.
295.	Basket Hilt Claymore	 The basket-hilted sword is the name of a group of early modern sword types characterized by a basket-shaped guard that protects the hand. The term claymore, from Scottish. Gaelic *claidheamh mòr*, "great sword") refers to the Scottish variant of the late medieval longsword, two-handed swords with a cross hilt, of which the guards were in use during the 15th and 16th centuries. An early German basket hilt sword, the Sinclair hilt, was named after George Sinclair who was a mercenary who fought in The Kalmar War

296.	Bunad	The bunad is a traditional Norwegian costume worn by both men and women. It can either come from established rural traditions or have a more modern design inspired by historical patterns and cuts.
297.	Ardvreck castle	Standing on a rocky promontory jutting out into Loch Assynt in Sutherland, north west Highland, Scotland, Ardvreck Castle is a ruined castle dating from the 16th century. The castle is thought to have been /................ constructed around 1590 by the Clan MacLeod family
298.	The Covenants of 1638 and 1643	National Covenant, a solemn agreement inaugurated by Scottish churchmen on 28th February 1638. It rejected the attempt by King Charles I and William Laud, archbishop of Canterbury, to force the Scottish church to conform to English liturgical practice and church governance. Solemn League and Covenant, (1643), agreement between the English and Scots by which the Scots agreed to support the English Parliamentarians in their disputes with the royalists and both countries pledged to work for a civil and religious union of England, Scotland, and Ireland
299.	Oliver Cromwell	 Oliver Cromwell (25th April 1599 – 3rd September 1658) was an English military and political leader who overthrew the English monarchy and temporarily turned England into a republican Commonwealth, and served as Lord Protector of England, Scotland, and Ireland.Cromwell was one of the commanders of the New Model Army which defeated the royalists in the English Civil War.
300.	Earl of Kinnoull	Earl of Kinnoull is a title in the Peerage of Scotland. It was created in 1633 for George Hay, 1st Viscount of Dupplin. The family seat is Dupplin Castle.

301.	The Battle of Auldearn	Was an engagement of the Wars of the Three Kingdoms. It took place on 9th May 1645, in and around the village of Auldearn in Nairn.
302.	Ord of Caithness	Where a narrow pass crosses a natural bastion of rock.
303.	General David Leslie	David Leslie, Lord Newark (c. 1600-1682) was a cavalry officer and General in the English Civil War and Scottish Civil Wars.
304.	Balvenie Castle	Balvenie Castle is a ruined castle near Dufftown in the Moray region of Scotland. It was built in the 12th century by a branch of the powerful Comyn family (the *Black Comyns*).
305.	Dunrobin castle	Dunrobin Castle is a stately home in Sutherland, in the Highland area of Scotland. It is the seat of the Countess of Sutherland and the Clan Sutherland.
306.	Skelbo castle	Skelbo Castle is a ruined 14th century keep, located on the high shore at the mouth of Loch Fleet in the Highlands in Scotland. The remaining wall is best preserved at the northern side of the castle.
307.	Skibo castle	Skibo Castle (Scottish Gaelic: Caisteal *Sgìobail*) is located to the west of Dornoch in the Highland county of Sutherland, Scotland overlooking the Dornoch Firth. Although the castle dates back to the 12th century, the present structure is largely of the 19th century, and early 20th century, when it was the home of industrialist Andrew Carnegie.
308.	Dornoch castle	Dornoch Castle was built around 1500 as the home of the Bishops of Caithness. Bishop Robert Stewart gifted the castle to John Gordon, 11th Earl of Sutherland land in 1557. The castle was rebuilt and included some additions after it was set alight in a feud between the McKays and Murrays in 1570. The castle decayed during the 18th century, but was restored in 1813–1814 to serve as a school and jail. In 1859-60 it became a court house, and was made the headquarters of the Sheriff of Sutherland.
309.	Pluscardine	In Morayshire.

310.	The Battle of Philiphaugh	The Battle of Philiphaugh was fought on 13th September 1645 during the Wars of the Three Kingdoms near Selkirk in the Scottish Borders.
311.	Broom	Brooms are a group of evergreen, semi-evergreen, and deciduous shrubs.
312.	General Monck	George Monck, 1st Duke of Albemarle, (6th December 1608 – 3rd January 1670) was an English soldier and politician and a key figure in the restoration of Charles II.
313.	Tynemouth castle	Tynemouth Castle is located on a rocky headland (known as Pen Bal Crag), overlooking Tynemouth Pier. The moated castle-towers, gatehouse and keep are combined with the ruins of the Benedictine priory where early kings of Northumbria were buried.
314.	The 3rd English Civil War	The Third English Civil War (1649–1651) was the last of the English Civil Wars (1642–1651), a series of armed conflicts and political machinations between Parliamentarians and Royalists.
315.	The Battle of Preston (1648)	The Battle of Preston (17th August – 19th August 1648), fought largely at Walton-le-Dale near Preston in Lancashire, resulted in a victory by the troops of Oliver Cromwell over the Royalists and Scots.
316.	The Thirty years war	The Thirty Years' War (1618–1648) was fought primarily in what is now Germany, and at various points involved most countries in Europe. It was one of the most destructive conflicts in European history. The origins of the conflict and goals of the participants were complex, and no single cause can accurately be described as the main reason for the fighting.
317.	Church of Scotland	The Church of Scotland, (Scottish Gaelic: *Eaglais na h-Alba*, Scots: *Kirk o Scotland*) known informally by its Scots language name, the Kirk, is a Presbyterian church, decisively shaped by the Scottish Reformation of 1560. But it's roots trace back to the beginnings of Christianity in Scotland.

318.	Transept	A transept is a transverse section, of any building, which lies across the main body of the building.
319.	Windsor castle	Windsor Castle is a medieval castle and royal residence in Windsor in the English county of Berkshire, notable for its long association with the British royal family and its architecture. The original castle was built after the Norman invasion by William the Conqueror. Since the time of Henry I it has been used by a succession of monarchs and is the longest-occupied palace in Europe.
320.		The English Civil War (1642–1651) was a series of armed conflicts and political machinations between Parliamentarians (Roundheads) and Royalists /............ (Cavaliers). It ended with the Parliamentary victory at the Battle of Worcester on 3 September 1651.
321.	The New Model Army of Cromwell	The New Model Army of England was formed in 1645 by the Parliamentarians in the English Civil War, and was disbanded in 1660 after the Restoration. It was intended as an army liable for service anywhere in the country (including in Scotland and Ireland).
322.	Roundhead	"Roundhead" was the nickname given to the supporters of the Parliament during the English Civil War. Also known as Parliamentarians.
323.	Denouement	The outcome of a sequence of events; the end result.
324.	The Battle of Wigan Lane	The Battle of Wigan Lane was fought on 25th August 1651 during the Third English Civil War. The Royalists were defeated, losing nearly half their officers and men.
325.	The Battle of Dunbar (1650)	The Battle of Dunbar (3rd September 1650) was a battle of the Third English Civil War. The English Parliamentarian forces defeated a Scottish army loyal to King Charles II.
326.	The Battle of Powick Bridge	The Battle of Powick Bridge, fought on 23rd September 1642, was the first major cavalry engagement of the English Civil War and it was a victory for the Royalists.

327.	Redoubt	A redoubt is a fort or fort system usually consisting of an enclosed defensive emplacement outside a larger fort and can be a permanent structure or a hastily-constructed temporary fortification.
328.	Haugh	Haugh is an Old English and Scots term referring to a low-lying meadow in a river valley
329.	Murchill (Murkle)	Murkle is a small scattered hamlet, made up of East Murkle and West Murkle located near Thurso, in Caithness.
330.	The House of Hanover	The House of Hanover (the Hanoverians) is a deposed German royal dynasty which has ruled the Duchy of Brunswick-Lüneburg the Kingdom of Hanover, the Kingdom of Great Britain, the Kingdom of Ireland and the United Kingdom of Great Britain and Ireland. It succeeded the House of Stuart as monarchs of Great Britain and Ireland in 1714 and held that office until the death of Victoria in 1901.
331.	Brabsterdorran	Brabsterdorran is an area of the civil parish of Bower in Highland, Scotland.
332.	The Royal Scots	The Royal Scots (The Royal Regiment), once known as the Royal Regiment of Foot, was the oldest, and therefore most senior, infantry regiment of the line in the British Army, having been raised in 1633 during the reign of Charles I of Scotland.
333.	William Augustus Duke of Cumberland	Prince William (William Augustus; 26th April 1721 – 31st October 1765), was a younger son of George II of Great Britain He is generally best remembered for his role in putting down the Jacobite Rising at the Battle of Culloden in 1746, and as such is also known as "Butcher" Cumberland.
334.	Hessians	German soldiers loyal to King George III who fought for Britain in the Revolutionary War.
335.	General Wolf	Major General James P. Wolfe (2nd January 1727 – 13th September 1759) was a British Army officer, chiefly remembered for his victory over the French in Canada.

336.	The Seven Years War	The Seven Years' War was a global military war between 1756 and 1763, involving most of the great powers of the time and affecting Europe, North America, Central America, the West African coast, India, and the Philippines The war was driven by the antagonism between Great Britain and the Bourbons resulting from overlapping interests in their colonial and trade empires.
337.	Sir Henry Clinton	Sir Henry (16th April 1730 - 23rd December 1795) was a British army officer and politician, best known for his service as a general during the American War of Independence.
338.	General Robert E. Lee	Robert Edward Lee (January 19th, 1807 - October 12, 1870) was a career military officer who is best known for having commanded the Confederate Army of Northern Virginia in the American Civil War.
339.	John Brown	John Brown (9th May, 1800– 2nd December, 1859) was an American revolutionary abolitionist, who in the 1850s advocated and practiced armed insurrection as a means to abolish slavery in the United States. He was executed but his speeches at his trial captured national attention.
340.	Queen Anne of Great Britain	Anne (6th February 1665 – 1st August 1714) ascended the thrones of England, Scotland and Ireland on 8th March 1702. On 1st May 1707, under the Act of Union, two of her realms, England and Scotland, were united as a single sovereign state, the Kingdom of Great Britain.
341.	Grand Master Mason of Scotland	Freemasonry is a fraternal organisation that arose from obscure origins in the late 16th to early 17th century. Freemasonry now exists in various forms all over the world, with a membership estimated at around six million, including approximately 150,000 under the jurisdictions of the Grand Lodge of Scotland
342.	The Scottish Lodges	There is evidence to suggest that there were Masonic lodges in existence in Scotland as early as the late 16th century (for example the Lodge at Kilwinning, Scotland, has records that date back to then).

343.	Siesia	Germanic origin.
344.	Gazetted	To announce or publish in an official journal or in a newspaper.
345.	Rognvald "The. Mighty"	Rognvald "The Mighty" "The Wise" Eysteinsson (son of Eystein Ivarsson) (b.830-d. 890)is the founder of the Earldom of Orkney in the Norse Sagas.
346.	Romsdahal	a county in the northernmost part of Western Norway.
347.	King Charles "The /.... Simple"	Charles III (17th September 879 – 7th October 929), called the Simple or the Straightforward, was the undisputed King of France from 898 until 922.
348.	The Battle of Hastings	The Battle of Hastings occurred on 14th October 1066 during the Norman conquest of England, between the Norman-French army of Duke William II of Normandy and the English army under King Harold II. It took place at Senlac Hill, northwest of Hastings and was a desisive Norman victory
349.	The Battle of Val es Dunes	The Battle of Val-ès-Dunes was fought in 1047 by the combined forces of William, Duke of Normandy and King Henry I of France against the forces of several rebel Norman barons, led by Gui of Burgundy (Gui of Brionne).
350.	Edward the Confessor	Edward the Confessor was king of England from 1042 to 1066. Edward's death was to transform Medieval England and led to the reign of the Norman William the Conqueror with all that his rule meant to Medieval England - castles, the Domesday Book and feudalism. His deep religious views gained him the nickname "Confessor"
351.	Cup-bearer	A cup-bearer was an officer of high rank in royal courts, whose duty it was to serve the drinks at the royal table.
352.	Cousland	The village of Cousland is in Scotland, in the county of Midlothian. It has a long and varied history documented as far back as 1110 when William St. Clair was the 4th Baron of Roslin.

353.	The First Crusade	The First Crusade (1096–1099) was a military expedition by Western Christianity to regain the Holy Lands taken in the Muslim conquest of the Levant, ultimately resulting in the recapture of Jerusalem.
354.	The Siege of Antioch	The Siege of Antioch took place during the First Crusade in 1097 and 1098. The first siege, by the crusaders against the Muslim city, lasted from 21st October, 1097, to 2nd June, 1098. The second siege, against the crusaders who had occupied it, lasted from 7th June to 28th June, 1098.
355.	Henry II	Henry II (5th March 1133 – 6th July 1189) ruled as King of England (1154–1189), Count of Anjou, Count of Maine, Duke of Normandy, Duke of Aquitaine, Duke of Gascony, Count of Nantes, Lord of Ireland and, at various times, controlled parts of Wales, Scotland and western France.
356.	The Battle of Northallerton	The Battle of the Standard, sometimes called The Battle of Northallerton, in which English forces repelled a Scottish army, took place on 22nd August 1138 on Cowton Moor near Northallerton in Yorkshire.
357.	The Church of The Holy Sepulchre	The Church of the Holy Sepulchre, also called the Church of the Resurrection by Eastern Christians, is a church within the walled Old City of Jerusalem.
358.	Dirleton	Dirleton is a village and parish in East Lothian, Scotland approximately 20 miles east of Edinburgh
359.	King Eric of Pomerania	Eric of Pomerania (1381 or 1382 – 3rd May 1459) was King Eric III of Norway (1389–1442).
360.	Fealty	An oath of fealty, from the Latin fidelitas (faithfulness), is a pledge of allegiance of one person to another. Typically the oath is made upon a religious object such as a Bible or saint's relic, often contained within an altar, thus binding the oath-taker before God.
361.	Nithsdale	Nithsdale (Srath Nid in Scottish Gaelic), is the valley of the River Nith in Scotland, and the name of the region.

362.	Flamborough head	Flamborough Head is a promontory of 8 miles on the Yorkshire coast of England, between the Filey and Bridlington bays of the North Sea.
363.	High chancellor	The Lord Chancellor of Scotland was a Great Officer of State in pre-Union Scotland. Holders of the office are known from 1123 onwards, but its duties were occasionally performed by an official of lower status with the title of Keeper of the Great Seal. From the 15th century, the Chancellor was normally a Bishop or an Earl.
364.	Earl of Douglas	The title was created in the Peerage of Scotland in 1358 for William Douglas, 1st Earl of Douglas, son of Sir Archibald Douglas, Guardian of Scotland. The Earldom was forfeited by James Douglas, 9th Earl of Douglas in 1455.
365.	Duke of Touraine	Duke of Touraine was a title in the Peerage of France, relating to Touraine. It was first created in 1360 for Philip, youngest son of King John II of France.
366.	Earl of Buchan	The Mormaer or Earl of Buchan was originally the provincial ruler of the medieval province of Buchan. Buchan was the first Mormaerdom in the High Medieval Kingdom of the Scots to pass into the hands of a non-Scottish family in the male line.
367.	Duke of Albany	Duke of Albany is a peerage title that has occasionally been bestowed on the younger sons in the Scottish, and later the British, royal family, particularly in the Houses of Stuart and Hanover.
368.	Dysart castle	The Sinclairs, built Dysart House (1755-1756) on the estate of Ravenscraig castle.
369.	Lord Chief Justice of Scotland	Known in Scotland as the Lord President of the Court of Session.
370.	Turnpike	A stone spiral staircase built within a wall, it narrowed access to one person at a time, and importantly whilst downward defence was easily accomplished, a right-handed swordsman had no way of attacking on a right-handed spiral stair. .

371.	1st St.Clair Charter	The first document is a letter of jurisdiction, granted by the Freemen Masons of Scotland to William Saint Clair of Roslin. The letter of jurisdiction is probably of a date1600-1.
372.	2nd St.Clair Charter	Purports to have been granted by the Freemen Masons and Hammermen of Scotland to Sir William Saint Clair of Roslin. Probably granted on 1st May 1628.
373.	Battle of the Boyne (1690)	The Battle of the Boyne (Irish: *Cath na Bóinne*, was fought in 1690 between two rival claimants of the English, Scottish and Irish thrones.
374.	Baronet of Alva	Alva is in the county of Fife.
375.	The Master of the Buckhounds	The Master of the Buckhounds was an officer in the Master of the Horse's department of the British Royal Household. The holder was also His/Her Majesty's Representative at Ascot.
376.	Sacrisity	A room for keeping vestments and other church furnishings, sacred vessels, and parish records.
377.	The General Assembly of The Church of Scotland	The General Assembly of the Church of Scotland is the sovereign and highest court of the Church of Scotland, and is thus the Church's governing body As a Presbyterian church, the Church of Scotland is governed by courts of elders rather than by bishops.
378.	The Corps of /............ Gentlemen at Arms	Her Majesty's Bodyguard of the Honourable Corps of Gentlemen at Arms is a bodyguard to the British Monarch.
379.	Poet Laureate	A poet laureate is a poet officially appointed by a government and is often expected to compose poems for state occasions and other government events.
380.	Tennyson	6th August 1809 – 6th October 1892) was Poet Laureate of the United Kingdom during much of Queen Victoria's reign.
381.	Apse	A semicircular recess.
382.	Baptistry	In Christian architecture the baptistry or baptistery is the separate centrally-planned structure surrounding the baptismal font

383.	Edward VII	Edward VII (Albert Edward; 9t November 1841 – 6th May 1910) was King of the United Kingdom and the British Dominions and Emperor of India from 22nd January 1901 until his death in 1910. He was the first British monarch of the House of Saxe-Coburg and Gotha, which was renamed the House of Windsor by his son, George V
384.	Momaers of Angus	The Mormaer or Earl of Angus was the ruler of the medieval Scottish province of Angus. The title, in the Peerage of Scotland, is currently held by the Duke of Hamilton.
385.	Mormaers of Strathearn	The Mormaer of Strathearn or Earl of Strathearn was a provincial ruler in medieval Scotland.
386.	Eric bloodaxe	Eric Haraldsson (Eric, anglicised form of old *Norse: Eiríkr*; died 954), nicknamed 'Bloodaxe' (*blóðøx*), was a 10th-century Scandinavian ruler. He is thought to have had short-lived terms as King of Norway and possibly as the last independent ruler of the kingdom of Northumbria (*c*. 947/8–948 and 952–5).
387.	King Haakon VI Magnusson	The Younger, Norwegian Håkon Magnusson Den Yngre (born 1339, Norway—died 1380, Norway), King of Norway (1355–80) whose marriage to Margaret, daughter of the Danish king Valdemar IV, in 1363 paved the way for the eventual union (1397) of the three major Scandinavian nations—Denmark, Norway, and Sweden—the Kalmar Union.
388.	Christian I	Christian I (February 1426 – 21st May 1481) was a Danish monarch, king of Denmark (1448–1481), Norway (1450–1481) and Sweden (1457–1464), under the Kalmar Union.
389.	The Battle of Halidon Hill	The Battle of Halidon Hill (19th July 1333) was fought during the Second War of Scottish Independence. Scottish forces under Sir Archibald Douglas were heavily defeated while trying to relieve Berwick-upon-Tweed.
390.	Titular earl	Existing in title or name only

391.	Magnus VII	Magnus VII (Magnus Ericsson), b.1316, d.1373 or 1374, King of Norway (1319–43) and Sweden (1319–63).
392.	Appellation	A name, title, or designation.
393.	Pantler	The servant or officer, in a great family, who has charge of the bread and the pantry.
394.	The Battle of Homildon Hill	The Battle of Humbleton Hill (or Homildon Hill) was a conflict between the English and Scottish armies on September 14, 1402 in Northumberland, England.
395.	The Peerage of Scotland	The Peerage of Scotland (Scottish Gaelic: Moraireachd na h-Alba) is the division of the British Peerage for those peers created in the Kingdom of Scotland before 1707.
396.	Fief	A fee (alternatively and rarely: fief, fiefdom) was the central element of feudalism and consisted of heritable lands (or revenue-producing property) granted under one of several varieties of feudal tenure by an overlord.
397.	Sir George Crichton	George Crichton, 1st Earl of Caithness (ca. 1409 - August 1454/1455), was a Scottish peer. Succeeding his father as sheriff of Linlithgowshire, he was knighted before 1438. He later served as Lord High Admiral of Scotland, sheriff of Stirling, and Keeper of Stirling Castle.
398.	Patrick Stewart Earl of Orkney	Patrick Stewart, 2nd Earl of Orkney and Lord of Shetland (c. 1566–6th February 1615) was the son of Robert Stewart, 1st Earl of Orkney.
399.	Knockinnan castle	It is said that Knockinnon Castle was started by William, 2nd Earl of Caithness who fell at the battle of Flodden in 1513 and so it was never completed.
400.	Fortalice	A defensive structure or position; a fortress or a small fort
401.	Berriedale Castle	In descending from the Ord of Caithness, Berriedale Castle was probably the first medieval fortification to be encountered, sitting on a tongue of rock projecting across the mouth of the Berriedale River. Berriedale Castle was developed from a 14th Century stronghold.

402.	Forse Castle	Forse Castle is a ruined building dating from 1200 in the hamlet of Forse in the Caithness region in the Scottish council area of Highland. It was the stronghold of the Sutherlands of Forse.
403.	Scrabster castle	Scrabster Castle became a property of the Sinclair family until it was passed to the Earls of Sutherland in the 1550s. Almost nothing now remains of the castle.
404.	Earl of Marischal	The title of Earl Marischal was created in the peerage of Scotland for William Keith, the Great Marischal of Scotland. The role of the Marischal was to serve as custodian of the Royal Regalia of Scotland, and to protect the king's person when attending parliament.
405.	Barmkin	Barmkin, also spelled barmekin or barnekin, is a Scots word which refers to a form of medieval and later defensive enclosure.
406.	Tower House of Dounreay	Dounreay Castle is situated on the foreshore at Dounreay and at the mouth of the burn known as the Mill Lade. It dates from the late 16th century, and is one of the few remaining examples of a Scottish Laird's castle from that period.
407.	Helmsdale castle	Helmsdale is a village on the east coast of Sutherland, in the Highland council area of Scotland. The remains that were demolished in the 1970's, were the location of the murder of the 11th Earl of Sutherland in 1567.
408.	Oriel window	Oriel windows are a form of bay window commonly found in Gothic architecture, which project from the main wall of the building but do not reach to the ground.
409.	Cadholl castle	In Caithness.
410.	Berriedale castle	Belonged to the Cheynes in the 14th century and was passed to the Sutherlands then to the Oliphants. In 1606 it was purchased by the Earl of Caithness (a Sinclair).

411.	Dirlot castle	Dirlot Castle was constructed in the first half of the 14th century and is another of Sir Reginald Cheyne's strongholds, possibly the smallest and perhaps one of the most intriguing of all his properties from a defensive point of view. The Castle lies near the village of Westerdale.
412.	Sir Robert Gordon of Sutherland	In Sir Robert Gordon's time during the 17th century the Clan Sutherland began to acquire the reputation for enthusiastic and pious Protestantism. This is probably what made the Gordon Earls of Sutherland begin to distance themselves from their Gordon of Huntly cousins who were Catholics and later Jacobites.
413.	Breadalbane	Breadalbane—from Scottish Gaelic *Bràghad Albainn*, "the upper part of Alba"—is a region of the southern/central Scottish Highlands in Atholl. Clan Campbell has a Breadalbane branch. It is retained in the title of Earl of Breadalbane and Holland, and later, the Marquess of Breadalbane. The *Breadalbane Gathering* is a popular 2/4 March tune for the Great Highland Bagpipes.
414.	Lord Berriedale	Title given to eldest son. Berriedale (Scottish Gaelic: *Bearghdal*) is a small village on the northern east coast of Caithness, Scotland
415.	Enochian Magick	Is a system of ceremonial magic based on the evocation and commanding of various spirits. It is based on the 16th-century writings of Dr. John Dee and Edward Kelley, who claimed that their information was delivered to them directly by various angels
416.	The Court of Session of Scotland	(Scottish Gaelic *Cùirt an t-Seisein*) is the supreme civil court and constitutes part of the College of Justice. It sits in Parliament House in Edinburgh and is both a court of first instance and a court of appeal.
417.	Barrogill	In Wick, Caithness.
418.	Lord Lieutenant of Caithness	The Lord Lieutenant of Caithness is the British monarch's personal representative in an area defined since 1975 as consisting of the local government district of Caithness, in Scotland.

419.	World War II	The start of the war is generally held to be 1st September 1939, beginning with the German invasion of Poland; Britain and France declared war on Germany two days later.
420.	The Gordon Highlanders	The Gordon Highlanders was a British Army infantry regiment from 1794 until 1994. The regiment took its name from the Clan Gordon and recruited principally from Aberdeen and the North-East of Scotland.
421.	The Seaforth Highlanders	The Seaforth Highlanders (Ross–shire Buffs, The Duke of Albany's) was a historic regiment of the British Army associated with large areas of the northern Highlands of Scotland. The Seaforth Highlanders have varied in size from two battalions to seventeen battalions during the Great War.
422.	The Cameron Highlanders	The Queen's Own Cameron Highlanders was an infantry regiment of the British Army formed in 1793. In 1961 it was merged with the Seaforth Seaforth Highlanders (Ross-shire Buffs, The Duke of Albany's) to form the Queen's Own Highlanders (Seaforth and Camerons).
423.	The House of Lords Act	The House of Lords Act 1999 was an Act of the Parliament of the United Kingdom that was given Royal Assent on 11th November 1999. The Act reformed the House of Lords, one of the chambers of Parliament. The Act removed the right to inherit seats.
424.	Fractional reserve banking	Fractional-reserve banking is a form of banking where banks maintain reserves (of cash and coin or deposits at the central bank) that are only a fraction of the customer's deposits.
425	Diaspora	A diaspora ("scattering, dispersion") is "the movement, migration, or scattering of people away from an established or ancestral homeland"
426.	Baileys	A bailey is the enclosed area around a castle. Baileys helped protect a castle.

427.	Barbican	The Barbican was an exterior castle defence situated at the entrance of the castle. The Barbican or 'death trap' was developed as another way to strengthen the main entrance.
428.	Portcullis	A portcullis (from the French "porte coulissante" or gliding door) is a latticed grille made of wood, metal, fibreglass or a combination of the three. Portcullises fortified the entrances to many medieval castles.
429.	Sally Port	A gateway permitting the passage of a large number of troops at a time.
430.	The War of The Rough Wooing	The War of the Rough Wooing (December 1543 – March 1550) was fought between Scotland and England. War was declared by Henry VIII of England, in an attempt to force the Scots to agree to a marriage between his son Edward and Mary, Queen of Scots. Scotland benefited from French military aid. Edward VI continued the war until changing circumstances made it irrelevant in 1550.
431.	The Lothians	Lothian (Lowden in Scots, Lodainn in Gaelic) forms a traditional region of Scotland, lying between the southern shore of the Firth of Forth and the Lammermuir Hills. In Lothian there is Edinburgh City, West Lothian, Mid Lothian and East Lothian.
432.	Keep	A keep is a type of fortified tower built within castles during the Middle Ages by European nobility.
433.	Scriptorium	Literally "a place for writing".

Images—Copyright Licences

Licensing—Paintings

*This work is in the **public domain** in the United States, and those countries with a copyright term of life of the author plus **100** years or less.*

*This image (or other media file) is in the **public domain** because its copyright has **expired**. This applies to Australia, the European Union and those countries with a copyright term of **life of the author plus 70 years.***

Licensing—Photographs attributed and unattributed

This file is licensed under the Creative Commons Attribution-Share Alike 3.0 Unported, 2.5 Generic, 2.0 Generic, 2.0 France and 1.0 Generic license, CC0 designation

You are free:
***to share**—to copy, distribute and transmit the work*
***to remix**—to adapt the work*

Under the following conditions:
***attribution**—You must attribute the work in the manner specified by the author or licensor (but not in any way that suggests that they endorse you or your use of the work).*
***share alike**—If you alter, transform, or build upon this work, you may distribute the resulting work only under the same or similar license to this one.*

Licensing—Photographs unknown authors
See A) above This file has been identified as being free of known restrictions under copyright law, including all related and neighboring rights.

Licensing—Others via Wikipedia under public domain no restrictions

With thanks to the following attributed & non attributed authors using one or more of the licences above

Author	**Image**
Castlesinclairgirnigoe.org	*Girinegoe Castle*
Celtus @ englishwkipedia	*Crest Badge*
Imars_Michael Shea	*Rollo*
Unkown—fwikipedia	*St Clair Sur Epte*
Tudorplace.com	*William the Conquerer*
Rampantscotland.com	*Malcolm III*
Richar Huseth—rhuseth@ev1.net	*Sinlcairs Bay*
Gsl wikidpedia commons	*Clan Map*
Tartansauthority.com	*Female Clan Member*
Lochcarron.com	*Green & Red Hunting and Modern Tartans*
Avenue	*Gorse bush*
revprsbbg.spot.com	*Firth of Clyde*
Richard Web	*Loch Long*
Brittanica.com	*Long Ship*
Dave Souza	*Largs Pencil*
Mintguy	*Monument to the Battle of Lewes*
Roger Griffith	*Loudoun Hill Stone*
Edmund Leighton 185-1922	*The Bruce addressing his troops*
Andrei nacu	*1st & 2nd days of battle at Bannockburn*
Finlay McWalter	*Bannockburn monumet*
Kim Traynor	*Statue of Robert the Bruce*
Unknown C15th artist	*Battle of Teba*
Tagishsimon	*Flodden Field*
Ipankonin	*Duke of Norfolk Shield for Battle of Flodden Field*
Adolf Tidemand 1814-1876	*Sinclairs Forces landing at Norway*
Author unknown +70 years	*Scottish Barn*
Leifern	*Monument at Otta*
Donald Bain	*Carbisdale Loch*
Richard Baker	*Ardvreck Castle*
Andrew Carrick Gow 1848-1920	*Cromwell in Dunbar*
Beringar	*Unidentified Scots flag & 3rd Captains Colours*
Machell Stace C19th	*Oliver Cromwell*
Phipli de Champaigne C17th	*Young Charles II*
C19th artist/authorMachel Stace	*Oliver Cromwell in the Battle of Worcester*
Source British Civil Wars/Author David Plant	*Map of the Battle of Worcester*
Blason familleHamilton & Blason ville ca Quebec & Lion Rampant & McDonnell of Antrim Arms/ Author Czar Brodie	*Earl of Caithness Arms*

Bletherskite	*Battle of Altimarlach Monument*
Godfrey Kneller C17th	*James II*
John Wootton C18th	*Battle of Sheriffmuir*
David Morier C18th	*1745 Rebellion*
Jeremy Atherton	*Interior of Rosslyn Chapel*
Colin Gould	*Castle Sinclair Girnigoe No1*
McKarri	*Castle Sinclair Girnigoe No2*
Mjgm84	*Castle Sinclair Girnegoe No3*
Unknown artiste/Author Mjgm84	*Castle Sinclair Girnigoe sketch No4*
Supergolden	*Rosslyn Castle from different approaches x 4*
Anne Burgess	*Exterior of Rosslyn Chapel*
Jack Spellingbacon	*Castle Mey*
Sian Abrahams	*Ackergill Castle*
Fergus Mather	*Keiss Castles old & new*
Author unknown	*Old Wick Castle*
Michael Beales	*Thurso Castle*
Brimms family	*Brimms Castle*
The following are the images within the Index	
Notingsnaid	*Crow Step*
tudorplace.com	*William the Conquerer*
Robert R McLan C19th	*Clan Chief*
Sodacan	*Lord Lyon Arms & Tudor Rose*
Photographer unknown C19th	*John Mahoney*
John Sullivan	*Aileach*
Lyall Duffus	*Huntly Castle*
Willaim Dobson 1611-1646	*Marquess of Montrose*
David Morier C18th	*Battle of Culloden*
Avenue	*Gorse flower*
Otter	*Ravenscraig Castle*
Kilnburn	*Dysart*
Unknown artist/Victoria & Albert Museum	*Mary Queen of Scots*
Mick Garratt	*Finlaggan*
audunn-marie.com	*Edinburgh Castle*
Finlay McWalter	*Stirling Castle*
Richard Webb	*Battle of Dalrigh location*
Patrick Mackie	*Mull of Kintyre*
Rama	*Claymore*
C17th artist/Author findagrave.com	*Oliver Cromwell*